A BOOK TO STIMULATE INQUISITIVE MINDS

"Eighty provocative questions and answers covering many interesting topics"

* Who were India's original people? * Primitive religious practices * Harappans * Who were the Aryans? * Decline of the Vedic gods and evolution of Hindu deities. * Where did the Jat tribes come from? * Emergence of castes * India's ancient languages and scripts * Meat and beef in ancient India * Evolution of Indian philosophies. * The importance of south India * The historic basis of the Ramayana and Mahabharat. * Influence of Buddhism and Jainism * How did the word Hindu evolve to become a religion? * The impact of Islam * Why have religions become so intolerant? * What enabled the British to succeed? * Has communalism ever been successful? ... and many more thought provoking subjects.

In Praise of Murad's 80 Questions

You must have wondered why religions as they are practiced today are so completely different from what their founders had hoped to make them. The founders had preached love, understanding and respect for people of other faith; their followers... look down upon and even wage wars against those who do not worship their gods. Many theories have been propounded to explain the degradation of religion but one of the latest and most perceptive that I have come across is Murad Ali Baig's Reflections in a Sacred Pond.

Khushwant Singh.
Column in The Tribune, Deccan Herald and others

A liberal's testament. Not many would dare to write a book nowadays on a topic like this one... However Murad Ali Baig does step out like a knight in the shining armour of a liberal knight... and then proceeds to demolish many cherished myths that have accumulated like cobwebs in the minds of educated Indians in the last few years...he does not spare anyone – jousts against Brahminical prejudices, Wahabi distortions (of Islam) and Sikh deviation. He spears through nationalist prejudices as well. He refutes the common belief that foreigners are responsible for the poverty in India. We may not agree with all his views, but it is a good read and provokes you to engage in a dialogue.

Parsa Venketashwar Rao Jr. Swagat flight magazine.

80 questions to reach the bottom of murky waters of origin of faith and religious systems in India. Who were India's original people? What were their early religious practices? How did Hinduism evolve to become a religion? What was the influence of Buddhism on Indian thought...What was the impact of Islam in India? Do all religions borrow ideas from each other? To find the answers plunge deep into the middle of historical and archaeological facts and stay off the shores of professional priests and propagandists. The author's efforts... succeeds in serving gulps of information... the thirst remains unquenched. However interesting bits of trivia and info keeps concentration afloat.

First City

Are the Bhils and Gonds Hindus? How did the British manage to defeat the Mughals? The author tries to encapsulate India's history, mythology and religion into the answers to 80 questions. The text could be interpreted as history by some, hearsay by others and heresy by the `faithful'. It does provide 80 topics for argument and introspection.

The Week

Spiritual lessons. It is a difficult (and thankless) mission that Murad Ali Baig has taken up in this book... in the sense that it surveys the Indian history and presents comments on well known sensitive issues in a way as to easily invite adverse reactions from all sections of society. What impresses us here is the authors daring – some would say reckless – treatment of the facts dealing with anthropological, geographical. political, economic, mythological and metaphysical issues.

Arun Gaur. The Tribune

This is a thought provoking book... The author has explored our past and questioned popular beliefs and opinions... that have led to the beliefs and superstitions that we harbour today.

Lakshmi Pillai. Jetwings flight magazine

Provocative, informative... a book of questions you had always wanted to ask about India... with eighty answers to argue about.

Gita Mehta

If people can learn how to find the glory of this spirit within themselves they will be freed from the bondage of sacrifices, penances and rituals. It will be the triumph of inner spirituality and the end of raucous religiosity.

Excerpt in The Times of India

This book is billed as a voyage through the ages to the present through a provocative series of 80 questions and answers reflecting and informing readers about Indian mythology and religion from a historical perspective. Baig does not question the importance of faith but outlines how religions have been altered by vested interests professional priests, rulers and the rich and the impact on Indian polity.

Business Standard

Murad Ali Baig showed how mythology and history do not gel... Baig brought out how myths associated with different religions to highlight the need for any discerning person to embark on a journey of exploration, to consider the possibility of tales one has grown up listening to being far removed from reality... The Ramayana could have happened anywhere. One should not rule out the possibilities of history. Questioning the origin of the scriptures Baig asked " Who wrote the Quran?" Even in Christianity the messages of Christ would have died down but for Peter and Paul. Buddhism would not have been a religion but for Ashoka. Baig never claimed that the possibilities he threw up were the final answers. But he emphasized the need for everyone to probe the possibilities.

P. Anima 'The Hindu'

"What Reflections in a Sacred Pond does~as much by its method as by its content—is to quietly and persuasively facilitate the path of rational and open dialogue on some of the most demanding issues of our time".

P.Gopinath, World Commission on Globalization

80 QUESTIONS
TO UNDERSTAND INDIA
HISTORY, MYTHOLOGY AND RELIGION

Dear Mia & Gavin
A few fragments of the
wonder that was India

Murad Ali Baig

Murad
16/12/2015

Foreword by
Khushwant Singh

Tara Press

Tara Press
(An imprint of India Research Press)
Flat No. 6, Khan Market, New Delhi - 110 003
Ph.: 24694610; Fax : 24618637
www.indiaresearchpress.com
contact@indiaresearchpress.com; bahrisons@vsnl.com

2009

ISBN 13 : 978-81-8386-093-2

Cataloguing in Publication Data

MURAD ALI BAIG
80 Questions to Understand India – History, Mythology and Religion
Includes bibliographical references & index.

1. India. 2. Culture. 3. History. 4. Religion.
5. Mythology 6. Question. 7. Travel.

1. Title.   II. Author

EARLIER EDITION PUBLISHED AS *REFLECTIONS IN A SACRED POND*

Printed for India Research Press at *Focus Impressions,* New Delhi.

Journey of The 80 Questions

It has been a very exciting year since *The Sacred Pond* was launched in early 2007. Its underlying theme of how the idea of God had been hijacked by the professional priests of all religions attracted a wide range of responses ranging from disbelief to approval. As I had been even handed to all religions and written with genuine respect and regard about all the prophets and founders of religion I fortunately attracted no Fatwas or dire threats from those whose long held religious opinions I might have challenged. Every religion has its bigots and wider knowledge about the real foundations of faiths is the only way that religious extremism can be countered.

I was asked to speak on this theme and to fourteen audiences ranging from 20 to 250 people and thus addressed over a thousand people provoking such keenly interested debate that many of the talks intended for 45 minutes lasted for over three hours. I was deeply flattered that my approach to this subject had the rapt attention of all the listeners who asked many very serious questions and seemed satisfied with my answers concerning a number of very controversial topics.

Based on these interactions as well as the responses and suggestions from many readers, I have incorporated two new chapters as well as a number of smaller points to the original text.

FOREWORD

Tyranny in Sacred Colours

Khushwant Singh

You must have often wondered why religions, as they are practised today, are so completely different from what their founders had hoped to make them. The founders had all preached love, understanding and respect for people of other faiths; their followers emphasise their own uniqueness and look down upon and even wage wars against those who do not worship their gods.

Many theories have been propounded to explain the degradation of religion but one of the latest and most perceptive that I have come across is Murad Ali Baig's 80 Questions (*Reflections in a Sacred Pond*) which I first saw in an earlier incarnation as *Tyranny in Sacred Colours: An Inquiry into the Paradoxes of India's Mythology, Religion and History.*

Murad does not question the importance of faith but outlines how religions have been altered by the vested interests of the professional priests of all religions and especially outlines its impact on India. He outlines how distortions, religiosity and superstitions that crept into all religions especially in Hinduism, Islam, Jainism, Buddhism and Sikhism as are practised in India.

He analyses the five participants in the practice of religion: the founder prophets, apostles, priests, rulers and the rich who became the patrons of religion and finally the common people who were persuaded to make offerings and sacrifices to insure themselves against the uncertainties of the future in life and the afterlife.

Murad takes the reader on a fast *Bharat Darshan* tour from its hoary past to the present, from the early societies of hunters, nomads and cultivators to more urbane civilised city life, the Aryans and their religion, a thousand years of Buddhism, revival of Brahmanical Hinduism, the impact of Islam, the Bhakti movement, the impact of Europeans and the spread of Christianity as well as the attitudes towards religion in post-independence India.

In this bewildering change of scenes one thing comes clear: in order to preserve their separate identity and assert their superiority over other faiths, the preachers of all religions understood that hate is a much stronger emotion than love. They practised it in the past: they practise it today.

In this work, Murad has changed the format from a series of statements to a Question and Answer format where readers can draw their own conclusions based on the evidence that he has provided. I suspect that caution has led him to this as writings on religion are always highly volatile and words attributed to him are bound to produce reactions. Fortunately, it is the questions that are provocative and he cannot be accused of bias when his answers equally affect Hindus, Muslims, Christians, Buddhists, Sikhs and others.

The answer to his last question is perhaps the most important for it shows how communalism has never been very successful politically despite the huge passions generated by religious and racial fanaticism.

ACKNOWLEDGEMENTS

My greatest debt is to my parents Tara and Rashid Ali Baig in whose eclectic home I was privileged to an amazing exposure to political affairs, history, culture, arts and travel to many exotic places.

Professor Mohammed Amin, who taught me medieval history, at St. Stephen's College gave this general interest in history new excitement, discipline and direction. Recently Amin Sahib spent many valuable hours going through my semi-final draft and made numerous corrections, suggestions and elaborations. Another very eminent historian, Dr. Romila Thapar had seen one of the early drafts and generously spent considerable time going through many of the points to correct some rather hasty early conclusions.

I also thank numerous friends especially Khushwant Singh for his generous encouragement on seeing an earlier draft, Jug Suraiya, Safwan Shah, Gita Mehta, Jaishree and Jairam Ramesh, Royina Grewal and Rachna Bhattacharya for helping sandpaper some of the rougher edges as well as Dipankar Bhattacharya who drew the excellent maps and illustrations that enliven the next.

My thanks especially to Anuj Bahri for his encouragement and advice and to his very able editor Debbie Smith assisted by Jehanara Wasi who had to wade through the corrections in the many revisions. They deserve my special thanks. Finally, my thanks go to my wife Vijayalakshmi Tannie who had to suffer endless discussions and arguments. My appreciation as well for her critical contributions and for her constant faith.

CONTENTS

NOTE : All spellings of names and places are in the form that they
are most popularly known.

INTRODUCTION

Few people realise that it is mythology that is the joker which has consistently distorted both history and religion in every country. The development of these myths and legends into scripture and history is actually easy to understand. Once upon a time, before there were films and TV, people in small towns and villages all over the world were entertained by wandering storytellers, minstrels and holy men with amazing tales of great heroes, beautiful heroines, awesome villains, terrifying demons and invincible divine forces. Not surprisingly, many small actual historic events would become magnified with each retelling to evolve into great legends. But myths are to a people what dreams are to individuals – colourful, fanciful and usually harmless outlets for the hopes, dreams, fantasies, angers and frustrations of their daily lives.

Over the years, these tales of victory, defeat, joy or sorrow were elaborated into theatrical events at celebrations of Holi, Dussehera, Eid, Muharram, Christmas, Easter, and the festivals of every land. So infectious and entertaining were these celebrations that the priests of all faiths were only too happy to weave these simple tales, as parables for the enlightenment of the people, into their scriptures as they evolved. So all scriptures, written long after the deaths of their founders, contain a huge baggage of mythology and customs that came to acquire almost the same sacred status as their core philosophies.

But when some priests declared that these myths were to be dogma, they created a body of inflexible tradition that separated their followers from the followers of other faiths. No prophet or founder prescribed any such dogma but dogma was to become divisive and created discord and conflict between religions and even between sects within the same religions. All the prophets were, in fact, rebels against earlier dogma and had been declared as heretics. Clerics forget that yesterday's heretics were to become the founders of new faiths. Buddha, Zoroaster, Jesus, Muhammad, Luther, Nanak and many others had all been branded as heretics by priests of older orders. Later their own followers were to declare their words as the final wisdom and call all new dissenters heretics.

Three hundred years ago, no one considered themselves Indian but as races like the Mughals, Afghans or Rajputs; castes like Brahmins, Kshatriyas, Vaishyas, Shudras, Banias, Chamars or linguistic groups like Bengalis, Marathas, Andhras, Tamils, etc. Geographic boundaries were fluid and the people of the Indian subcontinent were willingly subservient and loyal to their Mughal and later their British rulers. There were so many different identities that they had little sense of nation.

Three hundred years ago very few people considered themselves Hindu, as this word only vaguely existed. They considered themselves as Vaishnavas, Shaivites, Rambhaktas, Kabirpanthis and worshippers of Kali, Devis and numerous tribal deities.

It was only in 1826 that Raja Ram Mohan Roy used the originally Persian word Hindu as a unifying label to embrace all the varied forms of indigenous worship. Later Dayanand Saraswati, Vivekananda, Radhakrishnan and other reformers and philosophers gave the concept further shape and sincerely tried to integrate the many diverse faiths into a religion similar to the religions of revelation such as Islam and Christianity. Indian political leaders also wanted an equally distinct and well-defined Hindu religion knowing that religion had great political potential.

The so-called sanctity of religion made all those in political or administrative authority very careful in dealing with all religious practices that perhaps explains how tolerant police or other authorities are to the contravention of laws, rules or human rights as long as these are done in the name of religion.

This book evolved from a short essay called 'India Unvarnished' that I first wrote in 1991 in a furious four days after listening to the strong but ardent opinions of one of my Hindutva friends. A good friend, even if one who was deeply steeped in a rather romantic version of India's past that did not quite accord with what I had learned of history that had been my subject in college and a passion in later life. It is however paradoxical that much of the Hindutva vitriol against Muslims is owed to the highly exaggerated accounts by Muslim chroniclers, who in the Persian style of flowery prose, would pen words of lavish praise or condemnation. Many British historians also relied on these for their accounts of mediaeval India. These eulogies flattering the brutality or even the piety of Mahmud Ghazni, Alauddin Khilji, Aurangzeb and others are therefore very dubious. Sadly this love for exaggerated praise or condemnation continues to the present day leading to excessive hype as is evident even in the reporting on politics, film stars and even cricket.

These questions become all the more pertinent when a stormy controversy broke out after the demolition of the Babri Masjid in 1992. Many serious historians objected to the efforts of some scholars with clear Hindu Parishad leanings who were attempting to delete or rewrite portions of India's history textbooks that did not accord with their vision of India's glorious Hindu past.

A few dozen copies of the essay circulated to friends soon generated generous bouquets and furious brickbats showing that the issues selected were subjects of intense interest especially to anyone on the Indian subcontinent. Many emotive issues clearly needed to be studied dispassionately especially as such prejudices based on mythical or romanticised facts breed hurtful prejudices and destructive anger.

When my friend Safwan Shah put the 2001 version of the evolving essay up on his website it attracted hundreds of responses from all over the world. Despite a severe mauling by some, the many intelligent and detailed responses helped me to correct several mistakes and omissions and add many useful additional ideas and information.

Many critics also felt that my questions and answers were biased. Fortunately I was equally accused of bias against Hindus, Muslims, Christians, Sikhs and others so these criticisms roughly cancelled out. Others observed that the text was too simplistic, half-cooked and that I had provided no original research. I, therefore, need to say that I have not tried to present a complete record of all the historical facts about India, as to attempt that would require many thousands of pages. The purpose of this book is to stimulate interest so that readers can do their own explorations.

This little book attempts to examine some of the popular 'opinions' about our history to expose those that clash with historic facts or conflict with equally plausible alternative traditions to encourage open minded thinking unrestrained by orthodoxy or prejudice.

Historic thinking gets distorted in the prism of mythology especially when it becomes embedded into religious scripture. It is amazing how possessive people can get about their traditions. Some Hindu chauvinists seem to think that there is no Indian history except for that which is found in their select literary sources. These, unfortunately, were almost entirely written by Brahmin scribes over the ages in praise of their sages, kings, patrons and philosophies. So though they contain a huge body of useful historical material, they completely miss many important events of India's past. Major omissions include the entire Harappan civilisation, Alexander or even the existence of the Mauryan Empire. Surprisingly most of these accounts did not even mention Buddha or Buddhism and most Indians, till quite recently, were quite unaware that Buddhism had been the dominant religion in India for nearly a thousand years and was not only a religion of the mountain areas bordering Tibet.

The limitations of Brahmin literary sources were evident from the complete inability of all the Brahmin priests, who had been consulted, to decipher the Ashokan inscriptions. It was only from Buddhists in Sri Lanka and Burma, who were familiar with ancient Pali written in the Prakrit script, long forgotten in India, that James Princep was able to decipher them in 1837. Thus was found the key to open the glorious Mauryan chapter of Indian history. It is therefore not surprising that although the Buddhist period accounts for nearly a thousand years of India's known history it merits such little space in Indian history books.

But the Brahmin scribes raised their constantly evolving texts like the Vedas, Brahmanas, Upanishads, Ramayana, Mahabharata, Puranas, Shastras, Smritis, etc., to the level of sacred scripture making it sacrilege to even question the most patently absurd episodes and assertions. Later the passionate preaching of large numbers of barely literate babas and sages to their usually uneducated and gullible devotees created a body of opinion about India's history that over glorifies the past and breeds dangerous prejudices.

Few people realise that India does not even have a monopoly on the epic Ramayana. There are dozens of versions deeply loved as a revered part of their native traditions in many other Asian countries like Sri Lanka, Thailand, Bali, Cambodia and Vietnam. No Indian has a right to feel outraged by the beliefs of others. Unfortunately, with religion becoming a sensitive political issue, some members of the Hindu Parivar are bent on trying to create a glorified but inaccurate record of India's past that is no better than the distortion of Islam by the Taliban among poorly educated Muslims.

Many erudite Brahmin scholars undoubtedly gave India a great literary tradition but they had little interest or taste for the special disciplines of history. From the ruins of great monuments, British observers in the 18th and 19th centuries could see a faint glimpse about some great civilisation from the distant past but there was very little current knowledge of these ancient cultures before the accounts of a few Muslim chroniclers like Al Baruni and Ibn Batuta. The accounts of Greek and Chinese travellers were still not known.

The facts of India's history mainly became known from the researches by several remarkable European Indologists after the 17th century. Few people today realise that till then there were no books available in vernacular languages and that the Sanskrit texts, including the Ramayana and Mahabharata, that are so well known today, were till then only in the jealously guarded hoards of a few Brahmin scholars.

Though history is supposed to be a chronology of proven facts, many thinkers wishing to legitimise their strongly felt opinions, tried to twist, interpret or reconstruct them to fit their own preconceived ideas. It suited the British to be condescending about India's history to enhance their own sense of greatness. Communists and socialists interpreted history to support their theories about materialistic determinism. Politicians of all colours wantonly distorted history to pander to their vote banks. Many intellectuals were also very willing to sacrifice truth at the altar of populism.

Till a hundred years ago, as a result of Mughal and British rule most Indians, except for Muslim noble families and small groups of Brahmins were largely illiterate and most Hindus, barring the

Rajputs, were agriculturists, traders and menials with little self-esteem. So it was not surprising that the sudden awareness of India's great past culture filled a huge craving for knowledge and pride. So, rather in the Persian style of flowery exaggeration, many eminent writers responded by painting a thick gloss of excessive flattery, to accounts of India's undoubtedly great history and culture.

Perhaps the long period under Afghan, Mughal and British dominance had caused an over reaction of chauvinist pride about things considered to be essentially Indian. So there was understandable pride that India had invented the concept of zero or the game of chess but equal offence if things commonly considered Indian were proved to be foreign. Many are even offended by the incontrovertible fact that chillies were completely alien to India and only brought to Asia by the Portuguese.

The invention of the zero and chess shows that Indians were intellectually inventive but they were not nearly as mechanically inventive as the Chinese and Europeans even if they were quite good imitators. It has to also be understood that the transmissions of ideas, commodities and customs from one region to another has been a continuous process especially at times when national boundaries or even the sense of nation did not exist. In ancient times there were thousands of communities but no one who was Indian or non-Indian.

Many religious groups like the Jains, Buddhists, Christians, Jews and Muslims have been an intrinsic part of India's long history and Hindu tolerance had enabled them to coexist harmoniously. They all have their own cherished literary traditions, myths and legends and can be equally incensed by facts that conflict with the alleged words of their scriptures or beliefs.

The true definition of opinion is the absence of facts
...*for when there are facts there is no need for opinion.*

I Declare

I am a student of history and this study is based on a lifetime of extensive reading and equally wide field travel in a career of rural marketing that took me to a huge number of historic, religious and geographical sites in almost every district of India and gave me an invaluable exposure to the many people and their traditions throughout the country.

This short work examines some of the popular beliefs to try to confirm what is true, deny what is contrary to provable fact and to moderate opinions that are contradicted by equally plausible alternate beliefs. It has been written with a love for all cultures but mainly with a desire to stimulate open minded thinking unlimited by the barriers of orthodoxy or prejudice.

I know that it is dangerous to write about religions, especially in India, without inviting immediate controversy. And more so if I happen to have a Muslim name. So before I am accused of religious, ethnic or sectarian bias, I would like to say that my father was a non-practising Muslim, my mother a *Brahmo* from Bengal, my wife a Punjabi Hindu, my son-in-law a Jain and my daughter-in-law of Punjabi-Gujarati stock. I can therefore claim to be more representative of India than most people I know. I believe in a great cosmic spirit but deplore the self-appointed merchants of God who create so much discord and violence in the promotion of their own concepts of God.

I want to clearly state that I love and genuinely respect the prophets and founders of all religions but do not have the same regard for their professional priests who claim to be the sole selling agents of God and often promote division and discord against those who do not subscribe to their brands of God. So if some of the facts related in these pages disturb conventional thinking they are likely to equally shock or surprise Hindus, Buddhists, Christians, Jains, Jews, Muslims and Sikhs. These facts are not intended to disrespect their beliefs but to encourage people to understand that religions, like all man- made institutions, change over time and that the foundations of many common beliefs are not what many complacently believe today. The book also shows how the spiritual fundamentals of most religions are surprisingly similar.

Religions are much more than faiths. They all contain a small core of the philosophies of the original faiths but over the centuries develop many social customs and rituals added to it by armies of professional priests, mullahs or monks. Without exception, all religions carry a huge collection of customs and myths created around celestial events, and ancient traditions, as well as accounts of royal and religious personages who do not deserve to be treated with sacred reverence

There is no reason to consider these ideas controversial because there is a huge body of documented facts to show how all the religions and their religious myths evolved. And even if these challenge some conventional ideas readers need to open their minds to the many common threads and common prejudices that have made religions alternatively narrow and wonderful. The subject is huge and these books only attempt to skim quickly over the subject with the sole intention of making people see religious traditions objectively while also respecting the beliefs of others.

CHANGE IS THE NATURE OF THE WORLD

Few people realise just how quickly people can forget their history. A recent study among African tribes found that most of them could recall little before the time of their great grandparents. Earlier events were usually relegated to the realm of folk tales and legends. This perhaps explains why people like the Aztecs and Mayas so quickly forgot their once great civilisations after the Spaniards destroyed their cultural heritage. Conversely, this explains how quickly patently new customs, costumes, music and rituals become popular and are assumed to be part of some old tradition.

In all societies, even when science and historical evidence can better define past events most people, rooted in the recent past, are not happy when their cherished myths are questioned. They want to believe that the things and values of their present times have always been there and will never change

For several million years man could only progress as far as the strength of his arms and legs could take him. The domestication of animals, only during the past 8,000 years, enabled this motive power to be multiplied a few times. During the last 3,000 years man learned to harness the wind to propel his ships. But it was only during the past 400 years that man learned to release the chemical energy contained in coal, petroleum and later the atom to usher in the industrial age. Now man has learned to unleash the power of computers to hugely multiply the power of the human mind.

These inventions quickly made man the undisputed master of the earth and all its living things but man unfortunately did not learn how to restrain his ambition or greed. Primordial man took perhaps no more than 5,000 renewable calories a day from nature for all his food, clothing and shelter. A modern man in an industrialised country now consumes over 100,000 calories a day for the energy needed to produce his food with planting, harvesting, processing, packaging, transport and refrigeration; for energy to make his home, heat it, cool it and light it; for energy to make his automobiles and move them; for energy for his travels communications and pleasures. Most of this energy now comes from diminishing reserves of fossil fuels that are polluting the world while simultaneously depleting the forests and sullying the rivers, oceans and the atmosphere. Change is all around us but people are astonishingly blind to change and its consequences.

What is also surprising is that things that were once great wonders are so quickly considered commonplace. We can all recall the awe and surprise when cell phones, computers, televisions, radios, aeroplanes, gramophones, automobiles, refrigerators, telephones and electricity first entered our lives but the amazing thing is how quickly they all became assimilated into everyday living and people seemed to think that they had always been around.

Some of man's more significant inventions, that had dramatically changed human destiny, were perhaps the creation of a coherent language out of rudimentary sounds, the ability to make fire instead of having to carefully preserve fire sticks, making tools out of rough stones and the domestication of cereals that could be kept and eaten at later times. There were many others like the first domestication of dogs, sheep, cattle, horses, elephants and camels as well as the wheel, the use of pottery and the mastery of metals. There was also the magnetic compass that enabled man to sail far from the sight of land and paper to record the increasingly complex businesses of state and religion. There were also the inventions of weapons of war with better bows, swords, guns, tanks, aircraft, submarines and missiles that all accelerated human ambition and progress.

There was also a constant trend towards accelerated complexity. The speed with which mechanical, electric and electronic devices have multiplied and mutated in just one decade clearly demonstrates this amazing human genius. This trend was also clearly evident in the evolution of art, music, literature, philosophy, architecture, medicines, fabrics, costumes, fashions, cuisines, and in the technologies of war machines and building materials. This human genius for accelerating complexity quickly made all the original scriptures obsolete so new commentaries and revisions were constantly required. These later led to new ideas that the priests condemned as heresies until the heretics themselves became the founders of new faiths.

But while there have been many gainers, ambition and progress had also produced dropouts who resented change and sought refuge in the comforting myths of the past. Many sought spiritual or intellectual retreats far from the boisterous clamour of modern technologies, politics, music and entertainment.

Man has always been an anxious animal beset with fears about disease, hunger, attack by animals or enemies and about death itself so religions that evolved from earlier faiths, offering philosophies and rituals to allay such fears, were eagerly sought.

Most people want to think that their present situation has always been there. They want to consider the past, as a pleasant golden period from where there had been a steady descent into their present times of uncertainty and conflict. Unfortunately many people, especially the keepers of religious faiths, have selective memories to glorify their heroes or belittle their foes. They have all nurtured the myths of the past to help advance their ideas and ideals and have sought to fortify them with the supposed infallibility of sacred scriptures. For them, therefore, history has to be subservient to ideology and science and historical evidence must be opposed with scorn and mockery.

Unfortunately they all forget the immortal words of the Bhagavad Gita that says:

'Change is the nature of the world'. The only permanence of this world is its impermanence.

CHRONOLOGY

BC

12,000 – 10,000	Retreat of the last Ice Age
9,000	First cereal cultivation in Palestine.
4,000 – 2000	Cereal cultivation reaches India
2,700 – 1500	Harappan civilisation in North-West India
1,500 – 1,200	Probable arrival of Indo-Aryan people
1200 – 600	Early urban habitations in North India
600 – 400	Rise of Magadha
560 – 467	Mahavira
556 – 468	Gautam Buddha
580 – 529	Cyrus the Great
326 – 325	Alexander in Western India
321 – 185	The Mauryan Empire
268 – 231	Reign of Ashoka

AD

4 – 36	Jesus
78	Beginning of the Saka era with the Kushans
200	Beginning of South Indian empires
320 – 467	The Gupta Empire
399 – 413	Travels of Fa Hsien
450 – 600	The incursions of the Huns
570 – 632	Muhammad
606 – 647	Reign of Harshvardhana
630 – 644	Hiuen Tsang's travels in India
653	Arabs conquer Persia
711	Muhammad Bin Qasim's Arab incursion
780 – 826	Shankaracharya
997 – 1030	Ghazni's invasions
1047 – 1137	Ramanuja

1162 – 1227	Genghis Khan
1192	Ghori defeats Prithviraj Chauhan
1206 – 1526	Delhi Sultanate. Khiljis, Tuglaqs, Lodis,
1304 – 1377	Al Baruni
1340 – 1355	Ibn Batuta's travels to India
1398	Timur Lang sacks Delhi
1469 – 1539	Guru Nanak
1485 – 1533	Chaitanya
1498	Vasco da Gama reaches India
1526	First Battle of Panipat
1526 – 1757	Mughal Empire
1534 – 1613	Goswami Tulsidas
1540 – 1545	Reign of Sher Shah Suri
1556 – 1605	Reign of Akbar
1612	British in Surat
1630 – 1680	Shivaji
1658	Defeat of Dara Shikoh
1658 – 1707	Reign of Aurangzeb
1690	British found Calcutta
1757	Battle of Plassey
1761	Third Battle of Panipat
1799	Defeat of Tipu Sultan
1775 – 1818	Maratha wars
1869 – 1948	Mahatma Gandhi
1857	Mutiny of Company Sepoys
1939 – 1945	World War II
August 15, 1947	Indian independence. Partition.
1962	War with China
1965 and 1971	Wars with Pakistan
December 6, 1992	Destruction of Babri Mosque

CHRONOLOGY OF CIVILISATION

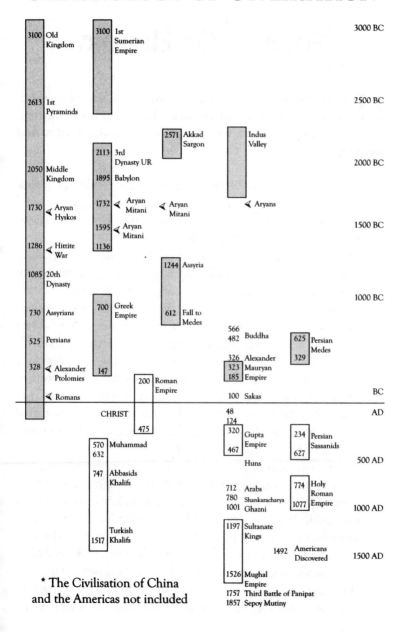

3100 Old Kingdom	3100 1st Sumerian Empire	3000 BC

2613 1st Pyraminds — 2500 BC

2571 Akkad Sargon

Indus Valley

2113 3rd Dynasty UR

2050 Middle Kingdom — 2000 BC
1895 Babylon

1730 ◄ Aryan Hyskos
1732 ◄ Aryan Mitani
◄ Aryan Mitani
◄ Aryans

1595 ◄ Aryan Mitani — 1500 BC

1286 ◄ Hittite War
1136

1085 20th Dynasty

1244 Assyria

730 Assyrians
700 Greek Empire — 1000 BC

612 Fall to Medes

566
482 Buddha

525 Persians

625 Persian Medes

326 Alexander
329

328 ◄ Alexander Ptolomies
147
323 Mauryan
185 Empire

200 Roman Empire

◄ Romans
100 Sakas — BC

CHRIST
48 — AD
124
475

320 Gupta Empire
234 Persian Sassanids

570 Muhammad
632
467
627

Huns — 500 AD

747 Abbasids Khalifs

712 Arabs
774 Holy Roman Empire
780 Shankaracharya
1001 Ghazni
1077 — 1000 AD

1197 Sultanate Kings

Turkish Khalifs
1517

1492 Americans Discovered — 1500 AD

1526 Mughal Empire
1757 Third Battle of Panipat
1857 Sepoy Mutiny

* The Civilisation of China and the Americas not included

SOURCES OF HISTORY

H ISTORY depends on evidence and there are several methods that enable scholars to evaluate the questions of history, mythology and religion to set their probable dates, locations and accuracy.

1. Fossils, the remains of stone tools, bones, buildings, coins, weapons, ploughs, sculpture, pottery, metals and other solid objects can now be fairly accurately dated by radio carbon, argon and other scientific methods.

2. The literature and oral traditions of all societies are important sources of information and give glimpses into past events. But they have almost always been the work of bards, courtiers, scribes and priests praising their kings, priests, deities and traditions with exaggerated prose or poetry. So they are almost always one-sided and, being paeans of praise to their patrons, usually neglect the concerns of the common people and mundane matters like industry, commerce, occupations, architecture, social conditions, diet, etc., that interest historians today. They add colourful flesh, blood and character to cold historical sources but often lack historic accuracy and so are very prone to repeated revisions over the years.

    Few people also realise that the very process of writing was so difficult in ancient times that the complex descriptions about Indian mythology, that are now widely read, had been very difficult to write till the Mughals introduced the Chinese invention of paper to India in the 16th century AD. The time and effort needed to inscribe texts on stone make Ashoka's inscriptions seem short and bare by today's flowery standards. Writing on birch bark (bhoj patra), leather, palm or papyrus leaves was only slightly easier. But these were all perishable and had to be reinscribed every few centuries. Thus many of the elaborations around almost all the old myths and scriptures only occurred in fairly recent times.

3. Astrology is a most unreliable source for history. Many writers and scholars have tried to date the events and personages of history through celestial events recorded in ancient texts or myths. Though seemingly impressive, this method is of absolutely no historic value because anyone familiar with astronomy can easily choose any date from the past, or even in the future and find comets, alignments of stars and other celestial events to 'prove' any chosen date for their gullible listeners.

4. The established dates of the first domestication of plants, animals, the use of copper, iron, ploughs, weapons, architectural technology, construction materials, building styles, pottery, coins and the first appearance of deities and forms of worship, can often indicate the time of their appearance. They also help to fix the probable dates of historical and mythical events and provide valuable internal evidence to support or contradict the oral and literary sources. The facts of history can also be ascertained by seeking parallels in surrounding countries where similar events or facts may have been more accurately dated. Bows, for example, were originally very simple straight bows. Then came much more complex double or re-curved bows followed with composite laminated bows and crossbows in later periods.

5. Myths are of very doubtful value as sources of history. Many are borrowed from other people while some seriously conflict with the ones popular in another country. Myths are, however, to a people what dreams are to individuals. Colourful and fanciful outlets for the hopes, dreams, fantasies, angers

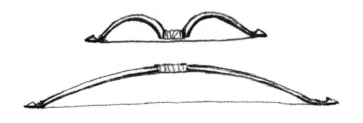

and frustrations. Such myths were mainly the creation of storytellers. And all good storytellers needed exaggerations and glorifications.

But myths, like dreams, allow free rein to emotions that can range from the romantic to the violent. So heroes were of amazing size, strength or cunning while the heroines were of dazzling grace and seductiveness and the villains were monstrously evil. Violence against enemies had to always be successful and the cause was always just. In myths such stories are charming and harmless but in the hands of the bigoted they can legitimise hurtful prejudices and encourage senseless anger and violence. And myths with heroic victors violently vanquishing despised enemies are also bad models for settling differences in the real world of families, corporations, states and nations.

Unlike the epics and myths of Greece, Egypt, Babylon, Persia, Rome and many other countries, that were accepted as charming but fanciful fairy tales, myths in the Indian subcontinent became part of popular religious traditions and have coloured and distorted the understanding of India's real history. As the Brahmin authors of these Indian myths raised them to levels of sacred scripture, comment or criticism of them could never be taken lightly. So instead of tolerant good humour, there is often self-righteous anger.

As with every culture, there is much to admire along with a lot to condemn. Many will not relish the puncturing of long cherished opinions but if wrongly founded opinions can breed intolerance, anger and violence, they need to be mercilessly exposed.

This little book endeavours to examine the factual basis concerning some of the popular beliefs. It also looks at events and personages of India's history without attempting to be judgemental. There are no final words in history where new evidence often alters past certainties.

80 Questions About India's Past are:

1. Was India One of the Oldest Civilisations?

Before a culture could be called a civilisation there were many early pre-urban habitations for many centuries after small bands of people gave up their long migratory existence as hunters and nomadic herdsmen and settled down at one place. Cereal cultivation was the defining event that enabled man to settle. Then small villages came under the domination of bigger ones till a still greater one demanded taxes and tributes from them in exchange for protection. Such taxes created the surpluses that paid for the creation of great cities and supported priests, scholars and entertainers in addition to the soldiers who though necessary were equally unproductive economically.

All civilisations evolved after large urban settlements developed with kings, palaces, priests, temples, soldiers, armies, crafts, literature, arts and culture. They all required big cities, a system of government, cultivation of cereals, pottery, metal tools, implements and weapons as well as domesticated animals for transport, ploughing and war.

Writing for literature and communications only came with civilisations. Social structures that had been simple and informal in tribal societies became multi-layered from kings and priests at one end and butchers and sweepers at the other, with soldiers, courtiers, courtesans, artists, musicians, artisans, craftsmen, tradesmen and transporters in between.

As the first known writing (Egyptian and Sumerian) first appeared 5,000 years ago, 99 per cent of man's history is known after that time. But, actually, perhaps 99 per cent of man's real history belongs to a time before it was recorded. By roughly 50,000 BC,

Cro-Magnon man had acquired modern man's brain capacity and bone structures that had evolved over millions of years. Man's ancestors, who seem to have first inhabited the rift valley of east Africa, migrated North down the Nile River to eventually populate the rest of earth. Egypt had an advanced civilisation with sophisticated technologies for building with stone over a thousand years before the Harappan cultures.

Anthropological studies show that primitive people today are not less intelligent than their literate urban counterparts but only culturally deficient. Their children are more alert, aware and interested than, for example, their American counterparts who spend several hours a day passively watching TV. Nature had been a great teacher till people gradually lost their sensitivity. With the advent of electricity, people seldom noticed the stars any longer. With the mass marketing of foodstuffs they lost their awareness of many edible plants and sensitivity to the wonderful world outside their habitations. All tribal people know the names and properties of hundreds of local plants, mushrooms, trees and even the sounds of the forests around them. They can read the language of the seasons and the glory of the stars in the night skies.

With the possible exception of small cultures like Mehrgarh, in Baluchistan, the main civilisations on the Indian subcontinent were not as old as the civilisations of Egypt or Babylon. By 3,100 BC these were advanced urban habitations with sophisticated, buildings, arts and culture. The earliest civilisation on the Indian subcontinent was the Harappan settlements that began about 2,500 BC. This civilisation was, however, older then those of Persia, Greece, Rome or Europe.

The Harappan culture thrived in north-western India from about 2,700 BC up to 1,500 BC. After its demise, there was a long gap till groups of small and less advanced early urban cultures began to appear in the Sutlej and Gangetic plains. The urban sites mentioned in the Mahabharata like the five 'Pats' of Inderpat, Panipat, Sonepat, Bagpat and Tilpat seem to have belonged to this pre-urban period at around 1,000 BC.

The first big urban cities in present-day India were probably Rajgir and Kosambi, on elevations above the then thickly forested and malarial Gangetic plain. These habitations are dated to around 800 BC. When the Gangetic plains were cleared and cultivated, Pataliputra was for many centuries one of the greatest cities of the world. It was the centre of Indian civilisation from about 400 BC to 300 AD.

It cannot therefore be claimed that India had the oldest continuous civilisation because there were huge gaps between the completely forgotten Harappan civilisation, some parallel cultures in the Sutlej region, the much later cultures of Pataliputra and those that developed in other areas.

2. WHERE DID HUMAN BEINGS COME FROM? WAS NOBODY NATIVE TO THE INDIAN SUBCONTINENT?

The scientific world now accepts from accurately dated and fairly inescapable scientific and anthropological evidence that all modern human beings originated in Africa. Though the scanty remains of one of the earliest homonids called Ramapithicus, very roughly dated to between the 8 to 13 million years ago, was found in the Pakistan Shivaliks, this line died out and was never the ancestor of modern man. Unlike apes, or monkeys without tails, homonids had thumbs opposed to their fingers, declining canine teeth and an enlarged frontal lobe for their bigger brains.

Our own ancestors, the Homo Sapiens evolved from homonids like Australopithecus and Homo erectus beginning about 7 million years ago. They came out of Africa and spread all over the world about 2 million years ago. Modern man, or Cro-Magnon, then displaced an older Neanderthal, who had inhabited earth for about 250,000 years till roughly 50,000 years ago at about the beginning of the last Ice Age. The Cro-Magnons were taller than Neanderthals but their bones show that they had bigger voice boxes. So speech and communications may have been the key to their success.

Human movement virtually froze during the last 40,000 -year-long Ice Age. The cold froze water on ice caps and mountains s well as thermally contracting the water in the oceans that seem to have dropped by about 113 metres. This lower sea level and ice bridges enabled many animals and people to travel from Asia to America and Australia.

Early homonids spread to Asia about a million years ago, to Europe and reached Australia about 40,000 years ago. They crossed over to the Americas about 12,000 years ago but inhabited the cold regions above the Arctic Circle only some 20,000 years ago.

After the last Ice Age ended about 12,000 years ago racial distinctions had developed in many different regions as climate had altered human characteristics. Those living in cold climates became fair, while others in the tropics needed darker skin pigment for protection from the sun. People in dry climates developed long noses to moisten the air going into their lungs while those in humid areas had short wide noses. The inhabitants of cold climates had short rounder bodies to best conserve heat, while the people of the open plains became tall with long legs. Being short, however, enabled the best survival for those who lived in dense forests or marshy areas.

But it was an immense journey that began with small groups of fur-clad hunters in their cold caves or timid travellers on the open plains. Man became a hunter and gatherer in the forests, then a nomad on the plains after he found that it was easier to tame flocks of sheep and herds of cattle than to hunt animals in the wild. Much later he became a cultivator in small village settlements. In more recent times came the advent of cities essential to civilisation.

Fairly accurately dated fossil remains of man's ancestors in many parts of the world indicate how and when they moved from Africa to other parts of the world. Science can also trace the evolution from the mitochondrial DNA (mtDNA) in studies of populations from all over the world. This rather complicated evidence shows that western-Eurasian lineages found in India average 5.2 per cent as compared to 7.0 per cent in Europe. They range from about 6 per cent in North India to about 4 per cent in Andhra but indicate considerable intermingling. The dating of these lineages also suggests a time between 9,000 and 12,000 years ago that roughly corresponds with the shift from the early to the late Stone Ages.

Unlike other species like elephants, horses, deer, cats and birds that did not change very significantly over time, hominids changed very rapidly and the changes during the past 12,000 years were the most rapid. Stone tools and scanty remains of very small habitations of Paleolithic humans have been found in India dating back to over 100,000 years but these were probably of pre-modern homonids and not, therefore, the ancestors of any modern people.

3. IS THERE ANY FOUNDATION TO THE KALPAS AND YUGAS OF INDIAN BELIEF?

Every ancient society speculated on the wonders of the heavens and created a complex cosmology that became part of their mythology. But scientific inquiry does not support most such myths. The idea of 4,320 million-year kalpas, each a mere day in the life of Brahma, is not a Vedic tradition. It only developed in the period of the, not so ancient, Puranas. It held that the age span of one kalpa was the time from the formation of earth to the present time. Each kalpa was divided into 4 yugas but even this division was many times longer than the length of man's entire existence. As modern man has only existed on earth for about 50,000 years, this period represents just 0.00001 per cent of the time of the last kalpa. The orthodox belief that Ram lived 900,000 years ago is equally absurd.

But India was not alone in cosmic speculations as many other civilisations had similar myths about cosmic cycles of creation, destruction and recreation. Actually there are some surprising similarities in the ancient cosmological myths of American Indians, Mayas, Australian aborigines and those of the Genesis.

This idea of kalpas is as far-fetched as the opinion, long believed in Britain, that the year of creation was 4006 BC. Reverend James Ussher, the Archbishop of Armagh, after a detailed study of Christian scriptures had even fixed the time of the event very precisely at 9 am on October 23.

Every society believed that their present time was fraught with troubles and they all hankered for a great and glorious golden age in the past. The idea of a Kalyuga appeals to many Indians in the recent times of stress and uncertainty. But as the yugas steadily descended from glorious early ones to the degraded present Kalyuga, it also promoted a very negative idea of good and bad and tended to legitimise bad conduct, immorality and fatalism. As philosophical speculations were paramount, ethics were considered much less important.

Modern science has been able to quite accurately map all the major occurrences of the past. If modern man's total existence on earth dates from just 50,000 years ago, there is absolutely not a shred of historic or geographic evidence that the yugas and kalpas could have ever occurred.

Today many Indians observe fasts on Tuesdays or will not purchase things of iron on Saturdays believing that such weekdays are auspicious or inauspicious despite the fact that the seven-day week was quite alien to India's ancient astronomical tradition. There had been a lunar calendar but the seven-day week was first known to Babylon. But in a world without boundaries, traditions from one country, following trade, quickly traveled to others.

4. WHAT WAS INDIA LIKE 5,000 YEARS AGO?

There is definite evidence from over 1,000 fairly accurately dated stone-age settlements that primitive stone-age people had inhabited the Indian subcontinent for about 100,000 years. There was a gradual shift from old Stone-Age (Paleolithic) to new Stone-Age (Neolithic) tools when the early inhabitants began shifting from being hunter-gatherers to cultivators of primitive cereals from 4,000 to 2,000 BC. The earlier tools were mainly coarsely shaped choppers and scrapers needed to cut flesh, break bones and scrape skin. The new Neolithic tools were finely chiselled blades, spear points, arrowheads and flakes that could be bound or glued together to make sickles to harvest cereals.

It took many more centuries for mature cultivation to develop and spread to all parts of the country. The world's oldest cereal cultivation site, so far discovered, is at Jericho in the Mediterranean area dated to about 8,500 BC. The eating of cereals needed a saddle quern for grinding the seeds, pottery vessels for storage and fire for cooking. These were the main markers of the advent of cereal cultivation. The shift from coarse Paleolithic stone tools to Neolithic tools was another marker. The dating of the evolving artifacts and tools marks man's advancement from hunters to cultivators. A hard and dangerous existence and scarcity of food kept the human bands small and scattered. India's total population was estimated at only about 20,000 in Paleolithic times.

Archaeological findings indicate that cities showing early cereal cultivation only reached maturity in north-east Afghanistan about 4,200 BC though the settlement around Mehrgarh at the foot of the Bolan Pass in Pakistan indicates that wheat and barley were being cultivated a little earlier.

From the dating of Paleolithic and Megalithic stone tools and the first appearance of pottery, cereal cultivation seems to have slowly spread to Baluchistan by 4,200 BC, Sind by 3,600 BC, Punjab and north Rajasthan by 2,800 BC, Maharashtra and Karnataka by 1,500 BC. Parts of the Yamuna-Ganges area came under cultivation with small settlements about 1,800 BC but mature cultivation only reached the middle Ganges area about 1,200 BC.

The introduction of the iron plough after 1,000 BC seems to have accelerated a big growth of population in North India following greatly increased food production. At this time India's coastal areas and river basins were thickly forested malarial swamps unfit for human existence. The habitation of coastal South India and Sri Lanka seems to have only begun about 400 BC.

5. How Did Food Resources Affect Man's Evolution?

There were not enough edible materials in most parts of the world to support large human populations till the domestication of cereals about 8- 10,000 years ago. Few people realise that the domestication of plants and animals was a necessary precondition for the growth of large human populations. The mapping of plant genes shows that there were no edible cereals and very few edible plants in India till about 5,000 years ago.

Meat from wild animals and birds as well as fish was therefore the only fresh food available around the year but killing game was not easy with primitive Stone Age weapons. A meagre diet with supplements of barely edible seasonal fruits, vegetables, plants and roots

made life very short, difficult and dangerous in thick forests inhabited by many dangerous animals. Remains of early humans preserved
in European bogs and in fossils show that they had enlarged small
intestines necessary to digest such harsh food. These later shrank,
when better food became available, to become the appendix.

Man first domesticated barley, millets and wheat about 8- 9,000
BC in the Mediterranean area around Palestine. Initially these were
wild grass seeds. Wheat was developed by man from 14 to 28 chromosomes to become edible and then to todays bread wheat with 42
chromosomes. The domestication of these cereals led to a rapid growth
of population in that area so people were able to spread out. DNA
mapping shows wheat cultivation spread at roughly one kilometre per
year. Though tiny native populations did exist before this in Europe,
India, China, Australia and the Americas their populations could not
grow till increased sources of food became available.

Cereal cultivation enabled man to abandon his wandering life
as a hunter or nomad and obtain most of the food he needed from
a few acres of nearby land. But as these crops had to be protected
from animals and other people, cultivators became possessive first
about their crops and later about their cattle, women and other
possessions. So possessiveness was probably the 'Original Sin' and
Adam's fabled apple was actually wheat. Adam's apple was clearly a
fable because wild apples were inedible till the Chinese invention
of grafting some 4,000 years ago. As cereals were the only vegetarian
food that could be stored and eaten at a later time, meat was man's
staple diet till cereals were domesticated.

Wheat, peas, olives along with sheep and goats were first domesticated in the Mediterranean areas of West Asia about 8,500
BC. A thousand years later, China domesticated rice, millets, pigs
and silkworms. Sugarcane and bananas probably originated in New
Guinea. Coffee came from Ethiopia. Sorghum (bajra) and yams
came from central Africa. Many commonplace plants like maize,
potatoes, tomatoes, chillies, beans, peanuts, cocoa, rubber and
pineapples only came to Europe and Asia after the discovery of
America. The Portuguese brought them to Asia about 400 years
ago. Cotton, sesame, cucumber and eggplant were native to India
as was the Zebu or Bos Indicus humped cattle.

Harappan sites show evidence of millets and barley and a little wheat. There is no trace of rice that seems to have come later to India from southern China. Coconuts too seem to have come from here. It is recorded that the Satvahanas imported coconuts from Southeast Asia about the time of Christ and deliberately propagated it throughout the West coast revolutionising the coastal economy and enabling it to support larger populations.

Even the domestication of animals has many surprises. Though dogs were domesticated first, the donkey was only domesticated about 4,000 BC in Egypt and the horse about a thousand years later in the Ukraine or the Caucasian area. Camels were tamed in Arabia and Central Asia by about 1,100 BC and elephants in India somewhat later.

The sources of food were insufficient to support large native populations in India till about 3,000 BC. Migrants from more agriculturally advanced surrounding areas gradually settled in India that had been a well-watered land compared to any in West Asia, as soon as the land began producing enough food to feed them.

Food sources also influenced social and philosophical concepts. But early hunters and nomads were very sensitive to nature and never took life casually. When they killed, they would often speak to the dying animal or bird and apologise with words to the effect that they were only taking life so that they and their children could live. They would also offer a few drops of blood in thanksgiving to the spirits of the land. They were very sensitive to nature and understood that death was a necessary condition for life and they never killed casually.

This concept is beautifully summarised in the words of an American medicine man or shaman:

"The shaman knows that he is a spirit that seeks a greater spirit. The Great Spirit knows death as Mother Earth knows life. We are all born from the spirit and once we have lived will return to the spirit. The shaman knows that death is the changer. We do not eat live food we kill our animals. If the seed or berry does not die when it is plucked, it will die in the teeth of the stomach. The shaman knows that it is death that furnishes us all with life."

6. WHO WERE INDIA'S 'ORIGINAL' PEOPLE?

There is archaeological evidence to show that the Indian subcontinent had small pockets of proto human habitation about 100,000 years ago and these were followed by people with several different racial origins. The first were probably the proto Austroloid people who may have come from Southeast Asia and the Negrito people who had probably came from Africa. The former had angular features and blackish skin, while the latter were smaller with rounder skulls and finer dark reddish skin. A 25,000-year-old fossil skeleton of an adult Negrito pygmy standing just 30 inches high was found near Baroda in 1935.

Later the Dravidian people seem to have come from West Asia after 3,000 BC followed by Caucasian people from the North-West in a series of waves from 1,700 BC right up to about the 6th century

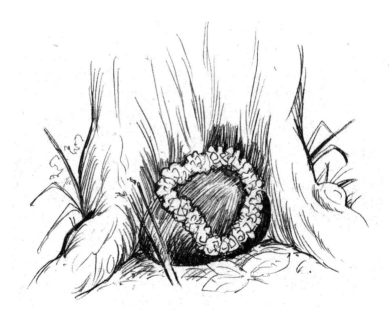

AD. There were also Mongoloid people who infiltrated in from the North-East. There were also the descendants of Egyptian and Arab traders who navigated the oceans long before the advent of Islam.

The Afghans, Turks and Mongols entered after the 8th century AD. There were no national boundaries so people moved freely to trade or to go wherever better food could be obtained or cultivated. The people of the Indian subcontinent are, therefore, the proud inheritors of many different racial strains.

7. Was Skin Colour Just An Accident Of Geography Or Was There Some Social Significance?

People who lived in the tropics gradually developed dark skin pigmentation with melanin to protect them from the harmful effects of the sun. Ultraviolet rays damage and age the skin and white people living in the tropics consequently have a high tendency to skin cancer. It is postulated that the people of the colder latitudes had grown coats of thick hair during the long last Ice Age and that the skin under it had become fair like the skin under the fur of a dog or a bear. When this body hair diminished as the climate warmed up it took a very long time before skin pigmentation could change.

Skin colour was primarily protective and should have had no social significance. But the lowly cultivators and craftsmen who worked in the sun were naturally temporarily darker than the kings, courtiers, courtesans and priests who worked in well-shaded palaces or temples. So dark skins became associated with menial work, while light skins were associated with the rich and cultured. These myths about race later encouraged colour discrimination. But if the Aryas were a fair race from a cold region, colour discrimination was probably also deliberately used as a device to try to prevent intermarriage with darker skinned local people.

8. Who Were The Harappans And What Were Their Cities Like?

In 1924 Sir John Marshall stunned the historical world by announcing the discovery of a huge ancient civilisation that no one had ever suspected existed though it had actually been first excavated by an Indian archaeologist Mr. J. M. Bannerjee. There was no record or reference to it in any ancient Sanskrit or other Indian text. In the succeeding years this civilisation was found to cover a staggering 1.5 million sq kms to cover a much greater geographical area than the civilisations of Egypt or Babylon.

There is archaeological evidence of several small pre-Harappan urban settlements dating to before 2,500 BC in the Indian subcontinent. There were several sites near Mohenjodaro and the Bolan pass as well as many in the Indus-Sutlej region along the course of a snow-fed river that may have originally carried the waters of the Yamuna before it changed course and turned East to join the Ganges.

It was an advanced urban culture with quite sophisticated cultivation and new copper weapons that seemed to have arrived suddenly in the Stone Age Indian subcontinent. Definite evidence at Mohenjodaro, Harappa and other sites show that new copper tools and old stone tools were being used simultaneously. This suggests that the newly arrived Harappans and the older indigenous people lived together. They seem to have occupied different parts of the cities. Possibly as the rulers and the ruled.

Their extensive planned cities covering the lower Indus, west Rajasthan and Gujarat introduced a new technology of building with perfectly measured bricks and planned cities with straight roads, drainage and rectangular houses opening into a central court yard. These bricks must have needed a lot of wood to bake them so the region must have been much wetter and more forested than it is today.

These Harappans seem to have been Dravidians who appear to have arrived in India from the West with an advanced urban culture because their urbanisation was far ahead of anything in the country up to this time. Similar seals found in Harappan cities, in Babylon and in ports on the Persian Gulf suggest considerable interaction between them. There is little evidence of pre-urban development at the lower levels of their cities. There is also some evidence that their arrival may have conflicted with the inhabitants of earlier pre-Harappan habitations as some were destroyed by fire. Their script has not been deciphered but their seals and art styles show similarities with those of Sumeria and Babylon with whom they may have had trade relations.

There are remains of 481 urban sites in Pakistan and 175 in India along the course of the proto - Saraswati that was close to the present seasonal river the Ghaggar in India and Hakra in Pakistan. Most of these are dated to a period after the main Harappan cities on the Indus. This culture was contemporary to the Harappan cities. Most of the structures were made from sun-baked bricks. Their pottery and seals indicate a mingling of cultures at a later period.

The Harappan civilisation only lasted a thousand years and the cities went into decline about 1,500 BC probably because of climatic changes that made the area too dry to sustain such a large population and tectonic changes that may have changed the course of the rivers. This period also corresponds with the probable arrival in India of a people who called themselves Aryas but there is no empirical evidence of any conflict between them. There is only one site showing dead bodies and signs of destruction. Some verses on the Rigveda speak of Indra being the destroyer of 'Puras' or cities including a city with 100 columns but this is insufficient evidence to support theories of a so-called Aryan invasion.

The main reason for the decline of their civilisation seems to have been insufficient water in the rivers to sustain their big urban settlements. Scattered groups of Harappans appear to have then moved South and East to wetter areas and their movements can be roughly traced from the dating of their distinctive red ware pottery at many sites where they settled. Ancient Indian cities never again achieved this level of sophistication in city planning.

9. Why was there no Bronze Age in India?

The implements and weapons found in most Harappan settlements were mostly made of copper. Though a few bronze tools and weapons have been found at the more recent levels of Harappan sites, there was no tin in India necessary to alloy it with copper to make the much harder bronze. Egypt, Babylon and ancient Greece had bronze. China had excellent cast bronzes dating back to 3,500 BC.

After the Harappan culture collapsed, India went into a long period of urban decline and it took many centuries for a new pattern of urbanisation to develop. When iron began to gain importance after 1,000 BC, most Indian cultures seem to have gone straight from the Stone Age to the Iron Age. The abundant surface mined iron ore resources in Bihar and Karnataka quickly led to the exploration of these areas and spurred the urban development of these previously heavily forested areas. In 1,000 BC India was an exporter of iron to West Asia. Bronze much later become an important metal for statues, bells and utensils.

10. WHAT WERE INDIA'S EARLY RELIGIOUS PRACTICES?

There are many scattered cave paintings of people, monkeys, snakes, birds and animals and a few stone objects. There is however, no evidence that these had ever been objects of worship. Elaborate burial sites in many parts of India, especially in South India, some with large stone megaliths, suggest that the rites of the dead were very different to the rituals practised today. The burial pits in many parts of India suggest that ancestor worship, as in many other early cultures, was probable.

Though there is one little seal at Mohenjodaro with a figure, similar to the god Shiv, in the form that he is presently worshipped,

A Seal from Mohenjodaro

surrounded by animals there is no indication of their religious practices. Like most of the other seals it may have only been a trader's seal. If there had been any religious significance, more such seals and idols would have been probable.

The pre-Vedic seal of a deity surrounded by animals is very similar to the present image of the god Shiv but this deity of animals is found in many other cultures as well including Cyrannus in pagan Europe except that the former has the horns of a buffalo instead of a crown of antlers. The large tank at Mohenjodaro may have been a sacred tank similar to the sacred tanks of Babylon. The tradition of sacred tanks in South Indian temples could also reflect such a Dravidian tradition but there is no proof.

European Pagan Deity Cyrannus

Anthropological studies among primitive people in many countries show many common trends. A prime example is the harvest celebrations corresponding to the changing seasons each spring and autumn. The worship of male and female fertility stones is another common trend. The belief in spirits that inhabited every mountain, rock, stream and tree that had to be given sacrifices or small offerings of food and flowers was also widely practised among all tribal people.

The earliest kings and priests were often people who claimed to have the magical ability to influence rain, health, good hunting and food while banishing droughts, pestilences and dangerous animals. In frenzied dance they would be believed to be possessed by spirits and could acquire the power to influence them. They all followed elaborate customs, rituals and sang hymns for their subjects and blamed some lapse on the part of their audiences as the cause for their occasional failure to produce miracles. Shamans who failed were often mocked and replaced by another candidate who seemed to possess greater magical power.

While the word Shaman is today widely used to describe the witch doctors, medicine men and others who presided at pagan religious ceremonies, the word was widely used by early Buddhists and is derived from the Sanskrit word Shramana or the Pali word Samana that mean a person who is very diligent about fulfilling religious duties.

There is no evidence that any of the heroes of legend could have had their legendary horses, glittering palaces, magnificent temples, etc., as depicted in the legends uttered or written about in later times. People led hard and dangerous lives in the pursuit of bare existence and it is unlikely that they had any organised religion or deep philosophy 3,000 years ago. Religions needed professional priests who only emerged when civilisations had reached a stage of maturity.

11. WERE THERE SIMILAR OLD RELIGIOUS TRADITIONS IN OTHER CULTURES?

Among primitive people, the physical world and the spirit world were believed to flow into each other. It was a great cosmic community of one's own people. Some who were living, many who had gone before and others who were still to come. Almost all the ancient legends of primitive people in Asia, Africa, Australia and the Americas speak of three worlds. The underworld from where man had originated from and was destined to "go back within". The terrestrial world where they lived their brief mortal lives and finally the world of the sky, which was the abode of the gods. These became enormously elaborated when a class of professional priests developed rituals, philosophies and myths that developed with economic and social progress in every culture.

People considered themselves as trespassers into a land of the spirits who ruled every mountain, stream, tree or material feature. They would offer small libations of flowers, food and the blood of their kills to placate them and prevent them from causing harm. This reverence to the surrounding spirits is beautifully described in the appeal of the American Indian chief Suquamish of Seattle to the US Government in 1851 protesting against their demand to sell their ancestral land. He said:

'How can you buy or sell the warmth of the land? If we do not own the freshness of the air or the sparkle of the water how can you buy them? We are part of the earth and it is part of us. So when the Great Chief in Washington sends word that he wishes to buy our land he asks much of us. For the land is sacred to us. This shining water that moves in the streams and rivers is the blood of our ancestors.'

It was very much later that man dared to imagine a heaven for human souls in this sky world that earlier had been thought to belong exclusively to the gods. There is an eloquent rendering of the Australian aboriginals' song of creation that is as lofty and beautiful as any in the Old Testament or the Vedas.

In the beginning the earth was an infinite and murky plain, separated from the sky and the grey salt sea and smothered in a shadowy twilight.

There was neither the sun nor moon nor stars. Yet, far away, lived the sky-dwellers: Youthful, indifferent beings, human in form but with the feet of emus, their golden hair glittering like spiders webs in the sunset, ageless and unaging, having existed forever in their green, well-watered paradise beyond the western clouds.

On the surface of the earth, the only features were some hollows that would one day be waterholes. There were no animals nor plants, yet clustered around the waterholes were pulpy masses of matter: lumps of primordial soup. Soundless, sightless, unbreathing, unawake and unsleeping... each containing the essence of life, or the possibility of becoming human.

On the morning of the first day, the sun felt the urge to be born. It burst through the surface, flooding the land with golden light and warming the hollows under which each ancestor slept.

Amazingly, despite vast distances in geography and time, the hymns to creation of the Baiga tribals of central India are remarkably similar:

In the beginning there was nothing but water, water, water. There was no voice of Deo (God), no voice of Bhut (ghosts), no wind, no rocks, no paths, no jungle. As the sky is now, so was water then. On a great lotus leaf that drifted here and there, sat Bhagavan (the ultimate cosmic spirit). There was no fruit or flower to his life. He was alone. One day he rubbed his arm and with the rubbings made a crow. He called his daughter Karicag told her to go and find some earth. He said, I am lonely. I want to make the world.

The crow flew and flew and flew till the last breath left its body and it fell with a thud onto the back of Kekramal Chattri (great turtle) who was sitting in the water with one arm on the bottom of the ocean and the other reaching to the sky. He said that they would have to find Ginch Raja (a worm at the bottom of the ocean) who had swallowed the earth. After a struggle they caught the sleeping worm and the turtle seized him by the neck and began to squeeze.

He vomited out earth twenty-one times in lumps the size of berries. First mother earth, then yellow earth, black earth, sinful earth, harvest earth, barren earth, earth that shakes... every kind of earth. A young virgin was then called to churn the earth that was then rolled out over the waters like a chapatti (unleavened bread).

The story of creation in the Rigveda has many similar elements: There was no non-existent and no existent at that time.

There was neither mid-space nor the heaven beyond.
What stirred? And in whose control? Was there water?
The abyss was deep.
Neither death nor deathlessness was there then.
There was no sign of night or day.
That One breathed without wind through its independent
power.
There was nothing other than it.
Darkness was there hidden by darkness, in the beginning.
A signless ocean was everywhere.
The potential that was hidden by emptiness - that One was
born by the power of heat.

The thoughts are similar to those in the Genesis of the Old
Testament that says:

In the beginning God created the heaven and the earth.
And the earth was without form, and void;
and the darkness was upon the face of the deep.
And the spirit of God moved upon the face of the waters.
And God said let there be light: and there was light.

All the early songs of creation have many common threads of
timelessness, a primordial soup or sea, the energisation through the
heat or light of the sun, occasional playful distant gods in the sky
and origins in the womb of the earth.

The 'shamans' presiding at religious ceremonies, who could intercede to the gods on behalf of man, were common to all tribal societies. They would get into apoplectic fits and appear to be possessed
by the invoked spirits who would speak through them with strange
voices. They were believed to gain the power to intercede with the
spirits and to give or take their messages to humanity. Their ecstatic
divine dance was expected to avert drought or disaster or provide
warning of impending danger. The 'Tandava' of Shiva, the whirl-
ing Sufi dervishes, even the oracles of Gelupka Tibetan Buddhists
and the 'medicine men' of the American Indian are examples of a
continuing faith in these 'shamanistic' practices.

They also had a major role in removing illnesses, as many believed that diseases were caused by mysterious spirits which had entered their bodies either from the curse, jealousy or ill-will of an enemy or as punishment for some wrong.

Shamans were also required to assure good weather and rain as well as remove evil spirits that had possessed some unfortunate person. They would also try to invoke divine assistance believed to be capable of protecting their friends or harming their enemies. This belief in the magical lasted well into the age of science. Despite the passage of time and the progress of science, 'shamans' as sadhus, fakirs, dervishes, babas, mendicants, etc., have continued to enthral the gullible in many cultures to this day.

The Ice-Age wall paintings in a French cavern at Trois Freres show a masked dancer with an antlered deerskin and a dancer imitating a mammoth whose tusks he imitates with one of his arms. Perhaps this may explain why the dancing Ganesh is also portrayed with only one tusk, as one arm of the dancer would have been needed to represent the much more important elephant trunk. Similarly, the monkey-faced Hanuman, flying through the sky, is depicted carrying a mountain in one hand as he leaps about. The dancing Shiva Nataraj was also probably the vestige of a similar old shamanistic tradition that was later absorbed by Brahmin priests into their evolving religion.

All these spirit deities promoted no philosophy except for seeking boons of power or wealth or for the removal of fears and afflictions of their devotees in exchange for sacrifices and rituals.

Ancestor worship was widespread and often led to the myths of heroes. It probably arose from a respect for the immortal souls of revered elders. People had a natural desire to invoke the blessings and guidance of their ancestors whose spirits were expected to have a continuing interest in the welfare of their progeny. The graves of any person of importance were filled with weapons, clothes, food, and even, occasionally, their wives, slaves, horses, etc., so that he could go back to the community of his own ancestors in a manner befitting his mortal importance. This belief eventually faded in most cultures as they evolved except in China where ancestor worship continues to this day.

As will be explained later, Egypt, arguably the world's oldest civilisation, had an almost morbid fascination with the after life and almost all their great monuments are tributes to their complex rites of the dead. As Egypt influenced other cultures, many of their beliefs and rites became part of other religious traditions.

There were many surprising similarities in the rites for the dead in different cultures. Most believed that the spirits went westwards, following the setting sun, and that the souls of the dead hovered around their bodies for periods of four days and than appeared again on the thirteenth or fortieth or forty-ninth day before finally departing.

The glorious sun had been worshipped by all the old religions. This 'Heliolithic' worship seems to have been widespread from the Druids of Europe, the Etruscans of Italy, to the Minoans and Mycenaeans who were the early inhabitants of Greece, and seems to have been well-entrenched in ancient Egypt, Babylon, Persia and the Indus valley. Perhaps the earliest and most eloquent written tribute to the glories of the sun is an inscription of Akhenaten, Pharaoh of Egypt in the 14th century BC.

Thy dawning is beautiful in the horizon of the sky,
O living Aten, Beginning of life.
When thou riseth in the eastern sky,
Thou fillest every land with thy beauty.
Thou art beautiful, great, glittering, high above the land.
Thy rays encompass the land, even all that thou hast made.
Thou art Re, and though thou carriest them all away captive,
thou bindest them by thy love.
Though thou art on high, thy footprints are the day.
Creator of the germ in woman,
Maker of the seed in man,
Giving life to the son in the body of his mother,
Soothing him that he may not weep,
Nursing even in the womb,
Giver of breath to animate anyone he maketh,
When he cometh forth from the body on the day of his birth.

Nearly a thousand years later, Persia's Zoroastrianism gave sun worship, perhaps its best preserved form and under the power of the great Persian Empire, Mithraism affected many later forms of worship. The worship of a sun god recognised the scientific reality that the sun was the source of all energy and growth, and the most primary of all natural forces. Fire was considered it's symbol as it was fed by the sun's energy stored in fuel wood.

The sun was, however, a constant and predictable sustaining force and never a source of any threat or danger. The unpredictable elements like storms, pestilence or fire were constantly feared and, therefore, received more fervent prayers to avert the possibility of their unpredictable fury. Teshab, the old Babylonian god of thunder was similar to the Etruscan Tinia and the Scandinavian Thor. The Vedic Tvastri, like Thor carried a great axe and forged thunderbolts. Rudra succeeded Indra as the Vedic god of storms.

12. WAS RELIGION JUST A MATTER OF MAGIC AND MIRACLES?

The word magic is derived from the name Magi, the class of priests of ancient Persia. All religions seem to have begun as magic rites that promised miraculous spiritual intervention in the affairs of men.

Primitive people living hard lives in dangerous and unpredictable environments sought miracles, magic and incantations that could give them good weather, hunting, crops, and remove heat, cold, sickness, pests, predators, enemies and evil spirits. They wanted miracles that could bless them and the power to curse their enemies. Shamans or witch doctors, who claimed abilities to provide such magical remedies, were the first priests.

These early faiths and spiritual traditions only became religions after a class of professional priests and monks assumed control of them. These full-time professionals wrote the hymns and scriptures, defined the rituals and chants and regimented the followers long after the founding prophets or sages.

Man, unlike other animals, is a transacting animal constantly exchanging goods and favours with parents and friends from early childhood. But man was also concerned and conscious about the uncertainties of the future in this life and in time beyond. So he needed a God to whom he could offer sacrifices or offerings in exchange for security, prosperity or peace. A concept of God that could enable man to deal with many unanswerable questions. So God may really be a creation of man and his uncertainties. especially among women who were most prone to anxieties in uncertain times.

In later times the priests of all religions used the supposed magic and the supernatural power of their mysterious hymns and magnificent ceremonies in huge sacred temples to awe the masses. These could make people believe that humble obeisance to their deities, kings and priests could secure boons for themselves and protect them from harm. Superstitions soon followed where people were made to believe that specific actions or inactions would attract misfortune through the wrath or disapproval of the gods. Superstitions were very addictive and soon overwhelmed the simple spirituality that was the base of all faiths.

With the maturing of religions came the elaboration of customs including celebrations of events in the supposed lives of the deities who were glorified as super humans with spectacular ceremonies for waking, putting to sleep, weddings and other very human rites of passage. Their idols, temples and treasures became hugely elaborated and people had to pay a huge price in time, effort and tributes to these glorified divinities. So simple faith soon degenerated into mindless religiosity.

When superstitions overwhelmed spirituality, many reformers appalled by the rapid encrustations of myths, superstitions and empty rituals questioned the foundations and started new reforming religions that sought to restore the original simplicity or to devise new philosophies better suited to man's evolving cultural and economic status. Buddha reformed and simplified the excessive Brahmin customs, sacrifices and superstitions. Christ reformed similar excesses of the Jews, Muhammad reformed Arab idolatry, Martin Luther reformed the excesses and indulgences of Roman Catholicism and Guru Nanak and Swami Dayanand reformed the caste and ritual excesses of later Hinduism.

Spirituality was the foundation of all faiths and superstitions were their tombstones.

13. WHAT DOES HINDU LITERATURE TELL US ABOUT INDIA'S ANCIENT HISTORY?

With the severe limitations of writing materials in ancient times, written texts appeared very much later than the original verbal traditions. Curiously, the oldest Indian scripts were almost identical to the Assyrian Mesa inscription of the 7th century BC while some similar to the Northern Semitic alphabet. These scripts first appeared in South Indian scripts presumably because seafaring traders had brought them. These Babylonian alphabets had originally been similar to the pin-shaped impression of a cross-section of cut reed that used to be pressed into tablets of wet clay that was later baked. Still later an iron stylus was used to punch or chisel similar shapes onto copper plates, rock slabs and pillars.

Later still an iron stylus was pressed on to pieces of parchment, bark or palm leaves or stamped onto copper sheets to create a similar 'pin man' impression. But these were slow to produce and very fragile. As they could decompose after a few centuries they had to be rewritten and were sometimes revised. It took almost a thousand years for this script to develop into Brahmi Lipi that later evolved into Ashokan and Gupta Lipi.

The Vedas, like the Zend Avesta of ancient Persia, had originally been written in the Kharoshti script that was written from right to left. This script later evolved into Persian and Arabic. These old texts were the hymns of the nomadic Arya tribe and tell very little about the history of any precise area of India. The oldest Kharoshti manuscript was found near Khotan in China North of Kashmir. The writers of the Ramayana and Mahabharata as well as ancient writers and poets like Kalidas and Kalhan also provide very scrappy details of India's ancient history. The oldest inscription in old Sanskrit was Rudradaman's inscription found at Girnar dated to the 2nd century AD. But Sanskrit was not written in the Devanagri script till much later. It was not the original but probably the fifth script used in India.

It was from Buddhist sources in the Prakrit script that India's early history could be understood because when writing devel-

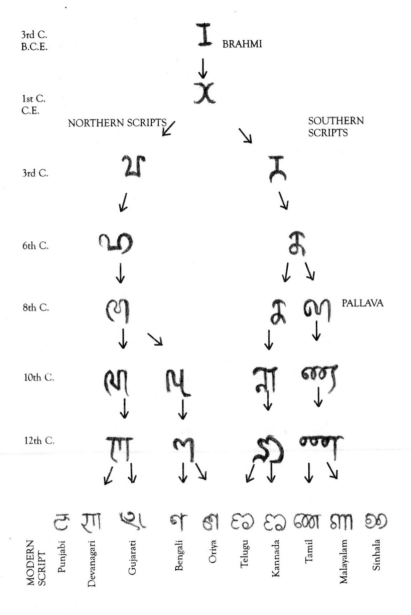

Evolution of Indian Scripts

oped, the Brahmins were a relatively small community in a predominantly Buddhist country for a thousand years from the 4th century BC to the 7th century AD. This is clear from the copper tablets granting land to monks and priests that not a single Brahmin god, temple or sacrifice is even referred to in the period between 300 BC to 100 AD. They only begin to find mention after the Sunga and Gupta periods. Sanskrit texts were transliterated into the Grantha and Nagri 'washing on a line' scripts only in the 7th century AD after which the Brahmin scholars abandoned all the earlier scripts.

The oldest known written tract in India was on the discourses with Buddha called the Silas written about a century after Buddha's death. British Indologists in the 17th and 18th centuries, even with the help of Brahmin scholars, were unable decipher the widely scattered Buddhist inscriptions of Ashoka written in Pali as none of the learned scholars they had consulted knew the old language. In 1837 James Princep, head of the Royal Mint at Calcutta, sent rubbings from Ashokan inscriptions to Burma and Sri Lanka where the Buddhist monks were able to read them immediately. Till that time no one even knew about the existence of Ashoka and the Mauryan Empire. Once the Pali texts were deciphered a huge chapter in India's ancient history opened.

With many Brahmin scholars making notes and commentaries in widely scattered areas the original texts could not always be consistent. In 1,030 AD, the Arab scholar Al Baruni after studying many Sanskrit texts on religion, philosophy, customs, laws, astrology, etc. stated: "The Indian scribes are careless and do not take pains to produce correct and well-collated copies."

14. WERE BRITISH AND EUROPEAN SCHOLARS BIASED?

European historians and anthropologists were fascinated by the history of Greece, Egypt and Babylon and only had a marginal interest in the history of the Indian subcontinent so it cannot be claimed that these mostly amateur scholars were greatly concerned about supporting or denigrating the culture of people in India. In the 18th century most Indians knew very little about this great past and the British were just traders and soldiers. Some scholarly individuals were however curious to unravel the riddles of history. Later, when the British gained power, Indology was often frowned upon.

The discoveries and startling findings of anthropologists and scientists about man's evolution were of universal interest even though they usually conflicted with the views of the clerics of all established religions. Darwin's theory of evolution, conflicting with the account of the Genesis in the Bible, appalled Christians who mocked Darwin for many decades. Muslim and Hindu scholars were equally disturbed by scientific or historical findings that conflicted with the myths found in many of their scriptures.

As there were no widely available books on Hindu religious traditions 300 years ago and most Indian scriptures were unknown except for oral accounts and the palm leaf, parchment, birch bark and copper plate manuscripts in the secret possession of some Brahmin priests. Few Indians today know that even the Rigveda had been virtually unknown until Coeurdeveaux, a French Jesuit missionary, discovered it in Benares in 1767 and had it translated. Similarly the discovery of the Upanishads was mainly owed to Aurangzeb's brother Dara Shikoh who first had them translated into Persian from which it was later translated into French and English before becoming known to Indian audiences.

Many Indologists like Warren Hastings, Sir William Jones, James Princep, Charles Wilkins, H. H. Wilson, Alexander Cunningham, Colonel James Todd, Sir Mortimer Wheeler and others investigated India's history with a sincere passion for unravelling the riddles of India's past.

Their pursuit was, however, mocked and discouraged by many of their British masters especially after the 19th century. Some of their findings and conjectures have had to be revised in the light of later excavations, literature and other new evidence but there is little doubt that their studies and conjectures were sincere efforts to unravel the riddles of India's past. It is chiefly to them that is owed our present-day knowledge of India's huge Mauryan, Buddhist, Harappan and Kushan history and many details of Indian culture including the Rajput traditions of chivalry.

15. WHO WERE THE ARYANS? WERE THEY A RACE, A TRIBE, A LANGUAGE OR JUST AN ADJECTIVE?

It is rather surprising that the origins or movements of races should generate so much religious emotion as the evolution of races should have little to do with religious beliefs. The Rigveda and, the probably older Persian book, the Zend Avesta, describe the adventures and beliefs of a tribe who called themselves Arya. They were one of a number of Indo-European tribes who spoke a language similar to old Persian and old Sanskrit.

Recent historical findings suggest that these people, usually called Indo-Europeans, may have originated from central Turkey about 6,000 BC, where they had developed into successful agriculturists. One branch moved north-west and another north-east. One of their tribes called themselves Arya in both the Zend Avesta and Rigveda. The word Arya is probably derived from the word Ara meaning plough. Later on, the word Aryan simply meant noble.

There is considerable evidence that a number of tribes speaking this old Indo-European language settled in the Caucasian area around the Caspian Sea, south of Russia and streamed southwards in waves between 1,800 and 1,300 BC. Well-documented records in West Asia show that many of their tribes like the Hittites and Kassites entered Turkey and destroyed Syria in 1732 BC. The Mittani attacked Babylon in the same year, while the Hyksos attacked Egypt in 1,730 BC. Their impact was so traumatic that the middle kingdom of the Pharaohs was utterly shattered and the carefully recorded history of the dynasties is blank for over two hundred years. The Dorians and Achaeans, soon after, went to Greece and the Italics to Italy. The Medes went to western Persia.

Their incursions seem to have initially been the peaceful movement of nomadic people with their sheep and cattle into sparsely populated areas where there may not have been any conflict for territory. Later as they gained strength and confidence, they swept through the territories of many great old civilisations.

The secret of the quick conquests of these Indo-European tribes lay in the fact that they were the first people to have domesticated horses. Earlier, horses were only a source of food. Initially their horses, like horses in the wild, were small and could not carry the weight of a mounted soldier. They were, therefore, yoked in pairs to a light bow fronted six-spoked chariot with a charioteer on the right and a warrior armed with a javelin and later a bow standing behind him.

Chariots of the Indo-Europeans

This distinctive chariot was the trademark of all the Indo-European tribes in all the countries that they conquered. The speed and impact of their chariots were fearsome against the donkey and oxen mounted armies of the great older civilisations. In one day they could cover four times the range of donkey or ox carts and their speed and shock terrorised their enemies. The cuneiform records in the clay tablets in West Asia and paintings and sculpture throughout the region give clear evidence of their devastating impact.

According to the early records they were dressed in leather from head to toe and had never tasted fruit. The life philosophy of this masculine race of self-professed warriors was to ride a horse, to speak the truth and to hurl a javelin. Later the bow and arrow was to replace the javelin.

16. WAS THE ZEND AVESTA OLDER THAN THE RIGVEDA?

The names of the gods of the Avesta were just different pronunciations of the Vedic gods Varuna, Mitra and Ahirman but these Avestan gods, or Ahuras, were to become the 'Purvi devtas' or old gods of the Rigveda. The Ahuras, were concerned with order of the universe and they were considered greater than the Daevas who were demonic deities mainly concerned with worldly issues like earth, fire and water. (This word Daeva is, incidentally, the origin of the English word devil).

By the time the Rigveda was composed, Indra had become the ruling deity and one-fourth of the verses of the Rigveda were addressed to him. He also had new companions like Rudra and Nasatyas. The Daevas of Persia seem to have evolved to become the sa-

Migrations of Indo-European tribes

cred Devas in India, while the Ahuras gradually declined to become the Purvi Devtas or Adityas, while still later texts further demoted them to the status of Asuras or evil demons. In both accounts, the early gods were the Dyuloka or gods of the heavens. Antariksha was the god of the atmosphere and Prithvi the god of the earth.

A significant passage in the Zend Avesta describes an earlier period when the Aryas had to leave their ancestral land called 'Aryenem Vaego' (Aryavarta of the Rigveda) Vaego means beeja or seed. So the word Aryavartha actually means seed of the Aryas. It is also significant that the Rigveda makes no mention of tigers, elephants, peacocks and other animals and birds distinctive to India though it does describe those of West Asia. Also significant is the fact that horses, so beloved to the Aryans only appeared in numbers in India after their incursions. There are a few traces of horses in the remains of settlements predating this time but no evidence of their domestication. Actually horses were never very successfully bred in India and were imported from Central Asia and later from Arabia right up to the end of the Mughal period.

17. WHAT IS THE EVIDENCE THAT THE ARYAS CAME FROM CENTRAL ASIA?

According to the Zend Avesta the Arya, tribes had to leave their ancestral land because the power of evil had made their land too cold. Modern science has found, from ice core samples in the Antarctic, a chronicle of climatic changes over the past 50,000 years. This and other geological evidence has confirmed that there had been a mini Ice Age around 1,800 BC.

Both the Zend Avesta and the Rigveda elaborately describe the geography of their ancestral homeland. It was described as 'a land in the North where the year is as a day', perhaps implying an Arctic region. A land with a sacred mountain of Hera Bezera (perhaps the 15,000 ft high Mt Baluka in South Russia) at its centre. The Meru mountains could have been the Pamirs where there are five mountains soaring to over 22,000 feet. Around it were the four seas - perhaps the Caspian, Aral, Black Sea and the Arctic Sea - as well as the three deserts (perhaps the Taklimatan, Dasht-e-lut and Kyzyl Kum into which the river Syr disappears).

The topography of India does not match these nearly identical geographical descriptions in the Avesta and the Rigveda. It is also significant that India's greatest river, the Ganges, is only mentioned once and that too as Ghangyah that could just mean the son of a woman called Ganga.

Most of the artifacts of the Indo-European tribes were made of wood and leather and perished but their distinctive grey ware pottery left clear evidence of their travels that can be fairly accurately dated. A few burial sites in the Caucasus and West Asia also yield evidence of their jewellery, costumes and other artifacts.

An analysis of the evolution of Sanskrit in India also shows that the language acquired many Dravidian and other local loan words over the centuries. If the Aryas had originated in India, as many Hindu chauvinists want to believe, these words and phonetic forms would also have migrated westwards to become a part of old Persian and other successor languages in West Asia and Europe. 'Echo words', similar to colloquial 'contract-shontract', 'aana - jana' are very much an Indian form and are frequently found in Sanskrit but not in any of the other Indo-European languages.

The Jain tradition of gods, demons and sages gaining great power through severe austerities and fasting is deeply imprinted in all India's religious traditions. This widely entrenched mythological tradition would also have been found elsewhere if the Aryans had migrated from India to other lands.

Migrations have always been quests for food or wealth. Nowhere in the world's history has there ever been evidence of people wanting to leave a rich, well-watered and fertile land for the arid semi- desert areas like West Asia or southern Russia. Conversely, the wealth of India, known to the ancient world as the 'land of gold', was a perennial magnet attracting hungry adventurers throughout the ages. There is no evidence of any mass migration from India at any time in history.

There are many tantalising similarities in the accounts of the Rigveda, the Ramayana and the Mahabharata with places and people of the Caucasian region. The Puranas declare that there had been an Uttara (Northern) Kuru and a Dakshina (Southern) Kuru. Most Indians believe that the epic battle of Kurukshetra (meaning battle at Kuru) had been fought near Karnal on India's northern plains. Most Indians are unaware that there is no river called Kuru in India but a river that is still called the Kuru that drains south of Baku, between Azerbaijan and Iran into the Caspian Sea. It .must have been an important river for the great Persian King Cyrus (Kurosh in Persian) was named after it. If the epic battle of the Mahabharata had been fought here, it might have been fairly close in both location and time to the epic Trojan War.

An absolutely definite historic event is the Treaty of Cappadocea in eastern Turkey signed between the Mittani King Mattinuza, son of King Dasratta and King Subiluliuma of the Hittites in 1,380 BC witnessed by their gods Varuna, Mittra and Indra. This King Dasratta was incidentally usurped by one of his sons and killed by another.

Perhaps the most interesting connections are found in the epic Ramayana. According to Valmiki's account, Ram's father Dasrath lived in the heavenly city of Ayodhya on the banks of the river Saryu. This could have also been a river that is still called the Syr Darya that flows through the Farghana valley in present- day Kyrghistan and Uzbekistan. It is north of the Pamirs (Meru) with a city called Andijan or Adhijan (possibly the legendary Ayodhya) as the capital of the area. East of it is Kashi (Kashgar) and west is Markanda (later called Samarkand). Babur was born there and considered it the most beautiful place on earth.

An early account of the Ramayana has it that Dasrath, meaning a small ruler with just ten chariots, met and fell in love with his second wife Kaikeyi when she tended his wounds after a local battle. Kaikeya means that she was the daughter of the king of Kaikay, or Caucasus, like the name Gandhari of the Mahabharata had been derived from Gandhara (Kandahar) where she had come from. As a small ruler he could not offer a big bride price to Kaikei's father but had offered to make the son of their union his successor. Thus Dasrath's agonising dilemma may not have been the demands of a scheming woman but being torn between his love of his son Ram and his moral commitment to fulfil his promise to Kaikeya's father. But if Kaushalya, Dasrath's first wife, came from Kosala, a kingdom in Central India, it would have implied a nearly impossible distance unless there was also a Kosala in ancient central Asia.

The names of the Caspian Sea over the centuries also contain fascinating traces of the origins of many tribes that now inhabit India. At the time of Herodotus in the 6th century BC, it had been called the Vrathian Sea after the Virks, one of the oldest Jat tribes. Later it was called Dadhi Sagar after the Dahae or Dahiyas and still later took the name of another tribe, the Gills and was called the Sea of Gilan. When the ancestors of the Gujjars were dominant, it was called the Badr al Khazar. Though the Gujjars are today considered a rather low tribe of nomads, they too had their days of glory and place names like Georgia and Gujarat honour a formerly great tribe. The Caspian Sea seems to have got its name from the name of a great sage called Caspili who was probably the Kashyap of the Puranas.

18. DID THE MYTHICAL RIVER SARASWATI ACTUALLY EXIST?

There are several possibilities. The Saraswati was the main river of the Rigveda that was described as pure from its source in the mountains till it emptied into the ocean. Today, satellite mapping and hydrological surveys indicate that the snow-fed waters of the Yamuna may not have flowed east past Delhi in ancient times. It may have once run south-west through Kurukshetra, Sirsa and Ratangarh to flow into the bed of the Luni River, South of Jodhpur, to empty into the Arabian Sea. Where it enters the Rann of Kutch it is still called Saraswati. It might have also flowed for some time on a course parallel to the Indus and close to the present Indo-Pakistan border. As there had been a mini Ice Age around 1,800 BC, the cooler climate would have also probably resulted in higher rainfall.

Ruins of many ancient habitations along this route also suggest that there must have once been a large perennial river like the Sutlej or Yamuna to support such large populations. This conclusion is supported by the absence of large cities along the present course of the Yamuna till fairly recent times. Traces of the ancient Pats of the Mahabharata like Indrapat, Bagpat, Tilpat, Sonepat and Panipat show that they had been small habitations at a very early stage of urbanisation. Even in the time of Mahmud of Ghazni, in the 11th century AD, Thanesar was the only city of any consequence

Probable course of the Saraswati

between the cities on the Indus and Mathura on the Jamuna and Kanauj on the Ganga.

It is postulated that seismic activity or siltation may have caused topographical changes to the relatively flat plains at the foot of the Himalayas. This may have caused the Yamuna that earlier probably flowed West into the course of the Ghaggar and Sutlej to shift eastwards past Delhi and flow into the Gangetic basin. Anangpal, the Tomar Rajput ruler built the first city of Delhi, Rai Kila Pitora, only at the end of the 10th century AD.

Without a perennial river the Aravalis were just another set of hills. With the Aravali hills to the South and a great river to the North, the site of Delhi made a perfect defensible position in the northern plains. If the perennial snow-fed Yamuna had flowed here a great city would certainly have been built here much earlier.

There is another possibility. Before the Indus plain, followed by the Sutlej/ Jamuna plain, became the seats of Arya habitation, they may have settled for many centuries in the valleys of present-day Afghanistan. Some evidence suggests that from 1,700-1,400 BC they may have settled in the region of the Halmand (the Avestan Haetumant and Arghandab rivers). The river Saryu is mentioned thrice and could have been the Avestan River Haroyu. Or Saroyu because Avestans always pronounced H as S, as in Hind and Sind or Hoama and Soma. It might have however been the present- day Harirud (Sarirud) river that flows west from central Afghanistan to later mark the Iranian border.

19. HOW WERE THE ARYANS DISCOVERED?

The discovery of the nearly forgotten Rigveda by the French Jesuit priest Father Courdeveaux, at Benares in 1767, followed by studies by dedicated Indologists like Sir William Jones, Charles Wilkins, H. H. Wilson, etc., showing links between Sanskrit and Greek and Latin created great excitement in Europe about their long lost Asiatic cousins.

Sanskrit had much earlier declined to become a nearly forgotten language of the Brahmin priests and their sacred texts like the Vedas and Upanishads were, till quite recently, only known to a very few. So paradoxically it was Western interest that revived an almost lost language and literary tradition. Encouraged by this many Indian scholars soon rushed to glorify the old language and literature as more examples began to surface around the country.

Later Max Mueller, who had never been to India, popularised the romantic vision of Aryans being a tall, blond, blue-eyed super race that so inspired Hitler and the Nazis. The theory appealed to many, especially in Germany, who were happy to discover a non-Hebrew heritage. It also appealed to many Hindus at later times, especially the Brahmins who claimed to be descendants of these noble Aryans. This theory became popular among India's higher castes and provided a racial justification of their superiority over the lower castes.

There were some dissenting views. A few historians have suggested that the Brahmins were originally a group of learned Dravidians who began as translators for the simple nomads and later took over their early religious traditions and, with the power of knowledge and priestly authority, became more Aryan than any Aryan.

It is surprising that the idea of an invasion should so trouble some Indian readers. Invasions, incursions, conquests and wars occurred in every country and in every epoch when people moved from one place to another. The movement from poor to richer areas or the arrival of stronger and more virile people into areas occupied by weak or slothful people was always a shock but they all stimulated change and progress. Wars advanced technology, encouraged trade and made people alert and better disciplined. The mingling of young powerful conquerors with the wiser but weary native people resulted in mutual benefit. The conquerors learned culture and luxury, while the conquered were stimulated to renew their energies.

The well-known conquests of the Greeks, Romans, Huns, Normans, Mongols and others caused no sense of horror among the chroniclers of later times. The conquerors and the conquered quickly adjusted and assimilated. The agony of invasion to Hindu sentiments is unique and seems to arise from a ridiculous idea that polluting foreigners should dare to contaminate a racially pure Aryan race that had been native to this sacred land. This myth does not allow any answer to when the invasions by the dark skinned Negritos, Proto-Australoids, Dravidian or others might have occurred. But to consider Aryans as invaders was quite unacceptable and strenuous efforts were made to distort the facts of history to try to fit them into a predetermined mythical mould.

Many historians with this opinion correctly point out that there is absolutely no hard evidence to show that the Arya tribes invaded India from the North-West. They claim that the Aryans had originated in India and then moved to the North and West taking their language Sanskrit to influence other races. But conversely there is also no evidence of any such westward migration.

The critics correctly point out that there was a large and mature Sindhu-Saraswati civilisation not only in the Indus valley but also in the region between the Sutlej and the Indus that dates back to nearly 3,000 BC, well before the time generally assigned to so-called Aryan invasions at 1,500 - 1,300 BC. The elaborate king lists in the Puranas, Brahmanas and other later texts have been used to try to extrapolate imaginary time frames but these are all highly specula-tive and inconclusive. The interesting accounts of the Bharata War and the Sapta Sindhu do not give any precise historical dates, loca-tions or other material details.

They point out that fire altars found at several sites like Kal-ibangan were similar to those used in Vedic worship. This is inter-esting but not conclusive evidence as fire altars are not uncommon in the rituals of many other people. They also question the link of the horse with the Aryans because the remains of the horse found in Harappan ruins and the clay model of a horse or perhaps a don-key found in Mohenjodaro. These examples are very few and the existence of horses does not prove that they were domesticated to drive the war chariots so feared by the opponents of the Indo-Euro-peans between 1,700 and 1,300 BC.

There is no hard evidence of Harappan collapse at the hands of any Aryan invasion and it is quite evident that the drying up of the old Saraswati or Ghagar/ Hakra river area had caused the end of large urban cities allowing numerous nomadic tribes to drift in to fill the vacuum. Except for one scene of mass slaughter at Mohenjodaro, there is no evidence that the entry of such people was a warlike invasion.

The geography and climate of India seems to have been very different 4,000 years ago. The North-Western area was much wet-ter and so more thickly forested than it is today as is clear from the wood needed to make the burnt bricks of the Harappan cities. The war chariots that the Rigveda so proudly speak about, that had been able to sweep triumphantly over the semi-desert areas of West Asia would have been unable to function in the marshy or thickly for-ested lands of ancient India and soon became items for myth and royal ornamentation. The Rigveda describes how they had to dis-mantle and carry their chariots while following the grassy foothills of the Himalayas as they moved eastwards up to the Kali Gandhak river after which the land was impassable.

They did not have iron till after 1,000 BC so cutting the thick forests was very difficult. Many verses in the Rigveda refer to the need to invoke the fire god Agni to burn a way before them. The account suggests that they had settled for a long time in the Indus-Sutlej region and gradually began to move East and South and merge with the local populations. The quest for the surface deposits of iron in Karnataka may have urged them to go to the South and there is no evidence of Brahmanical influence in the South till about the 2nd century BC.

20. DID THE AVESTANS HAVE CASTES LIKE THE 'VARNAS' OF THE RIGVEDA?

The Avestan priests were called the Arthvan (from the word Arth, thus meaning a person of essence). The Vedic word Brahmin seems to have evolved from it. Their warriors were called Rathesh-war (meaning charioteer from the word Rath, meaning chariot) and this was clearly the origin of the word Kshatriya. Their third caste was called Vastroyosh who were the husbandmen who did all the work and looked after their sheep and cattle. Phonetically, the word sounds rather similar to the Vedic word Vaishya, but they could have had no role as traders till the Aryas settled down from their nomadic ways many centuries later.

The Avestans much later added a fourth class of people who might have been captives, slaves or people picked up on their trav-

els. These being outside the caste hierarchy were called Hutoksha that sounds phonetically similar to the word Shudra, the name later given to the lower castes in India. The Avestans could not pronounce the sound S so Hutoksha would have become Sutoksha in India. The early accounts in both the Avesta and Rigveda speak of only three classes. When they abandoned their nomadic life and settled down to cultivation, the Vaishya became the traders and the Shudras did most of the agricultural and manual work in the fields.

The regimentation of castes into a strict caste system is not based on the Vedas but owes its real origin to Manu's Manusmriti that was probably written about the 3rd century AD and made much more rigorous after the 7th century. As Buddhism was the main religion of India during this period, these works may also reflect a reaction to Buddhist egalitarianism.

Strictly speaking there is only one Veda, the Rigveda. The Samaveda and Yajurveda were basically rearrangements of the hymns of the Rigveda with the addition of Brahmanical instructions for rites and ceremonies, priestly commentaries and additions that were added many centuries later. The Arthaveda came much later. The Brahmin priests later added Brahmanas as manuals of ritual to each Veda, then came the Arayankas and finally the Upanishads, that represented the philosophical core that were probably only composed after the 6th century BC and contained many later philosophies.

All these texts were constantly polished over the centuries. They contain many hymns of immense beauty and universal appeal as well as many that are petty, obscure and nonsensical. Some of the shlokas became part of a constantly evolving Brahmanical tradition while many others were ignored and forgotten. But the Brahmins, probably realising that much of the Veda was often quite nonsensical, tried to forbid non-Brahmins from reading them and also used the complexities of Sanskrit to conjure the most inventive interpretations to explain the many inconstancies. It was the Brahmins who gave these poetic accounts of an originally nomadic people a sacred status. They monopolised the absolute right to control all rites and ceremonies as well as all knowledge and writing.

21. If The Aryas Ate Meat How Did Vegetarianism Become Part Of The Hindu Tradition?

It would have been extremely difficult, in fact almost impossible, to have been a vegetarian in Vedic times anywhere in the world. Almost all the fruits and vegetables, so commonly available today, had not been domesticated and cereals, the only vegetarian food that could be stored to eat at a later time, were very scarce till about 4,000 years ago when they first appeared with the Harappans and then slowly spread to other areas.

Furthermore if the Aryas had been a nomadic people, they would never have stayed long enough at any place to cultivate cereals or any other crops. The wandering tribes would have certainly picked up wild seasonal fruits, vegetables, edible roots and leaves but these were very poor and unpredictable sources of food until they were especially domesticated for higher yields. And they were also usually very scarce in winter and summer. So meat and milk products must have been the main staples of their diets.

The Rigveda, as one of India's earliest texts, gives numerous examples of meat eating with verses giving instructions on how to slaughter, cook, cut and distribute the parts of horses and bulls at their sacrifices. Few people know about the Vedic Gaomeda, or cow sacrifice, was a standard ritual for important sacrifices like the Rajsuya yagna, or that the royal ritual of Ashwameda usually ended with the slaughter of the consecrated stallion and is described in rather gory detail in CLXII- verses 9 to 22 of the Rigveda.

The Rigveda did not give much importance to the cow though the bull and ghee, or clarified butter, were important. Horses were accorded great importance. Even dogs, as in all nomadic societies, were highly regarded. But Indra, the tawny bearded supreme Vedic god was specifically offered the best sides of beef. Only by the most extreme sophistry can the Vedic verses be interpreted to have any meaning other than the eating of beef. Hymns 86, verses 13 and 14 in book X can hardly be more explicit:

"Wealthy Vrasakpayi, blest with sons and consorts of thy sons, Indra will eat thy bulls, thy oblation that affecteth much. Supreme is Indra over all. Fifteen in number, then, for me a score of bullocks they prepare and I devour the fat thereof. They fill my belly full of food. Supreme is Indra over all."

There are frequent examples of meat and beef eating in the Rigveda. At one place Indra states... 'cook me fifteen plus twenty oxen'. Another important Vedic deity is Agni, who is called the protector of all men, and is also described as... 'one whose food is the ox and the barren cow'. The Gopatha Brahmana mentions twenty-one Yajna sacrifices. A bull (vrsabha) was sacrificed to Indra, a dappled cow to the Maruts, and a copper cow to the Ashvins and a cow was also sacrificed to Varuna and Mitra. There are numerous other examples in the Brahmanas, Upanishads and other sacred texts. The Dharmasutras list a number of animals and birds fit to be eaten including the cow. The cow was also the preferred dakshina, or sacrificial fee, to pay to Brahmin priests. When Vishwamitra came to visit Vashishta he ordered his disciples to kill a bull in honour of his guest.

Early Buddhist and Jain texts recount their horror about such extravagant taking of life and the wanton killing of cattle at their sacrifices. Several Vedic texts conversely express indignation at the disturbance of their sacrifices by the local Dasyus. The native Indian humped bull 'Bos Indicus', as portrayed in many Indus seals, may have been a pre-Aryan native object of worship that got absorbed by the evolving religion. The association of the Nandi bull with non-Vedic deity Shiva could be the result of such a pre-Vedic tradition.

But in ancient times, when food sources were scarce, even the Buddhists and Jains sometimes ate meat and even beef if these were placed in their begging bowls. The Samyutta Nikaya tells us that at the time of Buddha's visit to Sravasti, Presanjit the king of Kosala was to sacrifice 500 oxen, 500 male calves, 500 female calves and 500 sheep until dissuaded by Buddha. Jains were generally much more strongly against eating meat but the monastic rules allowed meat eating in extreme circumstances.

In the Upanishads, there is a specific injunction given by the father of the sage Nachiketa that milch cows should not be killed but that the old ones had to be killed. The Traita Brahmana talks of yagnas or sacrifices of bulls and cows. Verse 1-5-14-19 of the Apast-ambhadharma Sutra actually says that the cow is holy and is there-fore to be eaten. The only written prohibitions, concerning beef, to be found in any old text, concerned punishments for the theft of cattle belonging to the king.

Cows, like all female animals, were seldom eaten for the simple rea-son that they gave calves as well as milk while just one bull was enough to service many cows. It is for this reason that almost all meat be it mutton, pork or chicken was usually from well fattened males. Pork was however always of a wild boar as there were no domesticated pigs. There are however several texts in many Indian scriptures stating that barren cows that could not produce calves or milk must be eaten.

Valmiki's Ramayana has many instances of the killing and eat-ing of deer and other animals Sita even offered 100,000 cows and equal jars of wine to feed the Brahmins if the goddess of the Ganga were to bring her husband safely back from exile. It was while Rama went out to kill a deer that Ravan was able to abduct Sita. In the Ma-habharata, 2,000 cows were slaughtered every day in the kitchen of king Rantideva who used to distribute beef and food grains to many Brahmins. According to this text, the Vanaparvan, the river Carama-vati (Chambal) originated from the blood of the slaughtered cows. Draupadi offered Jayadratha and his companions 50 deer to eat.

Manu, in his law book, the Manusmriti says that it is a divine rule to eat meat on sacrificial occasions or while honoring the gods or guests. He attests that... 'animals were created for the sake of sacrifice and that killing for ritual occasions is non-killing because all sacrificial food attain higher levels of existence'.

The eating of beef or meat is also mentioned in ancient medi-cal texts. The treatise of Caraka Samhita, so important in Ayurve-da, lists 28 animals including cows, whose flesh is recommended for the cure of various ailments. It describes the benefits of beef for disorders of wind, catarrh and irregular fever. Caraka specifically recommends a gruel of beef gravy soured with pomegranates as a remedy for fever.

Meat and beef eating is often mentioned in the more recent Puranas. Sangham literature in Tamil Nadu has many instances of meat eating. Thousands of buffaloes were sacrificed every year at the Athanuramman temple in Salem. Similar slaughter used to occur in Kali temples in Bengal, Assam and Orissa.

Tribal, Jain and Buddhist traditions had a deep veneration for all forms of life including bulls and cows long before the Vedic tradition became established. The Brahmins seem to have incorporated this intense Jain and Buddhist aversion to all killing like many other local traditions that later became part of their continuously evolving religious code.

It seems certain that strict prohibitions against meat or beef did not exist anywhere in India till after the end of the Buddhist period. The Chinese travellers Fa-Hsien and Hiuen-Tsang who were in India in the 5th and 7th centuries AD, both comment on many strange taboos, unique to India, especially the Jain influenced prohibitions concerning root vegetables like onions and garlic. Their silence about beef that was widely eaten in China suggests that no taboo had existed at these times.

Jains as staunch vegetarians were especially averse to harming all life forms. They also considered that root vegetables such as garlic, onions, carrots and beets (potatoes only came to India 400 years ago) had several root clusters, to make them individual living organisms. So they forbade eating these, as it would result in taking many lives and of acquiring many more Karmas. They also forbade the eating of cabbages and cauliflowers whose tight leaves could contain hidden insects. As Jains influenced many other sects, their taboos as well as their tradition of austerity, gradually became a part of Hindu belief and customs.

Although almost all the ancient texts endorse or condone the eating of meat and beef this was modified by the Brahmins in more recent times that now ambiguously state the basis of very dubious literary authority that though the eating of beef had been permissible in ancient times it is forbidden in the present times of the Kalyuga.

The aversion to eating beef is much more a matter of local custom than anything that is offensive to the Vedas or other Hindu scriptures. This is evidenced through some Brahmins in the east and southern parts of India having no aversion to eating beef despite otherwise being very diligent in their belief and faith.

Among Hindus the cow only became sacred with the emergence of the Krishna cult in the Hindi-speaking areas of North India after the 12th century AD. Ramanuja began the Vaishnav Bhakti form of devotion but it was Jaideva's Gita Govinda followed by the preaching of Chaitanya (1485 - 1533 AD) that really established the adoration of Krishna with his gopis and cattle. It is not surprising therefore that archeological evidence in Vrindavan, that was the location of so much of the Krishna legend, does not have any structures of any great antiquity.

Because beef was commonly eaten by Muslims, cow protection was to become a political statement during the past 150 years. The first movement to protect the cow was by the Sikh Kuka (Namdhari) sect in 1870. In 1882, Dayanand Saraswati founded the first Gorakshini Sabha and challenged the Muslim practice of beef eating provoking a series of communal riots in the 1880s and 1890s. These were to later encourage further communal clashes where thousands were killed in Azamgarh in 1893, Ayodhya in 1912 and Shahabad in 1917. So eating beef moved from being just a matter of diet to becoming a defining icon of Hindu versus Muslim identity.

Despite strong religious sentiments among most Hindu's about cow slaughter, the practical realities of cattle breeding shows that cow slaughter is commonplace in almost every Indian village. The Government's livestock census of 2003 estimates that India has 285 million, or over 18 per cent of the world's cattle. Milch buffaloes and draught bullocks are important sources of milk, fodder, fuel, income and employment, even if they contribute little in India to meat production so important to the livestock industry worldwide.

This document clearly shows the actual numbers of cattle have been slowly declining and that deliberate culling is very widely practiced throughout India. UP, for example, has 17.7 million female buffaloes compared to just 4.9 million males and 16.9 million cows to 8.2 million bulls. In Andhra, there are 10.6 million female buffaloes but just 1.6 million males and 9.3 million cows to 4.7 million bulls. These statistics clearly show that despite the pious claims cattle slaughter is widespread.

Paradoxically, the keepers of India's cattle themselves perpetuate some of the worst crimes against cattle. Studies in Mumbai and

Delhi show that many thousands of pregnant cows and buffaloes are brought into 'tabelas', or cattle sheds, in the slums of Indian cities. As half the calves they deliver are males, and an economic liability, they are killed as soon as the mother's milk steadies.

22. WAS SANSKRIT THE MOTHER OF ALL LANGUAGES?

Sanskrit may not have been the original language of the Aryas but was nurtured in India as a sacred language of the Brahmins. It was actually the daughter of a still unnamed earlier language very similar to old Persian and old Sanskrit. The oldest Vedic texts were written in the Kharoshti script in which the Zend Avesta was also written. When Cyrus the Great ruled over West Asia in the 6th century BC, Old Persian was the official language of his empire and the script became the script of the Arabs. When the Arabs conquered Persia in the 7th century AD, a simplified script was imposed back on the Persians as the Old Persian script had become over complicated and ornamental over the centuries. So, paradoxically, it came full circle and shows that there is nothing intrinsically Islamic about the Arabic script.

There were many other ancient languages. People of Mongolia of the northern steppes spoke Altaic while the many old languages of Egypt, Babylon, Arabia, Assyria, Africa, Australia, China and the Americas had entirely different origins. As cultures mingled so did the loan words from one language to another. But the presence of many loan words does not mean that they are necessarily related.

The rapid dominance of the Indo-European tribes who spread quickly to Europe and India made their language the root language in these areas. Many of their loan words entered other languages while they too absorbed words from other languages. Old Sanskrit prevailed before 500 BC until the great grammarian Panini seems to have codified it. Modern or classical Sanskrit, as it is known today, only evolved about 400 AD and it was written in Nagri and later Devanagri scripts only after the 7th century AD.

As the Brahmins gained ascendancy, their now sacred language Sanskrit became the most voluminous body of texts and British Indologists understandably believed that they could be the best sources of India's ancient history. It was only later that they discovered that the older Buddhist and Jain texts actually contained much more historical information about ancient India.

The Brahmins had made themselves the self-appointed keepers of all learning and knowledge. They raised both philosophy and many common folk tales to the level of sacred scripture. They also elevated the Arya tradition into which they added many local and non-Vedic deities, philosophies, rites and concepts and gave them sacred status. On their own authority the Brahmins gradually abandoned many Vedic practices like the drinking of the intoxicating Soma and sacrifices of horses and cattle. They also abandoned Vedic gods like Indira, Varuna, Mitra, Rudra and Nasatyas and later elevated many local deities, especially Shiva and also Ganesha, Kubera, Kartikeya and Hanuman, in a constantly evolving religious tradition.

As people who made learning their profession, the Brahmins undoubtedly made a huge contribution to India's vast literary and cultural heritage but they were also dutiful servants of their rulers and compelled the masses to become obedient slaves of their royal masters. They wrote most of India's literature and imbued their works with such sanctity that the works of many mortal writers were raised to scripture to be considered sacred by the masses. Sanskrit, being a very old language, had kept evolving so many words acquired multiple meanings that allowed interpreters to twist them around when they found the texts inconvenient to the beliefs held at a later time.

A symbiotic relationship strengthened many local rulers who in return gave the Brahmins great importance and prestige as their reward. With the rich offerings from them and from their devotees, their magnificent temples, flourishing after the 7th century AD, became rich and opulent and were also the cultural centres of learning, literature, music and dance.

23. Are The Concepts Of Reincarnation, Dharma, Karma And Ahimsa And Deities Like Shiv, Krishna, Ram, Lakshmi, Parvati, Saraswati, And Ganga Found In The Vedas?

The philosophy of the Vedas, evolving from the original Rigveda, being originally the hymns of simple pastoral people, was rather rudimentary and mainly consisted of offering a Yagna, or prayers at a fire sacrifice, to seek boons or blessings. The early Vedas believed in a celestial abode of the gods and has no mention of reincarnation. All religions evolve over time. The Vedas were derived from an oral tradition and written and revised over many centuries. As they evolved, they began incorporating many deeply rooted concepts from indigenous, Jain, Buddhist and tribal philosophies like the concepts of reincarnation, Dharma, Karma and Ahimsa.

There was no trace of any deity resembling Shiv in the Rigveda though the Brahmins later tried to identify this possibly tribal deity with the Vedic Rudra who, known as the howler, actually bore very little resemblance. The only Krishna named in the Rigveda was no god but the leader of the demonic Rakshashas and the armies of dark Dasyus who Indra slew and skinned. The word Rakshasha was probably derived from an indigenous word Raksha, meaning to protect. This implies that the dark and dangerous enemies of the Aryas may have been the gallant protectors of the local inhabitants. The worship of Shiv as Mahadeva only became established by the Gupta period after the 4th century AD.

There is no mention of any hero called Ram or even the river Ganga. Saraswati was no goddess of the Vedas but their sacred river. Actually there were no goddesses among the thirty-three Vedic deities except the very unimportant Usha. The worship of goddesses or Shaktis began very much later when the concept of fertility goddesses associated with mature cultivation developed in very much later times.

Vishnu was a very minor god of the Rigveda and was very different from the great Vishnu of later worship. It was very much later in the Aitreya Brahmana that his image develops and the story of his striding across the sky in three steps emerges. Even Vishnu's epithet of 'Narayana', meaning one who rests upon the waters, was actually the epithet belonging to Varuna the Purvi Devta of the Rigveda. Varuna, like the phonetically similar Greek god Uranus, was the god of the atmosphere.

Although 25 per cent of the verses of the Rigveda were addressed to Indra there was a supreme deity beyond the gods called Daiyus similar to Zeus of the ancient Greeks. The Roman Jupiter was none other than Ju Pita meaning father Zeus.

24. How Can The Worship Of Gods And Goddesses Show The Economic And Social Advancement Of Their Worshippers?

It is difficult to claim any absolute co-relation, but an analysis of religious practices worldwide shows that religious traditions have usually evolved with man's intellectual and socio-economic development. Broadly these stages of religious consciousness usually go into five stages or five levels of religious consciousness:

Fear was a major element in religious consciousness as they developed. Early humans wanted spiritual protection from dangerous animals, sicknesses, pestilences and the many uncertainties of the future both in this life and in the life beyond. Later the priests of all religions used the fear of divine retribution for sins and the fears of the terrors of hell or damnation to keep their followers faithful. When people were fearing they were god-fearing.

Consciousness One: When early man was a timid hunter living in dark and dangerous forests, people believed that every mountain, river, tree, rock or other object contained a spirit like the Jivas of Jain belief. Spirits that were as real to them as the spirit in every living being. Some were benevolent, others evil and they could be male, female or in the form of animals, snakes, birds and beasts. Worshippers would seek the blessings of these spirits with little offerings of food, wild flowers and drops of blood from their kills. These were aimed to appease them to get good hunting or to ward off danger, illness or evil. Cave paintings and small, carved pebbles, stones and bones show many animals and occasional fat female figurines, perhaps fertility goddesses. This has been observed among hunter-gatherers in every land.

Tribal worship had no professional priests but men like African witch doctors, American Indian medicine men or Shamans in many early cultures. They would go into frenzied dance, often under the influence of intoxicants, and speak with the voice of the spirits. They believed that if they correctly observed detailed rituals, they could command the magic of the spirits to avert disasters and gain boons. They believed they could acquire the power to even control

the sun, moon, storms, rain and other elements. Small pockets of hunter-gatherers following such practices still survive in many cultures to this day and traces of their worship continue alongside more mature forms of worship. Even when man began to believe in one supreme God, belief in these spirits of the earth or the atmosphere continued to be respected in the form of goblins, elfs, angels or djinns.

Consciousness Two: When man found that it was easier to survive with captive herds of sheep or cattle than to try to surprise wild ones in the difficult forests, some of them left the woodlands to roam the semi-desert open pastures of the world with their herds. They had to travel long distances from their winter to summer pastures. Theirs was a man's world where they were able to see danger at a distance, and band together within the range of their voices.

They walked tall and proud and worshipped new elemental gods of the sun, moon, stars, wind, storms, thunder, rain and fire.

Their priests were simple poets and bards who originally had a social position below their patriarchal tribe leaders who led them to good pastures or to war. They composed hymns to the elements crucial to the lives they led and sang in praise of their gods and heroes. These songs and hymns contained their history, their objects of love and hate and were verbal expressions of all their aspirations. Even today, nomadic tribes like the Gujjars and Gaddis in India or the Bakhtiaris of Iran or the Tauregs and Masai of Africa still survive in many countries. The Rigveda seems to have been composed by bards at a nomadic stage of their evolution.

Consciousness Three: When people became cultivators they realised that human efforts were less important than the blessings of a good monsoon or flood so they began worshipping the woman as a symbol of fertility and fecundity in the shape of goddesses that now became the embodiments of good fortune. In Egypt, Babylon, India and many other river valley cultures, the worship of goddesses began to be observed at a stage after their cultivation had reached a state of maturity. These goddesses were usually benign but could also be fearsome and vindictive.

The popular image of the goddess Durga, like many goddesses in other lands, only became popular when cultivation reached a stage of maturity. But her depiction as the destroyer of evil in the form of a buffalo is not unique. Mithras, the god of Persians and even the Romans for some time, was depicted similarly killing a bull.

Consciousness Four: When man became a dweller of big urban cities, many thousands of soldiers, priests, artisans, courtiers, scholars, farmers, musicians, dancers, labourers, etc., jostled for position in increasingly densely crowded towns where their noise and disputes were a constant disturbance. So they needed moral or social laws to regulate their chronically unstable behavior.

This was also a time when settled villages began to grow into bigger urban cities where soldiers, priests, craftsmen and courtiers quickly relegated the cultivators to lower social esteem. Taxes from

smaller towns enabled a leisure class of priests, philosophers, scholars and artists to thrive without having to produce anything. Now magnificently robed priests presided in magnificent temples built by mighty kings to glorify themselves and their gods, with elaborate rituals, sacrifices, music, dance, art and literature. Their knowledge of writing, mathematics and astronomy also developed with the cities and gave the priestly classes awesome power to amaze and awe the masses. These joyous, awesome and sometimes depraved pagan gods and goddesses were to be frowned upon and mocked by the priests of the succeeding social religions.

The social religions of Buddhism, Judaism, Christianity and Islam began at the early stages of urbanisation and tried to regulate the human tendency towards strife and disorder even though they were based on beliefs of enlightenment or revelation. The eight-fold path of Buddhism, the Ten Commandments on Christianity and the five pillars of Islam were not as much concerned with Man's relationship with God as with Man's relation with his fellow men. Dharma now concerned what man did or should not do and not with what he was intrinsically. These urban religions later added orders of professional monks and priests dressed in sacred robes. It was only now that faiths became religions.

Believers were captivated not only by the magnificence of the huge religious structures but also by the art and beauty of the adornments, statues and idols as well as the entrancing and uplifting songs, hymns and chants at wonderful ceremonies. As such rituals were wanted at all rites of passage like births, marriages, deaths or the commencement of new buildings or projects, priests and rituals for religious endorsement were always in demand.

They and their places of worship readily incorporated many earlier local faiths into organised religions but they were not the joyous celebrations of paganism. Their faiths usually became more severe and sombre demanding that their followers strictly follow the tenets of their dogma to save themselves from the terrors of hell or a bad incarnation. Through the enlightenment of Buddha, and the revelations of Judaism, Christianity and Islam, the words of mortal men who wrote the scriptures were presented to their followers as the immutable and incontestable words of an omnipotent God.

Now regiments of professional priests and monks conducting religious ceremonies in temples, churches and mosques became socially and politically powerful. Full-time priests could now constantly refine and rewrite old customs into rituals, and old writings into their sacred scriptures and traditions turning them into inflexible dogma. Any deviation to their rules was quickly condemned as heresy with duly prescribed punishments.

Consciousness Five: The fifth level of man's religious consciousness came when people sought a personal contact with their conceptions of a cosmic spirit without temples, churches and mosques and guidance from their priests. They sought to identify themselves with their ideas of a supreme creator with simple spiritual devotion. This was soon seen as a threat to the organised religions. Interestingly, the Gnostic Christians were hated by the orthodox Catholic priests, the priests of Mecca scorned the Muslim Sufis and the orthodox Brahmins similarly despised the Bhakti and Vedantic saints.

Though there may have been five such stages of religious evolution, there was considerable overlapping of the traditions and the dwellers of towns and villages often observed different deities, rituals and beliefs. All religions, therefore, evolved as man developed socially and economically and the appearance of different deities and customs give broad indications about the time of their development. Except in the interpretations of their priests, the traditions of no religion have ever been the fixed or immutable words of any sage or prophet.

Prayers had been part of worship in every stage of religious consciousness. The word prayer is derived from the Latin word 'precarious' meaning 'to obtain by begging'. And though some forms of prayer are the simple adoration of the worshipper's conception of God, prayers in practice have been usually observed as a process of begging the deities for boons or favours. It was usually a ritual of beseeching the divinities for luck, love, fame, fortune, health, children, promotions, etc.

As the priests gained control of religious faiths to create religions they claimed that they were God's representatives on earth and demanded that the offerings and tributes to the gods to be routed through them. They all created fear in worshippers minds that any deviation from the rituals that they prescribed would attract the wrath of the heavens and subdued dissent with beautiful chants, songs and magnificent ceremonies. Buddhist prayer had originally been a simple adoration of Budha with just the entreaty to make oneself strong enough to overcome one's own problems but it soon degenerated into blind worship.

Behind their sacred robes the priests of all religions could with the same dedication seek to deliberately enslave their followers and condition them to surrender their minds, their wealth and even their bodies. These rich tributes and sacrifices gave all places of worship unimagined patronage and power as well as incredible wealth. And, to defend these valuable estates the priests unhesitatingly resorted to hatred, hypocrisy, mockery, sophistry, duplicity and cunning.

An interesting commentary about religious consciousness is the example of Genghis Khan in the 12th century AD who, though tolerant to Buddhism, Christianity and Islam, only believed in the all pervasive Eternal Blue Sky. When he occupied Bukhara, he rode up to the large mosque in the centre of the city and asked if it was the palace of the sultan. When informed that it was the house of God he quietly asked how it was possible for God to be confined in any building. He then asked what the book in the hands of a priest was and was told that it was the words of God. He again asked how the words of God could possibly be confined to any book.

25. WHAT WAS THE IMPACT OF SUFIISM?

The Sufi saints had a especial impact on the Indian subcontinent and helped shape many devotional Bhakti faiths, Sikh philosophies and Islamic thought. They were surprisingly the main contributors in bringing many people willingly into the fold of Islam.

Though Sufis are now considered Muslim, their history goes back to long before Islam. When Alexander conquered Persia the Greeks called Persia the land of Sofie. The word Sufi simply means a length of rough unstitched cloth that was to be their only personal possession. They despised all priests, rituals and places of worship believing that a spark of the divine resided in every human heart. The English words sophist and sophistication are derived from this detached attitude to life. Though many Sufis later gave a deep spiritual depth to Islamic thought they were philosophers and not religious bigots. Not surprisingly, many Sufi shrines are places of worship to people of many faiths.

Sufis, like Christian Gnostics and the Hindu Bhakti mystics all believed in a simple direct worship of god or cosmic spirit without the intermediaries of temples or priests and developed a following in protest against the widespread tyranny of the priesthoods of most religions. They all lived very simple lives and sang joyous hymns to a great cosmic spirit greater than all the gods of religion. They despised the offerings, sacrifices and penances demanded by priests and were therefore predictably mocked and hounded by them as blasphemers, heretics and traitors to their revealed and sacred gods, rituals and traditions.

26. WHAT IS THE HISTORIC BASIS OF THE RAMAYANA?

There must have been some historic core to all mythological epics. Like Homer's account of the Trojan War of ancient Greece, storytellers with the retelling and glorification of many old stories continuously expanded the events of small tribal skirmishes to epic proportions. When Troy was discovered by Schliemann and later dated to 1,180 BC it proved to be very much smaller than the glorious city described in Homer's heroic account written some five hundred years after the event.

The Ramayana is undoubtedly one of the greatest stories ever written and the film Star Wars I is actually a futuristic interpretation of this great tale. There are, however, many different traditions of the story of Ram in India and abroad. The most popular versions of the Ramayana are the accounts written by Valmiki usually dated to about 300 BC but probably only put into writing after 400 AD. In Valmiki's work, Ram was a great mortal hero but no god.

There were several other oral accounts of the great legend before the celebrated version of the robber turned writer, Valmiki. This legend also has many versions and revisions. There is no certainty about whether his account is older than the Mahabharata. As many historians believe that the southern movement of the Aryas only began about 800 BC the events of the Ramayana must have occurred after this date if the events of the myth had occurred in peninsula India.

The Indian legend names a number of places in India like Ayodhya, Chitrakoot, Dandakaranya, Lanka, Panchavati, Videha, Kosala, etc., that have now become an intrinsic part of the Indian legend. There is no empirical historic evidence about the exact location of any of these places. People in all countries have a habit of naming new places after venerated old ones in the places that they had left as evident from the names of many English towns in America, Canada and Australia.

The events of the epic Ramayana may have also occurred in places very far from the boundaries of British India that most Indian's consider as the only India that ever existed. But it is also possible that the events might have occurred in Central Asia where a Syr Darya, phonetically similar to the Saryu, flows through Kirghistan, Turkmenistan and Uzbekistan.

The possibly older Buddhist Jataka tales, however, have a completely different story of Ram who they believe to have been an earlier incarnation of Buddha. The story of Ram is also a part of the equally ancient Jain tradition where they believe that a noble Jaina like Ravana could not have been an eater of human flesh or a drinker of blood. Theirs is a tale of tragedy of a great and noble person undone by his unrequited love of Ram's wife Sita. Another spin to this story is the tradition that Sita was actually Ravana's daughter who he had been forced to abandon. She rose from the earth under Janak's plough, and at the end of the epic, returns to the soil. In many versions of the Ramayana, Sita was Ram's sister and not his wife.

According to Jain tradition, Ram, as an evolved soul, was not capable of taking life, even that of Ravana, and that it was his brother Lakshman who kills his enemies. When Ravana hurls his ultimate weapon the discus, or Chakra, it tamely returns to Lakshman's hand and becomes the instrument of Ravana's death. As a result, Lakshman goes to hell, while Ram finds release (Kaivalya).

In Sri Lanka, the myth of the Ramayana is told in reverse with Ravana portrayed as the great hero and Ram as his evil, blue faced, invading adversary from the North. There are many different versions of the great epic in Bali, Cambodia, Vietnam and Thailand. In the latter, Hanuman is a paragon of loyalty but not of virtue being a playful seducer of women.

There is no historical proof to substantiate any of these legends but Ram was the hero of one of the world's great myths. Many scholars believe that the internal literary evidence suggests that the first and last book of the present-day versions were interpolated at a much later date. Valmiki's Ram was a very human hero but the later glorifications gave him the attributes of a god. Actually he was only raised to being an incarnation of Vishnu in recent times especially after Tulsidas wrote the Ramacharitramanas. Goswami Tulsidas (1,534 to 1,623 AD) who had lived at the present-day city of Ayodhya wrote this lyrical work whose colourful and evocative poetry fired the imaginations of people and uplifted a badly bruised Hindu pride. This occurred in the late Mughal period and at time when very few Hindus had any knowledge of, or belief in, their rich earlier culture and craved for an authentic Hindu hero.

The present-day city of Ayodhya used to be called Oudh at the time of Buddha who lived most of his life in the region close to it. He spent 25 years teaching at Savatthi that is located just 58 kms north on the Rapti river. So many Buddhist pilgrims including Fa Hsien and Hsuen Tsang frequently visited the area in the 4th and 7th centuries AD. These accounts detail the many Buddhist monasteries as well as the numerous Viharas of the Brahmin heretics. But of Ram we hear no word except for a place called Ramagram on the little Gandhak river not far away. If Tulsidas had not lived at Ayodhya, the legend of Ram's birthplace may have been identified elsewhere. Lal Krishan Advani's exhortation, at the time of the Babri Masjid demolition, that Hindu sentiment was more important than history is not tenable. How can the sentiments of any one religion be appeased at the cost of the sentiments of all the others? If every religion and race pleaded for the unattainable on grounds of sentiment nothing would be spared.

Only after the Ramacharitramanas was Ram raised to the status of a god throughout North India. As a god, Ram was now worshipped, like Christ in the Christian fashion, as a living, feeling, compassionate and almost human deity with compassion for his devotees and not as just an abstract idol in stone.

In the intervening period, many interpolations were also added to the story. The story of Sita's banishment may not have existed in the original version but may have been added much later. Indian women have been made to suffer for centuries following this cruel and chauvinist example. Scenes from the Ramayana were popularised through miniature painting, first introduced to the courts of Indian rulers by the Persians from where it spread to many lesser courts. Later much more sophisticated European painting techniques were added that enabled artists to emotionally portray many scenes from this great story and add to its popularity. Devotional music with songs of adoration by many pious singers made the worship even more emotive.

27. Was Ram The Epitome Of Honour And Nobility And Ramrajya The Ideal Society?

Ram was portrayed as the epitome of honour in terms of the rather patriarchal values of the time that the Brahmin scribes at later times wished to project. Valmiki's account of the reunion of

Ram and Sita after his defeat of Ravana, however, leaves readers in no doubt that his Endeavour was not a romantic quest to regain his beloved wife but was primarily aimed to redeem the grave insult to his personal honour after the abduction of his wife.

Instead of warmly welcoming back his long lost love, he receives her in an offhand way that suggests suspicions about her chastity and conduct while in Ravana's captivity. He then callously banishes this loyal and loving wife, even in her pregnancy, despite her earnest endeavour to try to prove her innocence through a trial by fire that she herself had proposed.

There are also feminine versions of the great legend sung by local women in Andhra, Bengal, Karnataka and many other parts of India where his chauvinistic values are mocked. These folk versions contain songs with feminine themes extolling issues like Kaushalya's pregnancy, Ram's birth, Sita's puberty, wedding and pregnancy and Ravana's sister Surpanakha's revenge that take a higher place than the heroic victories of the men in the legend.

There are similarly several non-Brahmin versions sung by lower castes that have a completely different focus. They mock Ram's treacherous killing of Bali from behind and his killing of Sambukha simply because he was a Shudra who dared to perform austerities. Brahmins have defended this offensive action with an obscure myth that these austerities had caused a Brahmin boy to become sick. E. V. Ramaswamy, in 1956 collected extensive literary data to show that Ram was weak, vain, indecisive and fickle while it was Ravana who was truly noble. But unlike folk tales in other countries, the Brahmin priests and scribes made the Ramayana into a powerful religious and social statement to define individual and group values.

28. What Is The Historic Basis Of The Mahabharata?

The Mahabharata is undoubtedly one of the greatest epics ever written detailing a long tale of courage, betrayal, cowardice, joy, tragedy, romance, developing almost all human emotion and moral values. It compares with the Greek Iliad but there is no way in which the dates and sites of the events can be accurately determined.

But the Mahabharata is not the oldest legend because the father of almost all legends is the very much older Babylonian legend of Gilgamesh that is the probable source of many later legends like the story of the deluge and the forbidden fruit. The first recorded version of this is a cuneiform inscription on a black rock that is dated to 1800 BC.

The time and place of the events of the epic Mahabharata are uncertain and there are numerous local traditions. The inhabitants of the remote Jaunsar Bewar area North West of Mussourie in Garhwal believe that the Kauravas were their ancestors and they still worship Duryodhana in a number of temples dedicated to him in every village. Many other areas in India also have numerous myths concerning local sites supposedly visited by the heroes of the great legend. If the Pandavas had actually visited all the places that people believe they had been to, it would have entailed many lifetimes of travel and not just 14 years of exile.

Paradoxically all the Mahabharata sites have yielded evidence of human occupation but that nothing has ever been found at any of the sites named in the Ramayana. This strongly suggests that the Mahabharata was actually based on events that might have occurred in India but that the Ramayana could have either been purely a fable or else that it was a record of events had occurred at other places, perhaps even in the Caucasus region. On the basis of excavations most archaeologists believe that the Mahabharata sites can be dated to around 1,000 BC but no reliable date can be given to the Ramayana but internal evidence suggests that it probably belonged to an earlier period.

29. WHAT WAS THE INFLUENCE OF BUDDHISM ON INDIAN THOUGHT?

After the mysterious Ashokan inscriptions were finally deciphered in 1837, an awareness of India's thousand-year-long Buddhist history became known for the first time and from these Pali sources it was possible to reconstruct the facts about the early history of India about which Sanskrit literary sources shed almost no light.

Buddhism held sway over most parts of India for over a thousand years from the time of Ashoka in the 3rd century BC till after the time of Harsha in the 7th century AD and influenced many philosophical ideas in all later Indian religions. Though it may have initially been a revolt against the oppressive Brahmin practices especially their lavish sacrifices of horses and bulls, it propagated the concepts of Karma, Dharma, Ahimsa and reincarnation that were to later became intrinsic parts of Hindu philosophy especially through the Upanishads written long after the original Vedas.

Buddhism was a joyous religion that introduced the idea of compassion to the religious world. A concept that may have also influenced Christianity, as joy and love were concepts alien to the rather austere Judaist tradition that Jesus had declared was his mission to reform. During his many years in the wilderness, he might have traveled to India and been influenced by it. Many believe that he had lived in Kashmir that was Buddhist at this time. He might even be buried in Kashmir for there is an old grave and a well-maintained tomb at a place called Rosabal outside Srinagar that is still venerated because Jesus is also revered as an important Muslim saint.

Buddhism preached that hatred can never be appeased by hatred but only by love. It asserted that the only lasting victories were the conquests of the heart because victories on the battlefield only caused the defeated to lie down in sorrow waiting for revenge making future peace impossible.

Significantly Buddhists and Jains were not, strictly speaking, religions as they did not believe in a supreme creator but that every man and woman would get the rewards and punishments for their good and bad actions in this life and in future incarnations. When their souls evolved they could achieve Nirvana or a breathless, soundless, inert nothingness.

Buddhism was also more a philosophy than a religion because it did not originally concern itself with metaphysical or other worldly matters. It's monks were scholars rather than priests and, at later times, many Buddhists even recruited Brahmin priests to perform their rites of birth, marriage and death.

Buddhism was a simple and practical philosophy for life and social cooperation.

The four cardinal virtues of Buddhism were:
1. Friendliness to all
2. Joy
3. Compassion
4. Equanimity

These were so simple and clear that there was little scope for interpretation. Friendliness to all meant a positive, open and trusting relationship with all people. Joy demanded that everything in life was done with total heartfelt commitment. Compassion was not pity but a big hand that could grasp the fist of another's anger, jealousy or greed and bring it down to a state of harmony and balance. With these achieved the fourth level of equanimity, or being undisturbed by good or bad events, was possible

The four cardinal vices of Buddhism were:
1. Injury to life.
2. False speech.
3. Taking what is not given.
4. Base conduct in physical relations.

These four sins allowed very little latitude. Injury to life not only meant killing but also inflicting pain and even injury by wounding words. The injunction against false speech was very difficult because it excluded white lies and half-truths. Taking what was not given, even if it was, for example, a property owned under law, attracted the sorrow of an evicted tenant. All these sins were believed to generate Karmas that weighed upon the soul and chained the individual in a continuing cycle of rebirth.

Later Buddha's 'Laws' were elaborated with ten obligations, the eight-fold path, five precepts, and many others that, like the ten commandments of the Jews, were a long list of Do's and Don'ts. But this tradition of social and moral precepts was new to the religious traditions in India where to 'Be' had been considered more important then to 'Do'.

Buddhists did not originally worship God, or a supreme cosmic spirit, to overcome their problems but looked to the Bud-

Ashoka's Empire

dha to give them the inspiration to achieve their goals. Buddhist prayer had usually been an entreaty to make oneself strong enough to overcome one's own problems and emphasised the importance of helping others instead of seeking divine favours for oneself. In the beginning there were no statues of Buddha. Later, however, worshippers began to worship representations of his feet and it was only after the Greek satraps at Gandhara and Taxila that beautiful statues of Buddha began to be worshipped.

Interestingly the name Taxila was derived from the words Taksha Shila, a place where according to Buddhist legend, Buddha, in an earlier incarnation, when he was a Bodhisattva, sacrificed his head.

In the later period, after the 3rd century AD, the simple purity of Hinayana (lesser vehicle) Buddhism became corrupted by a huge multiplicity of supernatural deities, Bodhisatvas, rich temples, elaborate ceremonies and the metaphysics of Mahayana (greater vehicle) that had borrowed many elements from competing Brahmanical traditions.

Fa Hsien in the 4th century and Hiuen-Tsang in the 7th century write about the pomp and ceremony of Mahayana Buddhist celebrations at many places during their long visits to India. Fa Hsien's account, for example, describes huge processions of deities at Pataliputra, six centuries after Ashoka, with twenty big floats over 22 feet high covered with colourful silks with the images of numerous Hindu gods and Bodhisatvas. At the corner of each float were niches with statues of Buddhas surrounded by Bodhisatvas and all the gods. These were dragged through the streets crowded with rejoicing worshippers casting flowers before them. The Brahmins may have been particularly offended with the portrayal of their gods as being subservient to Buddha.

Superstition and ritual had by now overwhelmed the simple spirituality of the early Buddhist belief and practice. This eventually led to its downfall when Shankaracharya, in the 8th century AD, propounded the inventive interpretation that Buddha was not a rival divinity but just another incarnation of an even greater Vishnu. Thus Buddhists were soon embraced into the ever-encompassing arms of Brahmanism.

30. HOW DID JAINISM INFLUENCE HINDUISM?

The influence of Jainism was no less significant. Mahavira, the 24th and last of the Jain Tirtankhas, like Buddha, was a prince and lived in roughly the same time and the same locations and had fairly similar traditions. As the scriptures of both Buddhists and Jains were written many centuries after the founders, some historians speculate that Gautama and Mahavira may have actually been the same person. Jainism was, however, much more rigorous in its prohibitions about killing and infused a reverence for severe austerities and fasting that was to later influence all Indian religions.

Like Buddhists, Jains did not believe in God or a great cosmic creator. They worshipped their Tirtankhas, or ford crossers, who were guides to help others to cross the great river between life and death. They were role models as Jinas or moral warriors and as examples to emulate.

The Jains propounded the idea that there was a 'Jiva' or living subject residing inside the heart of every object, including inanimate objects, like a stone, or a hill. The number of senses they possessed ranked the Jivas. A stone could only feel and not cry out if it was carelessly kicked. Plants had a stronger sense of feeling and some sense of smell. A worm had the sense of touch and taste but could not see. Animals could feel, hear, smell, taste and see. Men and angels also had the sixth sense of intuition.

The Jains believed that injury to the Jivas produced a Karma that forced one back into a cycle of rebirth and the extent of karmic injury was proportionate to the number of senses affected. Thus kicking a stone caused a single injury while killing a human did injury to six senses. This mainly accounts for the Jain aversion to root vegetables as every onion, carrot or garlic had root clusters that were each regarded as a number of individual living things.

Apart from killing, they believed that harsh words, disrespect, anger and greed also injured one's karma. One could not rid oneself of the accumulations of Karma with Punya or good deeds but only through austerities. So Ahimsa (non-killing), Satya (truth) Asteya (not-stealing), Brahmacharya (celibacy and abstinence from adultery) and Aparigarha (limiting possessions) were regarded as Karma reducing. A great virtue was made of 'walking out of life' by voluntarily starving oneself to death.

Like all religions, Jainism, Buddhism and nascent Hinduism borrowed from each other. And like them all Jainism also gradually lost its early simplicity and innocence and became cluttered with a huge baggage of myths, rituals and superstitions.

31. WAS THE INDUSTRY AND COMMERCE ENCOURAGED BY BUDDHISM AND JAINISM THE REAL BASIS OF INDIA'S GREATNESS?

Buddhism, as well as Jainism actively promoted by commercial guilds encouraged industry and commerce that the Brahmins despised as 'arth', or earthly, and thus impure and undesirable. It was actually this trade and commerce of the Buddhist era that contributed to so much of the greatness of ancient India. Many of their monasteries and viharas show that they were deliberately located at trade centres especially on the trade routes to distant markets.

After the sudden decline of Buddhism after the 8th century, many Buddhists gradually drifted towards a low superstition- riddled Hinduism and may have brought their own icons like Ganesha and Lakshmi into the Hindu fold. The earliest representation of Lakshmi is a statue carved on the Toranas or gateposts of the Buddhist Sanchi Stupa dating to the 2nd century BC that much predate any Hindu representation.

It is postulated that these late period Buddhists may have been the ancestors of the Bania, Chettiar and other trading communities who were unknown to history before the time of Harsha. It is also postulated that the festival of Diwali, dedicated to Lakshmi, may have originally been a Bania festival while Dussehra was a Kshatriya festival and Holi a tribal or low caste festival.

Industry, trade and commerce unfortunately, leaves behind little evidence in history but the temples, palaces, sculptures, arts, literature and other examples of cultural achievement survive for future generations to admire. Industry and commerce that enriched the mass of the people were the real foundations of all great empires of the world while the arts and culture that flourished during the dying periods, were their tombstones.

But it has to be said that culture was also the lifeblood of every race and when it was destroyed, as the Spanish had so ruthlessly done in Central America, people lost all pride in their old traditions and became utterly rootless and lost.

The historical importance of industry and commerce is illustrated by the example of the Mongols. Though Genghis Khan created the largest empire of history in just 25 years, it created no great buildings or culture but it was their encouragement of industry and trade and the transmission of technologies from China to the west over the next two centuries that created the lasting importance of the Mongol empire and even simulated the renaissance of Europe.

World history clearly shows that progress and prosperity thrived at times when countries threw open their doors to new people and ideas and withered when the doors were closed for racial, religious or other reasons. When Indian orthodoxy had barred Indians to travel to polluted foreign lands it made the country vulnerable to foreign domination. The same had been the experience of Muslim countries before and after the 13th century, ancient Egypt, medieval China and Japan till the Meiji revolution. Now paradoxically numerous young Indians who are flourishing with new technologies in foreign lands are leading the country to a new era of prosperity.

32. WAS THE MAURYAN EMPIRE INDIA'S FIRST ORGANISED STATE?

It was the first Indian Empire after the long forgotten Harappan civilisation uniting a number of large urban cities of North central India after the gradual collapse of the Harappan civilisation some 1200 years earlier. Though the Mauryan empire lasted just 238 years from 323 to 185 BC it was to profoundly influence India's future.

The founder of the empire, Chandragupta Maurya had probably never met Alexander who did not enter the geographical area of present-day India. The furthest eastern extent of his daring foray was up to the Sutlej in present-day Pakistan from where he traveled down the Indus to the sea for his return to Babylon.

After cementing a matrimonial alliance with Alexander's successor, the Greek satrap Seleucus Nikator, Chandragupta Maurya created the first true empire in India with his capital at Pataliputra in Bihar. As an important Greek princess could only have married a person of high status like Chandragupta or his son Bimbisara, there is the interesting possibility that the great king Ashok might have been part Greek.

For a long time Ashoka's identity could not be determined from his numerous and far-flung inscriptions on pillars and rock edicts because he had called himself Piyadasi meaning the beloved of the gods. Later when British indologists were able to decipher the Pali translations and compare them with the surviving quotations from Megasthenes' account called Indica, scholars were able to piece together details about the empire. Later Kautilya's Arthashastra was found to provide further elaboration.

The wealth of the Mauryan Empire was sustained by land taxes and by extensive trade through a series of imperial roads surfaced with earth covered logs to provide a firm surface in all weathers. One was the Uttarapatha going northwest through the Ganges basin to Afghanistan while the Dakshinapatha opened the south-western trade routes to the Narmada valley, the ports of the Arabian Sea and later down the Godavari River to the East coast. Massive clearing of forests also brought in revenue from people who were settled on them.

Perhaps influenced by his Brahmin chief minister Chanakya, or Kautilya, the empire forged a new political system of subsidiary alliances with numerous vassal kingdoms or Samanthas. These were regularised to bring in rich tributes at great state ceremonies. Strict surveillance and an elaborate spy system kept them in line. Many temples, with loyal Brahmin priests posted in them, were erected in the territories of adjoining rulers who spied for the empire and contributed to Mauryan suzerainty.

This strongly centralised command and control system integrating large territories and many different races marked a departure from the numerous independent tribes and small city kingdoms or republics relying on the voluntary participation of individuals that had earlier prevailed in India.

The Mauryas were evidently casteless because the inhabitants of India had no caste at all till the Brahmins enrolled them into a caste system that they later created and managed. There is no record of the Mauryas ever being made Kshatriyas though the practice of ceremoniously raising petty warlords to rulers was widespread in ancient times. The Brahmin priests gained great power by legitimising the position of almost any robber baron who had seized power.

Though the Brahmins were always Brahmin, caste codification really began after the Manusmriti in the 4th century AD.

The Brahmins performed magnificent ceremonies and sacrifices like the Ashwameda, where a sanctified horse was allowed to roam freely daring any neighbouring ruler to stop it. Thus confirming the primacy of the horse's owner. But the most important were the elaborate rites and sacrifices for kingship. The Rajasuya yagnas were magnificent coronation ceremonies that legitimised a ruler's worldly power. The Brahmins also raised the new kings to a virtually divine status including alleged descent from mythical deities of the sun or the moon.

These ceremonies were to make the Brahmins very much sought after by rulers throughout India for thousands of years. They were even sought by the kings in the countries of Southeast Asia to raise almost any ruler's status and power to nearly divine levels. In return, Brahmins gained huge prestige as well as power and worldly goods. The new sovereigns now elevated to the caste of Kshatriya, predictably endowed many lands and temples for them in gratitude.

Throughout India's history, the Brahmins faithfully served their rulers by subjugating the tribals and lower castes and making them obedient slaves to the higher castes. This was a symbiotic relationship where the rulers gave patronage while the priests tamed the masses making them docile and obedient subjects. The two places of importance in any ancient city were the fort or palace of the ruler and the temple of the priests.

Evidence from all over the country clearly shows that the earlier sedimentary kinship ties with voluntary participation were insufficient to make people work hard enough or fight hard enough to create the surplus that the state needed. India's magnificent temples, palaces, art and culture were the products of a surplus created by the sweat, tears and blood of people mainly enslaved by a merciless caste system. The extensive Brahma Danas, or land grants, to Brahmins throughout India over the centuries give clear evidence of this widespread symbiotic relationship between the Brahmins and the rulers.

Many rulers throughout India's history were thus legitimised and elevated to the class of Kshatriyas. Even Shivaji, the great Maratha warrior of the 17th century, was thus raised to Kshatriya status. The local Brahmins had refused to perform the ceremony for a Bhonsle belonging to a casteless agriculturist community that they scorned. So some obliging Brahmins, imported from the Sisodias of Udaipur, were persuaded to perform the coronation ceremony in 1674. This elevation changed the nature of Shivaji's struggle that began to be more than just a political rebellion against an oppressive Mughal Empire. They later gained added strength by proclaiming his endeavour as a fight for Hindus against Muslim rule.

33. WAS RELIGION THEN THE CREATION OF PRIESTS AND RULERS? WHAT ABOUT THE SAGES AND PROPHETS?

Tribal faiths only became religions after regiments of professional priests or monks elaborated spiritual traditions and organised them into well-defined rituals, scriptures and dogmas that they managed.

There were generally five main creators of all religions:
First came the **founding sages** or **prophets** who sometimes through a vision, dream, revelation or enlightenment gained a new insight into harmony or truth. They all lived simple lives and wanted no idols, temples or places of worship. They were simple people who loved all humanity and advocated peace.

Second came the **apostles** who spread the word of their sages or prophets. They wrote down and elaborated on the words and philosophies of their founders that later became their religious scriptures. They were the marketing managers of their carefully crafted brands of god and they also provided their religious orders with distinctive costumes, symbols and disciplines. It was Ashoka who made the message of Buddha into a great religion. Peter and Paul raised Christ from a poor Palestinian Jew to a Christian god. It was the first four Khalifs who spread the message of Muhammad from Spain to China in just 60 years. But for the elaborations by the later nine gurus, Nanak would have been just another Indian sage.

Third came the **priests** who were the dedicated soldiers or salesmen of their brands of god. The word priest is used here in the sense of all the professional keepers of religious places and practices. Every religion had different disciplines, traditions and rites of admission. There were many differences between the customs of initiation and practice of Christian priests, Jewish Rabbis, Buddhist monks, Islamic mullas and maulvis, Hindu pundits and purohits, etc.

The message of all the prophets and sages were imbued with joy. But the priests shrewdly understood that hatred was a more powerful uniting factor than love. When people loved together there was always rivalry but that there was always unity when people hated together. Hatred was the core of religious fervour uniting believers against the perceived enemies of every faith. Throughout the world, it was the greed for power and wealth of the rulers instigated by their priests that caused more people to die for religion than from almost any other cause. In more recent times the Nazis, with almost religious zeal, made Jews into hate objects to unite their cadres.

Priests fanned the fears of their followers with dire predictions of suffering in life or after death if their words and rituals were not assiduously followed. So many million priests in every land who contribute nothing to economic or social advancement have all offered peace and salvation from the very fears and anxieties that they helped create.

The priests knew that magnificent temples, magical rites, majestic costumes and ceremonies could awe the masses into becoming hard-working, peaceful and obedient servants of their rulers. The priests of all religions asked their followers to suffer in this life for a future reward in heaven, reincarnation or a Promised Land. It was a case of paying now to fly later.

Fourth came the **patrons**. The rulers and rich merchants rewarded the priests for taming and disciplining the masses. They generously gave the priests magnificent places of worship, glorious or fearsome idols, dazzling clothes and jewellery and lavish land grants with which they could support their places of worship as well as their followers. They also protected the priests from protests by the enslaved masses.

Finally came the ordinary **believers** who accepted their duties to priests and the deities they promoted and made the donations, offerings, sacrifices, pilgrimages and penances as prescribed by the priests that made the places of worship so rich and powerful. Devotees willingly made these sacrifices thinking of them as spiritual insurance policies against the uncertainties of the future both for this life and for the life hereafter.

All the prophets and founding sages wanted people to live with joy, harmony and compassion but the priests and patrons realised that religion had to be a serious business if they were to succeed in enslaving the masses. So all frivolity, intoxication, colour and spontaneity were frowned upon or extinguished. In their hands all the humour and joy went out of the lives of the people they dominated and religion was driven from joyous spirituality to sombre, jealous, superstitious, vengeful and sometimes vulgar religiosity.

34. HOW DID SUPERSTITIONS AND DEVICES TO MITIGATE SINS CREEP INTO RELIGIOUS TRADITIONS?

In all religions, the priestly classes, as devoted merchants of their brands of God, quickly discovered just how vulnerable people were to the very fears and anxieties that they themselves had so assiduously created. Followers of all faiths wanted protection from the many uncertainties of the future in this mortal life as well as in the feared life after death and were therefore happy to make sacrifices, go on pilgrimages offer penances and donate generously. These offerings enriched the priesthoods while assuring the support to their patrons the kings and rich merchants as their followers were soon brain washed into becoming docile and obedient subjects.

Christian priests, for example, fostered the myth that 'Christ had died for our sins' and that the church could forgive all mortal sins provided there was repentance , confessions and penances that were never the requirements of Jesus. Catholic popes, bishops and priests were soon offering 'indulgences' or transactions where they, on their own authority, would guarantee remission of sins or even places in heaven in exchange for generous donations, construction of churches or other good works. These were to became so blatant that they led to the Protestant revolt. Needless to say there were numerous practices that were considered auspicious like touching wood, a symbolic touching of the cross, and others that were considered inauspicious. The sale of amulets, religious icons, etc also provided good business and supporters among all religious orders.

It was substantially the same experience in all religions. The numerous superstitions, rituals and gaudy pageants in Mahayana and Tibetan Buddhism were a wide departure from the very simple early tenets. Brahmin priests quickly seized upon the originally Jain concept of Punya as a ready balm for the Paap or the sins troubling the consciences of their followers. Though Jainism had originally only considered actions that could help or comfort others like providing food, water, shelter, gentle speech as being sin mitigating, the Brahmins quickly defined numerous other good deeds as being capable of diminishing the impact of sins even to the point of assuring spiritual purification. So feeding cows or Brahmins, bathing in the Ganges, being a vegetarian, going to holy places and building new temples were encouraged.

Even more pernicious than the materially useless pilgrimages, donations to Brahmin or the building of ornate temples was a strange practice of punya by proxy. Here the priests allowed donors to 'earn' punya even if the prayers were actually recited by a professional reciter or if a pilgrimage was actually done by a proxy pilgrim who was paid to do the task. Quite recently a new practice has emerged in north India with thousands of 'Kanwarias' taking holy Ganges water to their home towns or villages. These acts of piety are mostly the earning of punya for other people who pay them to do the job.

In this way, all religions soon degenerated into mindless religiosity where the spiritual messages of the prophets or founders were replaced by empty rituals and superstitions. But it was just these colourful practices with bright decorations and sacred music that kept poor and ignorant followers captive to the religions.

35. HOW DID HINDUISM EVOLVE TO BECOME A RELIGION?

Strictly speaking, Hinduism is not a religion. Calling it a way of life is also far too simplistic. Originally the word Hindu was just a geographical expression covering all the people living beyond the River Indus (Sindhu) that had been the 19th province of Cyrus the Great in the 6th century BC. As the Persians could not pronounce the sound S and called it H, the word Sindhu became Hindu. So Hindu was a Persian word and just a geographical expression with no religious significance.

Though the word Hindu had been loosely used by the Mughals and British to describe all the non-Muslim native people of India, the use of the word Hindu to describe a religion is actually owed to the great social reformer Raja Ram Mohan Roy (1772 - 1833) who coined the word in 1826. So Hindu was a 'catch-all' phrase to embrace thousands of local religious traditions worshipping Vishnu, Shiv, Ram, Krishna, Ganesh, Hanuman, Durga, Kali, Lakshmi and a plethora of other local and tribal deities.

So although most of the religious traditions of India had been diligently managed over the millennia by highly dedicated orders of Brahmins, there had been many sages but few individual prophets who had specifically laid down a distinct new philosophy. The religious tradition evolved continuously in response to challenges of economic and social change with many sages and Brahmin writers appearing at intervals to give it new direction.

The Vedas had many beautiful verses that continued to be chanted as well as the worship of fire, veneration of the bull (later the cow) and many other customs. Many of them, including the elaborate ceremonies with an intoxicating Soma, were gradually abandoned.

Vedic worship had no place for deities like Shiv, Ganesh, Lakshmi, Parvati, Saraswati or the concepts of reincarnation or Karma central to Hinduism today. None of the thirty-three gods like Indira, Rudra, Nasatyas or Usha with the solitary exception of Vishnu are worshipped any longer. The Vishnu of the Rigveda was also very different from the Vishnu of present-day worship. Early Hinduism, therefore, had a bloc of Vedic texts without any specific author, prophet or sage. It soon had an army of professional priests and a complex system of rites and rituals. Vedic philosophy was basically a transaction where boons were sought with Vedic prayers at fire sacrifices.

The Brahmin priests made the long secret Vedas the supposed

fountainhead of all religious and spiritual knowledge and custom. By enshrining it and many subsidiary commentaries like the Brahmanas, Arayankas and Upanishads with a cloak of sanctity the priests could claim great divine authority.

The original tribal inhabitants of India, with simple animistic spiritual traditions, that still survive in many hill and tribal areas had these Brahmanical beliefs, rituals and customs thrust on them. When, out of persuasion, superstition or fear, they accepted these beliefs along with the attendant rituals and sacrifices presided over by the Brahmins, they were considered to be Hindu. But the Brahmins readily absorbed many popular local traditions into their constantly evolving religious authority

So essentially, present-day Hinduism can be best described as a religion of the Brahmins, by the Brahmins and for the Brahmins. Though Brahmins today account for about 5.7 per cent of the Indian population, they very successfully persuaded most other groups to follow their practices to the point that many of the lesser castes created by them have tried to ape them in following strictly Brahmin customs and taboos. The Brahmins were pragmatic professionals who readily absorbed all local traditions that they could control and so manage thus Hinduism of today has evolved far beyond the original Vedic beginnings.

36. WHAT WAS THE IMPACT OF ALEXANDER'S INVASION?

Alexander entered the present-day territory of Pakistan in 326 BC. This was the first absolutely accurate and verifiable date in India's long history. His long march of conquest through Syria, Egypt, Iran, Bactria and Afghanistan before India was a daring adventure that fired the imagination of the world for many succeeding generations but few know that his inspiration was Cyrus the Great, the Persian emperor, whose footsteps he followed for much of his epic odyssey.

Alexander's campaign against the king of the Puravas who the Macedonians called Poros was actually a most useless exercise of military ego as he had no interest in conquering the land, looting its treasures or enslaving its people. Nor did his grandiose scheme of reaching the mythical encircling sea, that he believed lay to the South, succeed.

His armies were, however, exhausted and depleted after many years on the march with severe losses through wars and sickness. The thick heavily forested terrain of India, especially with monsoon downpours, was also daunting to armies accustomed to easier travel over the dry semi arid land of west Asia. His Indian adversaries were not organised kingdoms but numerous stubborn independent bands of freewheeling warlike tribes who were a source of constant harassment.

Alexander was severely wounded by a huge arrow that pierced his breastplate while fighting the tribe of the Mallas who inhabited the area between the Indus and west Rajasthan. This wound was probably from the famous Indian seven-foot long bow described in the Greek accounts. It had to be handled by two people and projected a heavy spear like arrow that could penetrate any armour.

His demoralised and depleted soldiers were desperate to get back and were now unable to return the way they had come with many hostile enemies ranged behind them. So they tried to escape through the sparsely inhabited southern route. They went along the thinly populated Baluchi and Persian coast partly by sea and partly by land. But the cruel Makran desert destroyed half the remnants of the once proud army. Sick in body and heart, Alexander died soon afterwards in Babylon. Malaria may also have also been a cause. It was an ignominious end to one of the most daring adventurers in human history.

Alexander's foes were not Indian or Hindu. At that time there were no national boundaries and Buddhism was on the ascent. The many independent tribes of western India do not seem to have had any particular religious conviction at this time. The Greeks raised several temples and statues of their goddess Athena and were interested in local religious practices. These early accounts speak of a Krishna like deity similar to their own Heracles being worshipped. While pockets of Brahmins were known to have been active in almost every area, the numerous Greek accounts do not show that the tribes opposing Alexander were aware of Shiv, Vishnu or any of the deities or customs of present-day Hindu belief.

The Greek impact on the Indian subcontinent was marginal except for the Greek soldiers and their allies from the Caucasian areas who were to later settle in India's north-western region. These Greek satraps, who succeeded Alexander, brought their art and culture and increased the trade links. Then came the arrival of several Sythic tribes who could now easily pass through defeated Persia and were destined to have a great impact on India's future.

There is no evidence in India of stone buildings, pillars or statues before the time of Alexander. Pataliputra, the magnificent Mauryan capital had been made of wood. After the Greek satraps settled in the northwest, they built temples of Apollo and introduced stone carving that they and the Persians had probably learnt earlier from the Egyptians and Babylonians who had earlier built huge pillared colonnades and big statues had been unknown to the western world till the 6th century BC. The Gandhara (Kandahar) art introduced a fusion of Greek style with Indian costumes, features and other stylistic elements. Local craftsmen, however, very quickly mastered the techniques of stone carving many of the early stone buildings in India imitated the traditional patterns of their old wooden structures.

The first Hindu temples of stone in India are only dated to the 5th century AD. The early temples like those at Mahabalipuram, South of Chennai, were carved out of living rock or in caves like Ellora until the South Indian temples introduced pillars and beams with huge temple towers soaring into the skies after the 7th century AD. These were built without any cementing medium like lime mortar that Muslim rulers and their Persian architects introduced to India after the 12th century. These changing building technologies and evolving styles help historians to estimate the dates of many ancient structures.

37. Who Were The Jat Tribes And What Was Their Significance To India?

After Alexander and the Mauryas, western India remained in a state of political instability for a long period of nearly 500 years until the short 147-year Gupta period beginning from 320 AD. Before this the scattered local kingdoms were swamped by many waves of people originating from the Caucasian area bordering the Caspian and Black seas after Alexander defeated the Persian Empire that had earlier blocked their routes to the South.

Many other tribes followed the Parthians and Scythians till the Kushan (Kuie-shang) Empire loosely united many in a vast region from Afghanistan to Varanasi and Malwa from the beginning of the Christian era till about 150 AD. Chinese accounts describe these people as white faced with long noses and thick beards so they may not have had the typically Mongolian features of the people living in these areas today. The description corresponds to a statue of Kanishka in the Mathura museum with a long broadsword. Kanishka was their greatest king and he loosely ruled a huge empire from Central Asia to north-west India. It was from his reign that the Saka era, so important to the Puranas, is said to begin. Most historians date this to 78 AD.

Many such tribes loosely known as Yue-Chi/ Git-ti in China, Jats in India, Jatts/Zotts in Arabia, Djati in Egypt, and Goths/Jutt in Europe poured out of Central Asia. The word Jat only became linked with Indian castes at a much later date.

Jat tribes in 600 BC

About 244 Jat tribes are now known in India. These Jat tribes came in several waves. The oldest tribes were Virk, Dahiya and Kang but many others like Bains, Chauhan, Dhillon, Gill, Maan, Parmar, Rawat, Rathor, Sandhu, Siddhu, Tomar, Tur, etc., can be traced to places of their Caucasian origins as far back as 600 BC. One of their clans, the Hsung-Nu, or the Huns, shook the last of the great Roman and Gupta empires in the 5th century AD.

After the 9th century AD, one of their clans, the Turs, seem to have became the powerful Turranis or Turks who were to later play such an important role in history of India and West Asia. Though most Turs later embraced Islam there were Hindu and Buddhist Turs as well. Most of the Jat clans used to have rather shallow religious traditions and gradually came under the influence of Islam in Central Asia after the 12th century. Genghis Khan (1162 - 1227 AD), from the related Mongol tribes, was no Muslim but a devotee of the great Shaman who worshipped the Eternal Blue Sky and the golden force of the sun. It was only in the time of Timur Lang (1336-1405) that many Jat, especially the Tur tribes became Muslim and the Turks became a powerful force.

These Jats tribes were hardy groups of cultivators and herdsmen, who had very little religious interest and many, to this day, do not subscribe very actively to religious customs or ceremonies. In India, most of their tribes did not come under Brahmin sway and many Jat villages still do not have any temple. They retained many customs completely alien to the Brahmin tradition like the marrying of widows of their brothers, equal sharing of property and total disinterest about caste or religious customs.

Consequently, Brahmin influence has never gained a strong foothold in the Jat-dominated areas and very few old temples were constructed in their territories west of Mathura till recent times.

38. Was The Gupta Empire Really India's Golden Age?

Indian thinkers and historians familiar with a British Empire in India a Mughal one before that and several earlier Turk and Buddhist Empires understandably looked for an equally great Hindu Empire in India's early history. Perhaps something like the glorious

Ramrajya of literature and mythology. As the first Indian Empire, the Mauryan Empire was mainly Buddhist, the Gupta Empire, some 500 years later, seemed to be the most suitable candidate especially as many important Hindu deities first appeared in this early Puranic period. So some historians rather over-enthusiastically proclaimed it as a glorious Hindu empire.

The empire only lasted 147 years from 320 to 467AD. By now advanced cultivation and urbanisation had shifted west from Pataliputra to Benaras and Allahabad up to Mathura. The area west of Mathura including Delhi and Punjab seem to have still been mostly wild and undeveloped.

Within a fairly small core area of this kingdom competing rulers were eliminated. Outside this area the Gupta kings undertook extensive military expeditions but, in the pattern of the Mauryan kings, reinstalled their conquered rulers as their viceroys in Samantas and received tributes as marks of submission. North Indian historians glorify Samudragupta's conquest of the South but this feat was no greater than a seldom remembered conquest of North India by the Chola king Rajendra I in the 11th century.

There is evidence of considerable cultural advancement, better coins and sculpture during this period with the development of many respected guilds (srenis) of bankers, traders, and artisans. Statues of Buddhist, Jain and Hindu deities suggest that Buddhism was still strong though early Hindu deities were beginning to appear.

Before the Gupta period several Brahmin kings, loosely described as the Sungas, had ruled over parts of North India and some of their names are mentioned in the complicated genealogies of the Puranas.

The Chinese traveller Fa Hsien who visited India between 399 and 414 AD reports that that the Gupta Empire was a period of peace and prosperity. At this time Buddhism was the main religion in North India with over 500 sangramas teaching Hinayana doctrines to thousands of monks at each institution.

The Gupta Empire was completely overrun by the Huns by 467 AD and then splintered into many smaller kingdoms. Hiuen-Tsang who visited India 230 years later details the 72 kingdoms that existed in the country at the time though some accepted the temporary suzerainty of greater rulers. These, however, were temporary alliances and no great empire to unite them had yet emerged.

39. What Was India Like At The Time Of Harsha In The 7th Century Ad?

Harshavardhana was just sixteen when he ascended the throne at Kanauj on the Ganges in 606 AD and ruled a large North Indian kingdom from Gujarat to Bengal for 41 years. His benign reign is well known to Indian literature mainly because of the lyrical praise in the works of the poet Bana that is an important part of Sanskrit literature. But it was no Hindu Empire because Harsha was Buddhist.

Harsha was a poet himself and loved philosophy and literature along with great pomp and show. He had a huge train of attendants including Buddhist monks and Brahmin priests. Brahmins were evidently so envious of his patronage of Buddhists that a group attempted to assassinate him and were exiled. When he died without heirs, the empire fell to pieces.

According to Hiuen-Tsang (596 -664 AD), who spent 16 years in India from 629 to 645 AD, there were as many Buddhist monasteries as Hindu temples in his kingdom. Harsha's was not however a period of perfect peace and order. Hiuen-Tsang was twice robbed by bandits and once nearly sacrificed to the goddess Durga by a band of river pirates on the Ganga. At this time it seems that orthodox Brahmin priests did not approve of the worship of Durga and Kali who seem to have then been the deities of robbers and thieves. This tradition continued with the Pindari Thugees even 1200 years later in the British period.

Hiuen-Tsang was not the first Chinese traveller to India. Fa Hsien visited the country between 399 and 414 AD during the Gupta period. A century later came Hoei-Sen and Sung-Yun. What is remarkable about these travelers is that they did not come to India to preach their faith but were sent to learn about Buddha and India's spiritual knowledge to enrich China's own religious tradition. Hiuen-Tsang studied Sanskrit at Nalanda and became so knowledgeable about Brahmin scriptures that he thoroughly defeated a renowned Brahmin scholar in a public debate on spiritual values and the latter, after losing the keenly contested discussion, had to become his disciple.

He incidentally observed that the Hindu tradition of death at Benares being a passage to heaven had, at that time, only applied to Hindus who committed ritual suicide by drowning themselves in the Ganga and reports that 90 per cent of elderly people ended their lives in this manner.

Hiuen-Tsang travelled the entire country in his quest for knowledge and has left a remarkably detailed and generally accurate account of the people, places, rulers and their philosophies. He returned to China with 657 works on Buddhism, many sacred relics and numerous other works on Indian philosophy, mathematics, astronomy, medicine and sciences. These were carefully stored at Xian and were to be one of the most valuable sources of knowledge about this period of Indian history.

Though he was a firm believer in Mahayana Buddhism, he very thoroughly studied Hinayana as well as Vedic and all other Indian Sutras, Shastras and philosophies and recorded their ideas with surprising detachment and objectivity. He remarks on the continued vitality of Buddhism even 1,200 years after Buddha's death and had little inkling that this strongly entrenched religion would collapse in India within a century and become virtually obliterated in the succeeding years.

Hiuen-Tsang's detailed records show accurate descriptions and distances between all the places that he visited. It was the single most important source of information about India in the 7th century. It was from his records that the precise locations of many temples at Bodhgaya, Lumbini and many other places could later be accurately located and excavated.

40. IS PRACTISED HINDUISM THEN MAINLY A RELIGION OF THE PURANAS?

Although the huge mass of 400,000 shlokas, or verses, in the 18 main Puranas are full of contradictions and gigantic exaggerations, the Brahmin priests quoting selectively from them gave them a religious import almost equal to the Vedas. As they were composed in many far-flung areas, they incorporated many local and tribal deities and myths and ideas into their constantly evolving literary tradition.

Vedic hymns and some Vedic concepts and rituals were retained with new rituals for the worship of the new deities and philosophical ideas including an array of animal deities like Ganesh, Hanuman and Garuda. Female deities like Parvati, Lakshmi, and Saraswati and much later Durga and Kali began to gain importance. Many old Vedic deities like Indra, Surya, Yama, Agni, Vayu and Soma were demoted from deities of primary worship to mere mythical characters. They also synthesised many philosophical concepts borrowed from Buddhism, Jainism and other faiths in a continuously evolving religious stream.

Elaborate literary and internal evidence compiled by S. V. Ketkar, shows the Puranas were mainly composed between the 4th and 10th centuries AD. The Brahmin scholars constantly rewrote and embroidered the traditions of the Vedic gods and introduced thousands of entirely new ones whose names are not found in any Veda.

Several beautiful and elevating Vedic hymns were retained in new religious ceremonies but a highly complicated mythological universe with thousands of gods and goddesses replaced the early Vedic deities. The dominant Vedic gods like Indra and Nasatyas vanished from history and were never again worshipped by Hindus.

41. WAS THE VISHNU OF THE PURANAS DIFFERENT FROM VEDIC VISHNU?

Vishnu was a very minor god of the second rank in the Rigveda. The early Vishnu, though a close companion of Indra, only merits six verses out of the thousands of verses of the Rigveda. In the much later Brahmanas, he was given legends and attributes quite unknown to the original Vedas. He gained further popularity and power in the oft rewritten epic Mahabharata. Even his popular epithet Narayana, meaning 'moving upon the waters', was originally a title that belonged to the old Vedic god Varuna who, like Uranus, was the Greek god of the atmosphere. It was only with the Puranas that Vishnu gained pre-eminence over most other deities and first as Vasdeva became Prajapati or creator and the supreme god.

It has to be noted that the Puranas were written well after the Christian age so the Jewish idea of a Messiah, who would appear to save the world, may have only entered into Hindu thought with this influence. The tradition of the ten, sometimes twenty-two, avatars or incarnations of Vishnu who would arrive at times of trouble in different forms was unknown to Indian thought before the Christian communities began to develop in South India.

The early philosophies of Buddhism, Jainism and early Vedic Hinduism from the Vedas till the Upanishads were concerned with Samkhya or an abstract cosmic force. It was much later that the Bhakti cults, based on devotion to God as a person, began to evolve after which a totally new aspect of Vishnu in his various 'avatars' or incarnations became popular. The numerous stories of the many Puranas popularised this process.

42. WAS SHIV ALSO A TRIBAL DEITY RAISED TO A GOD IN THE PURANAS?

Deities like Shiv and several proto Shivas seem to have been objects of tribal worship in many different areas of India before the Brahmins incorporated many local forms of worship and brought them into the fold of their ever expanding religious tradition. An ascetic lord of animals was a common motif of many tribal cultures in many countries and is even found in European Paganism. There were a number of spirit deities including Ganesh, Kubera, Kartikeya, Murugan, etc., who in earlier times were sometimes regarded as companion spirits of Shiv, sometimes as his progeny and later as aspects of his multifaceted power.

Shiv, also called Pashupati or lord of animals, resembles the Harappan seal of an ascetic surrounded by animals but with a new vehicle the Nandi bull. In the present form of his worship, Shiv most resembles the ancient Tamil deity Murugan who many locals in south India still regard as the supreme deity. Murugan's favourite weapon was a Vel or trident that was to also became the symbol of Shiv. However, Murugan, also called Subramanya, had a peacock as his mount. The priests of Murugan, to this day, go into a Shamanistic dance similar to Shiv's Tandava ecstatic dance as depicted in many south Indian statues and bronzes. Shiv was also known as Mahadeva or the supreme deity.

43. Was Ganesh Also A Creation Of The Puranas?

Ganesh is today a beloved elephant-headed deity of almost every Indian home. He is also known as Ganapati, or the master of the many malevolent and mischievous imps and demons. His blessings are, therefore, fervently sought at the beginning of any prayer, journey or enterprise to ensure that the evil power of his many troublesome spirit companions does not interfere with the worship or the efforts of any devotee. The practice is rather like paying spiritual protection money to the boss of a spiritual mafia to ensure that they do not create trouble.

Rock carvings and a small 5th century statue in the Gupta period suggest that an elephant effigy might have once been a tribal deity until it was brought into the fold of the Brahmin faith. The first large stone sculpture showing Vishnu rescuing Prithvi from the underworld is found at the Udaigiri caves near Sanchi and Vidisha. They are dated to the 7th century AD. The first literary reference to Ganesh is in the 8th century Tamil text, the Malatramadhava.

Wider worship began after the 10th century AD. But it was

only in the past century after Lokmanya Gangadhar Tilak, in 1903, taking inspiration from a local a fishing custom that celebrated the end of the monsoons, began the big Ganapati processions to compete with Shia Muslim Muharram processions, that Ganesha gained such widespread popularity.

Early Puranic accounts had Ganesh as the son of Ambica, sister of Rudra. Later he became the son of Parvati, the consort of Shiv. There are more than a dozen contradictory and sometimes obscure myths about his creation though the version in the Matsa Purana is the one that is most widely accepted today.

In the Skanda Purana, Shiv in a moment of generosity had decreed that all worshippers going to the temple of Somnath would get easy access to heaven and this made it crowded with too many undesirables. This provoked Uma's curse that produced an ugly guardian of heaven in the form of Ganesh. This account must have, therefore, been written after the temple of Somnath was established and as this could not have been before the 7th century AD, so the antiquity and authenticity of this, like many Puranic stories, is therefore rather questionable.

In still another Puranic account Parvati worshipped Vishnu seeking a son and Vishnu decided that he would himself become the eagerly awaited baby. When the gods came to congratulate Parvati, Shani (Saturn) lowered his eyes because his jealous wife had cursed him so that anything he looked at would perish. At Parvati's insistence he looked at the baby's head and it flew to the heavens. Parvati then cursed him so he became lame. Vishnu then replaced the missing head with one that he cut off from a sleeping elephant. The Shiv Purana has an even more bizarre account. These stories are all delightful but none should be treated be treated as sacred.

44. WERE THE GODDESSES PARVATI, LAKSHMI, SARASWATI AND DEVI ALSO PRODUCTS OF THE PURANAS?

The worship of female deities only developed from fertility goddesses after cereal cultivation reached a mature phase in different parts of India. There had been a number of benign or fearsome tribal goddesses with many different local names and some were elevated to objects of Brahmin worship. Many were initially espoused to the male gods of earlier worship and later raised to objects of devotion themselves.

The idea gradually developed that male deities were inert, passive and potential, playing the celestial games of the gods and that they needed a female principal to energise them and release their powers to create life. Male deities had usually been distant and abstract while female ones, were not only symbols of female energy, fertility and fecundity but could be objects of love and adoration.

No Devi, or Mahadevi is mentioned in the Vedas but they appear in the much later Mahabharata with a variety of names and rose to great eminence in the Puranas. She was elevated to become the wife of Shiv and daughter of Himavat. She came to acquire two characters both mild and fierce. As Uma or Parvati she was mild but as Bhavani or Durga and later as Kali she was fearsome, destructive and terrifying.

In the Rigveda, the word Lakshmi was just an adjective for good fortune but in the very much later Arthaveda she was personified as a woman of lucky and unlucky character. Still later, Lakshmi and Sri were made the two wives of Aditya. By the time of the Puranas she was elevated as the goddess of good fortune, the daughter of Kama and wife of Vishnu.

In the Rigveda Saraswati was clearly no goddess but an important river "She who goes on pure from the mountains as far as the sea." A river lauded for its fertilising and purifying powers. Her position as Vach or goddess of speech only appears in the Brahmanas and in the Mahabharata still later. By the time of the Puranas she becomes the goddess of learning and a spouse to Brahma, a God who failed to get any great following.

45. WHY IS THERE SUCH VIOLENCE IN PURANIC MYTHS AND HOW HAS THIS AFFECTED INDIA'S FUTURE GENERATIONS?

The Puranas contain a huge baggage of myths and legends. Some were elevating, some amusing, some obscure and many that were very violent. As most of these stories were intended to be recited for the amusement and instruction of listeners the need to exaggerate was understandable. Unfortunately when the Puranas began to be considered as scripture they became very destructive examples to emulate in real life.

The Brahmin authors of the Puranas were very hostile to the gentle concepts of Buddhism and Jainism that had been the ruling religions during the period when the Puranas were written. The Brahmins mocked and challenged all Buddhist or Jain beliefs and undoubtedly hastened the end of Buddhism and put Jainism into decline. Their strong but gentle traditions and their concepts of compassion and understanding faded from popular belief.

This attitude is vividly illustrated by the story of Vena, the righteous and wise ruler of Anga, told in several of the Puranas. Influenced by a Jain teacher he said:

"I follow the true religion. My god is Arhat and I teach the religion of mercy for everyone. I do not believe in useless ceremonies or of reading the Vedas. What purpose do yagnas and sacrifices serve? All that happens is that the Brahmins get a good feast. The religion of the Vedas prescribes the killing of animals, but are not animals living beings as well? What is this Varna system you talk of? A real Brahmin is determined by his actions and not by a mere accident of birth."

According to the Padma Purana, Vena adopted this 'evil religion' and had to suffer terrible indignities and pain for deviating from the "path of righteousness."

The Krishna of the Puranas was very different from the wise and gentle Krishna of the Bhagavad Gita. His violent destruction of Keshi, Kamsa, Poundraka and other demons is described with gleeful detail. Other heroes of the Puranas similarly gloated at the sufferings of their demolished foes. There are many instances of righteous indignation followed by savage destruction in many of the Puranas. Even the meditating sages like Kapila were prone to violent and destructive anger when disturbed.

One of the earliest post-Vedic accounts concerns the athletic hero Parshuram who with his battleaxe and bow is reputed to have led the Arya conquest of the south. He unflinchingly severed his own mother's head at his father Jamadagni's command after the latter felt that his wife Renuka had lost her chastity simply by becoming engrossed in sensual thoughts.

When Kartavirya Arjun stole a magical cow from his father's hermitage Parashuram killed him but the latter's vengeful sons retaliated by killing Jamadagni. The infuriated Parshuram then vowed to clear the earth of Kshatriyas for 21 generations. According to the Harivamsha, the sage Kashyapa then made him vacate the land he had conquered from them. The ocean god Varuna was persuaded to withdraw from the coast creating a long strip of land on India's South West coast where the Brahmins were settled.

With religious endorsement to such barbaric violence, victories were no longer a triumph of ideas and ideals. Violence aided by a multitude of heavenly allies and magical weapons was praised and so encouraged. But such violence and righteous anger was permitted to a Brahmin but to no lesser caste. And the greatest crime for any Hindu was to kill a Brahmin.

The idea of Karma had evolved from Buddhist and Jain roots to later become central to Brahmin philosophy and glorified the actualisation of spiritual potential in every person. But at a common level it also encouraged individualism to the point of stubborn selfishness. The instances of a teenaged boys today throwing acid or kerosene on a girl who rejects their advances shows that the new moral conscience is without any feeling of ethics, compassion or moderation.

Myths of violence were also the probable outcome of frustrations and suppression during many long periods of India's history. It is understandable that at such times, the poor fantasised miraculous remedies for their sorry plight and horrible punishment for their oppressors. India's social tradition made people accept their individual troubles with stoic fortitude but they were quick to anger at any slight to their traditions or community.

While such violence may have been fairly harmless in myth it was to later become explosive in the hands of mobs with brute strength, modern weapons or inflammatory materials. This Puranic tradition of achieving goals through violent action sadly remains an inspiration for many who believe that violent behaviour is condoned by mythological, and thus, religious endorsement. It is perhaps the explanation for the bloody riots that periodically erupt and for the crude and violent means adopted by many as soon as they get into positions of political power.

Today the ordinary Indian cinema, as well as many popular TV serials, unfortunately also imprint many such violent stereotypes onto the minds of India's impressionable and often uneducated masses. Sadly, as the Puranic and earlier myths have become so entangled with popular religiosity, people have tried to ape their mythological heroes. While myths allowed gigantic exaggerations, they were bad examples for real life where, as in physics, every action creates an equal and opposite reaction. The gentle Buddhist concepts of compassion and conquest by love and of seeking win-win situations between adversaries were completely forgotten.

In the periods of India's decline such exaggerations may have been morally intoxicating but in times of India's strength, where mature restraint was needed, they were recipes for trouble. Psychologists know that rage and infuriated action against others is often an infantile response from those who lack the strength, education or confidence to maturely oppose or influence their rivals or adversaries.

The violent destruction of the Babri mosque, the atomic explosions of Pokhran, and the Gujarat riots instead of paving the way for a triumphant Hindu state resulted in a backlash that were setbacks to India as a nation and paradoxically tarnished the BJP as a political force.

46. Was South India The Real Cradle Of Hindu Culture And Philosophy?

Most of North India had been in a state of endemic economic instability and political turmoil for 500 years after the end of the Mauryan Empire and was then overrun by many waves of Scythians (Sakas), Parthians, Kushans and other tribes.

North India then had a brief 147 year Gupta Empire followed by another long politically unstable period of 600 years with the Palas of the East competing with the Gurjara Pratiharas of the North

Prefabricated pillars, beams and panels

and the Rashtrakutas of the South until the Afghan and Turkish invasions in the 12th century AD. During this period, the courts of South India, that was less politically disturbed, quietly grew and flourished with rich trade, cultural achievements with religious and philosophical development.

The early Sangam poetry and anthologies show that the early southern kingdoms were loose federations of a number of scattered tribes in different regions (Tenai). They mainly cooperated through loose kinship ties but they could not provide the devoted servitude and surplus labour necessary to create the great temples and palaces of the future. The enslavement of the masses by the priests for their rulers changed this and the great southern kingdoms could now develop. The kingdoms of the Cholas, Pandyas, Cheras and Pallavas began to emerge after the 4th century AD and steadily grew and expanded till the 12th century. The 9th century saw a frenzy of temple building.

The Brahmins raised many previously casteless South Indian rulers to the status of divine kings and soon enslaved the masses through new bonds of ritual and caste. The kings now gained a large number of docile and industrious workers who produced an agricultural surplus that enriched them and enabled them to have the leisure and surplus to employ artists and sculptors to build their magnificent temples.

A new technology of temple construction also developed. Unlike the earliest Indian shrines in caves or carved out of living rock, a new system of pre-fabricated pillars, beams, supporting brackets and carved panels began to appear after the 7th century that were much easier and quicker to build even though they look as if built as one massive rock structure.

The museum of Mathura clearly shows that the early forms of Hinduism were beginning to compete with the stronger Buddhist and Jain traditions of the area between 200 BC and 600 AD. By the 10th century the Hindu deities had clearly gained the upper hand. By this time, the Brahmins had codified and frozen almost all forms of art into regimented Shastras with the result that creativity became stifled and repetitive even though the culture seemed to have become most prolific.

The southern kingdoms allowed considerable political and intellectual decentralisation and many independent thinkers and philosophers flourished. Notable among them was Shankaracharya (788 to 820 AD) who gave Buddhism a mortal blow by propounding the ingenious idea that Buddha was no religious rival but actually an incarnation of Vishnu and incorporating many Buddhist ideas and concepts within a redefined Shaivite Hinduism. It is quite amazing that in 32 years, or roughly 16 adult years, he wrote as much as would have taken any other mortal six lifetimes and still found time to travel throughout India vigorously challenging Buddhism.

Ramanuja (12th century AD) similarly gave a powerful new focus to a more devotional Vaishnav Hinduism to make it the most widely practised form of Hinduism.

47. WHEN DID KRISHNA AND RAM BECOME OBJECTS OF WORSHIP?

The Krishna of the Rigveda was very different from the revered Krishna of much later worship. He is mentioned as the leader of the dark Dasyus who Indra, the supreme Vedic god, slew and skinned. His tradition seems to have developed over time from early accounts of a tribal leader and developed over time. His literary tradition surfaces in the Mahabharata with Sisupula's diatribe when

Yudishthira makes him chief guest, Draupadi's scornful remarks about his sister Subadhra and references to his dark skin indicates that he was of low caste and of non Arya-stock.

His role at a later time in the Mahabharata as the reciter of the Bhagavad Gita raises him to a much higher status. The grammar and other internal evidence suggest that the Bhagavad Gita was added to the original Mahabharata long after the main story had been written. And, even in this great epic, Krishna in the early part of the narrative is depicted as a crude and destructive person quite unlike the clever and wise Krishna of the Gita.

In Ved Vyasa's Mahabharata, Krishna was never portrayed with greater power than that of any mortal man. In fact, Vyasa even has Krishna mocking the Vedas by saying...

> "Beguilingly flowery is the speech uttered by the foolish who adhere to the doctrines of the Vedas and claim that naught else has verity."

But the later versions laud his miraculous deeds. Krishna then disappeared from the traditions of North India and gained an entirely new legendary life in the prose and poetry of South India and in the works of Haala in the 1st century AD where he first became an object of erotic romance. His story is sketchy and contradictory in the Puranas, but the Harivamsha added an enormous baggage of 18,000 verses of new and mostly erotic material. There is, surprisingly, no mention of Krishna in the Katha Sarita Sagar, the ocean of stories, written at the end of the 10th century AD even though it contains all the main Indian legends up to that time.

Jaydeva's Gita Govinda written in the late 12th century elaborated a tale of Krishna's romantic dalliances with the gopis or cow tending maidens of Vrindavan. It was to quickly capture mass appeal in the declining days of the Mughal Empire by offering a beautiful new object of adoration. The Hindu psyche that had become demoralised after 600 years of Afghan and Mughal dominance now rejoiced with this new icon in the form of a playful, mischievous and wise new deity. But it was only in the 16th century that Chaitanya (1485 to 1533) of Bengal popularised the almost forgotten folk cult of Krishna.

It was only now that the probable influence of Christianity may have entered Hindu iconography with beautiful lifelike statues and colourful paintings in the style of Jesus that were much more emotionally appealing than the lifeless idols to Vishnu, Shiv and other deities.

Like Krishna, Ram was raised from a hero of legend to a deity only in the late Mughal period. Ram, in Valmiki's old epic, was no more than a mortal man but after Goswami Tulsidas (1534-1623) wrote the lyrical Ramachiritramanas depicting a heavenly Ramrajya, he became an object of devoted worship but mainly in North India. It was only from this time that Krishna and Ram began to be worshipped as deities in their own rights.

48. WHAT ABOUT SANATAN DHARMA OR PURE HINDU PHILOSOPHY?

Priests of all faiths are usually bad historians especially if they have fixed ideas or prior commitments to use myths of the past to support their ideas or convictions. No religion can claim to have had an unbroken religious tradition despite the proud claims of their priests and devotees. As religions were created by men they changed constantly with changing social and economic pressures and they all gave and borrowed many philosophies, ideas, customs, rituals and myths from each other. There never was any divine original Sanatan Dharma of an unchangeable, static, pristine purity as some philosophers and many bigots have tried to portray.

A prosperous Gujarati Brahmin, born as Mul Shankar called himself Dayanand Saraswati, and founded the Arya Samaj in 1875. He propounded the idea of an eternal, elevating and nationally integrating Sanatan Dharma. This modern reformer sought to cut the encrustations of ritual, superstition and caste that had accumulated and sought to redirect Hindus to the purity of original Vedic practices. It, however, fell far short of absolutely defining Hinduism that remains a widely varied pluralistic faith practised in many different ways by many Indian communities.

Hinduism was thus an amalgam of many different elements including Vedic texts and commentaries, Jain and Buddhist philosophies, tribal deities of local worship, puranic myths and Bhakti devotionalism. Brahmin priests were, however, a constant factor even though they were open to adapting to diverse local customs and integrating new deities, ideas and rituals as long as these could strengthen their positions.

49. So What Are The Main Hindu Philosophies?

The numerous philosophic and metaphysical speculations of numerous Brahmin sages over the centuries gave Hinduism one of its richest treasures and its greatest claims to fame. To detail these will need several volumes but here is a very brief summary. From the simple sacrifices and entreaties to the many elemental gods seeking boons in the early Vedic hymns, concepts concerning the nature of creation and the soul kept evolving through the Brahmanas and Arayankas and were perhaps best expressed in the 108 Upanishads that probably evolved at about the time of Buddha and Mahavira.

Concepts like Atman, Karma, Samsara, Vaisesika, Sankhya, Yoga and Mimansa were all explored in great detail and crystalised in Vedanta that meant the end of the Vedas.

Sankhya, attributed to the ancient philosopher king sages Kapil and Janak was one of India's earliest philosophies. It believed in a supreme creator but one who did not intervene in human affairs and did not subscribe to the concept of a personal god. It believed that the consequences of good and bad deeds would be felt in one's own lifetime or in the next incarnation. This philosophy was to deeply influence both Buddhism and Jainism.

Shankara (788 -820 AD) rejected the concept Dvaita or a cosmic duality and opted for Advaita or monism or the belief in one sole cosmic creator. This was in many ways a heresy to earlier Hindu thought that had always had a multitude of deities. Shankara was perhaps influenced by the 'One Great God' idea of Judaism and Christianity that had by now reached south Indian shores. He was a brilliant debater who vanquished many intellectuals of the time and composed commentaries on the Brahma Sutras and the main Upanishads to harmonise numerous earlier concepts. He also propounded the novel idea that the material world was

Maya, or an illusion, and that the great impersonal cosmic spirit that also encompassed every individual soul was Brahman, the only reality. As in Christianity, Shankara wanted to establish seats of religious authority and established Dhams or religious seats at Badrinath in the North, Dwarka is the West, Puri in the East and Rameshwaram in the South that continue to be venerated by most Hindus.

Vaishnavism later added Bhakti or more devotional forms of thought and worship. Ramanuja probably from 1017 (or perhaps 1047) to 1137 AD defined the cosmic spirit as a much more personal being full of love for his creations. It was only now that devotion to human deities like Ram and Krishna began to take shape. These concepts were to be best propounded in the Bhagava Gita. In more recent times Bhakti worship was redefined in the even more devotional worship of Krishna and Ram who were regarded as incarnations of Vishnu.

In the Bhagavad Gita, that was essentially a discourse between the hero Arjun and Krishna, and was probably added later into the constantly rewritten accounts of the epic Mahabharata, and was a philosophy for positive action also appeared. The concepts of Satva, Rajas and Tamas now encouraged believers to rise out of their 'tamsic' ways and not become overwhelmed by sorrows or hedonism and to control their destinies by becoming 'rajsic' or positive and even strive to attain a higher 'sattvic' or spiritual plane.

While the basic Vedic rites were yagnas or sacrifices at fire altars, the new devotional faiths worshipped idols, inside which the spirits of the deities were supposed to reside. So puja, or an adoration of the deities with prayers, flowers, music, hymns, rituals, ceremonies and the seeking of boons was now to become the common practice.

But such elevating intellectual philosophies tended to skim over more material issues like social morality and ethics. So high intellectual beliefs did not impact on the consciences of ordinary people. At a common level, the attainment of personal Karma was akin to selfishness. Unlike the moral mindset of Buddhism, there was seldom any feeling of a strong moral outrage or stigma against unethical practices like usury, insult, sexual exploitation, loot, greed, gluttony, sloth or violence.

50. What Is The Importance Of Ayurveda And Yoga?

Every advanced civilisation responded to the numerous health needs of its people with remedies that had evolved as the people developed. In most cultures the priests were important practitioners because patients often wanted their alleged magic and spiritual powers to add to the prescribed tonics, pills and potions. As in many early societies, people believed that illnesses were the result of evil spirits or the curses of enemies that could be blocked by divine power promised by the priests.

Ayurveda, where Ayur means life and Veda means knowledge, is an important school of Indian medicine with one of the richest traditions of herbology but has acquired almost religious sanctity especially among the Brahmins who were the main early practitioners. But the medical traditions of the Chinese, Greeks, Egyptians and other cultures were no less significant.

Over the centuries people, in every country, had observed the ways sick animals had treated their ailments and noted the medicinal properties of many plants as well as how they probably worked on people. The ancient Egyptians have left the most complete record of the early medical practices including an unprecedented knowledge about surgery. Their experience with mummifying corpses was also applied in surgery among the living. They also had a very well-documented record about the medicinal properties of many plants and other substances.

Ayurveda laid down a huge body of texts with knowledge exploring the role of the senses, the physical and mental natures of patients as well as role of elements like space, air, fire, water and earth. It recognised that disease was also influenced by emotional states including fears, anxieties, grief, heredity and many other factors. Ayurveda contained one of the most comprehensive examinations of the properties of thousands of plants and herbs from India's huge treasure house of flora and fauna.

Unani, meaning Greek, medicine is also widely practised on the Indian subcontinent. It had evolved in Baghdad during the time of Haroon Al Rashid in the 8th century. Beginning with the importance of balancing the three, sometimes four, 'humours' or body fluids it also fused many concepts from Egyptian and Jewish medicine until an important hakim or doctor, called Ibn Datt, obviously originating from India, added Ayurvedic herbology.

The Chinese had pioneered acupuncture and acupressure and had once been the world leaders in pharmacology. The Mongols fused these with many other streams of medicine. They exported doctors to the West and Persia and imported Muslim surgeons who were superior in surgery. The Chinese practice of pulse diagnosis became especially popular in Islamic areas as less physical contact was required especially for the treatment of women. It soon became part of other schools of medicine including those in India.

All these schools of alternate medicine were scoffed at when modern medical practices became established. But they remain popular because they believe that health is not achieved just by killing the invading bacteria or virus but that the body as a whole has to stay in balance and harmony with all these invaders. So building resistance and strength is more important than drastic remedies that can also have negative side effects.

Many regimes of exercise were also found to help health, physical development, muscle tone and to reduce aches and pains especially among the older people. The Chinese had Tai Chi that they considered as efficacious as Indians considered yoga. Both had evolved over many centuries to remedy many ailments but the Brahmins made yoga into almost a scripture with near scriptural sanctity.

51. WERE THE RAJPUTS ORIGINALLY HUN OR JAT TRIBES?

The word Rajput is virtually unknown to Indian history or literature till the 7th century AD. It may have been derived from an old Persian word Vishpuhr meaning the son of a king. It is recorded that, in the 7th century, there was a huge fire sacrifice or yagna conducted at Gaumukh near Mount Abu in Rajasthan by a celebrated Brahmin sage who called himself Vishwamitra. (More than thirty other sages had earlier also called themselves Vishwamitra). At this purification ceremony four previously casteless Jat or Hun tribes were raised to the rank of Kshatriya (probably derived from the Avestan word Ratheshwar meaning charioteer) with new genealogical links with mythical ancestors linked to the sun or the moon (Suryavanshi and Chandravanshi). The Huns were not of Mongolian stock and the white Huns were fair, tall and with long noses. These new 'fire born' tribes were elevated to a new caste that people were made to believe were superior to the trading and working classes.

Kshatriyas, who as a caste, had virtually died out during the thousand-year Buddhist period were now virtually reinvented. From now on, the Brahmin priests gradually took complete control of many Jat clans who they raised to a new class of Rajputs and managed their religion and customs. It was a symbiotic relationship that gave the Brahmin priests protection, wealth, power and enormous prestige in exchange for exalted status for Rajputs. The clans to first convert were the Parmars, Parihars, Chauhans and Chalukyas (Chulik/ Sulik). Many other clans soon followed as being a Rajput was so much more respectable than being a casteless local chief.

These new Rajputs soon developed an elaborate new code of chivalry and military pride. They were sometimes called Brahma Kshatras at this time. Many other Jat clans gradually followed their example and were raised one by one to high Kshatriya status. Some other Jat tribes remained unconverted and casteless until some of them adopted Sikhism, which also abhorred the excesses of the Brahmanical caste system and Brahmin religious and social dominance.

52. WERE BUDDHISTS AND JAINS PERSECUTED?

There was a heady period of vigorous Brahmanical revivalism that gathered strength after the 7th century AD. Many local rulers, probably at the goading of their Brahmin ministers and priests, began to ruthlessly exterminate the previously dominant Buddhist and Jain faiths. No doubt the rich lands and treasures of their monasteries and temples also gave material incentives to this new religious fervour and many Buddhist and Jain stupas and monasteries were destroyed and Hindu temples established at their sites. Similar material motives had actuated religious persecutions in many lands including those by the nobles in England during the much more recent period of the Reformation.

Mihirikula, the Hun ruler was converted by Brahmins in 515 AD and soon unleashed a wave of violent destruction on Buddhist monasteries in Punjab and Kashmir. Kalhana's Rajatarangani relates that crows and birds of prey would fly ahead of his armies in anticipation of the slaughter that lay ahead.

Hiuen-Tsang describes the influence of a South Indian Hindu queen on her husband who ordered the execution of many thousand Buddhists including 8,000 in Madurai alone.

Vira Goggi Deva, a South Indian king, described himself as: "A fire to the Jain scriptures, a hunter of wild beasts in the form of the followers of Jina (Jains) and an adept at the demolition of Buddhist canon."

Hired Brahmin killers tried to assassinate the Buddhist ruler Harshavardhana, who ruled in Kanauj from 606 to 647 AD. As a Buddhist, he was unwilling to take life and so banished 500 Brahmins involved in the conspiracy to a remote area South of the Vindhyas.

Graha Varman Maukhari, married to Harsha's sister, was treacherously killed by Sasanka, king of Gauda (Bengal). He also proudly destroyed many stupas and cut down the sacred Bodhi tree at Gaya.

Chandradip, a Buddhist ruler of Kashmir, was killed by Brahmins in 722 AD. His successor Tarapida was killed two years later. The newly anointed Brahma-Kshastra rulers usurped power in the kingdoms of Sind and Kota.

The old tribal shrine at Jaganath Puri was usurped by Vaisnavas and still displays gory murals recording the beheading and massacre of many Buddhists.

The huge Buddhist complex at Nagarjunakonda was destroyed. According to Shankara Dig Vijaya, the newly anointed Brahma-Kshastra kings ordered every Kshatriya to kill every Buddhist young and old and to also kill those who did not kill the Buddhists.

A Jain temple at Huli in Karnataka had a statue of five Jinas (Jain heroes) that was re carved into a Shaivite temple with five lingas. Nepalese and Kumoani documents record that Buddhism had been the prevailing religion of the Himalayas until Shankaracharya deliberately destroyed them in the 8th century. There is no reliable evidence that Shankaracharya actually directed this persecution but what is likely is that grasping local rulers may have used his name to lend legitimacy to their destruction and looting. Many local hill rajas now invited Brahmins to their domains to get themselves elevated to the rank of Kshatriyas. And many were encouraged to attack Buddhist monasteries.

There are records stating that the followers of Buddha were ruthlessly persecuted, slain, exiled and forcibly converted. Though many converted rather than face death, humiliation or exile. It is reported that the attackers tested their faith by making them perform 'Hinsa', or the sacrifice of live animals, that was abhorrent to Buddhists and Jains. Many bhikshunis, or nuns, were forcibly married and the learned Grihasthas were forced to cut off the distinguishing knot of hair on top of their heads. It is on record that 84,000 Buddhist works were searched for and destroyed. The originally Buddhist Himalayan shrines at Badri and Kedar were then converted into shrines of Shiv and Vishnu.

It is believed that Shankara introduced pilgrimages to these holy places in the Himalayas for the first time to prevent their relapse into Buddhist or animist ways that were earlier practised. As sufficient local Brahmins could not be found who were willing to preach in such remote places he imported Nambudri Brahmin priests from Kerala who, to this day, officiate at Badrinath, and Kedarnath.

Later as the mountain settlements grew other Brahmins like the Joshis and Pants from Maharashtra, Gairolas from Bengal and Negis from Gujarat were also invited to settle in the hills. A constant influx of Hindu pilgrims ensured the presence of many traders, priests and rulers who had a vested interest in sustaining the pilgrimages to these sacred spots. So conversions have had a long history in India and are not exclusive to Islam and Christianity.

53. WAS THERE A DARK AGE BETWEEN THE 8TH AND 12TH CENTURIES AD?

Perhaps the impact of the Huns had been as devastating in India as it had been in ancient Rome. For 600 years from the end of the Gupta period till the beginning of Turk rule in India after the 12th century, North India gradually slipped backwards into a muddled anarchy of warring local rulers with some rulers like the Rashtrakutas, Gujara Pratiharas and Palas attempting wider conquests This period is not known for many notable historic personages or events. The area between Mathura and Afghanistan seems to have become a barren and poorly populated tract. Kanauj and numerous other kingdoms flourished further East but, with the exception of Thanesar, the huge area between Mathura and Lahore seems to have become a poor scrub jungle.

Most of the fertile districts of present-day Haryana, Punjab and western UP were barren. They developed much later with irrigation technology introduced by Persian engineers under the Turks and Mughals to irrigate the great river plains of Punjab and the Ganges. Much later there was an even more extensive network of canals created by British engineers.

Land grants to temples became increasingly frequent after the 5th century and many temples and even a few surviving Buddhist monasteries gained control of numerous villages and were given rights to govern and even punish their inhabitants. So rather like the Permanent Settlement in British times, the power of the rulers was delegated and dissipated. Each community around a temple ruled by priests became insular and inward looking. Industry and trade with other towns declined and the great guilds of earlier centuries shrivelled as well as the flourishing earlier trade with Rome, Egypt and China that had made Indian crafts and culture so prolific. This decline is also evident from the reduced number of gold and silver coins that had earlier been necessary for trade and for royal salaries.

By the 8th century the Brahmins had succeeded in gaining complete social supremacy and with the active support of the Kshatriyas or Brahma Kshatras, that they had created, gained a total stranglehold on all learning. This social dominance is evident from the fact that though India is strewn with thousands of magnificent temples there are virtually no palaces until much later times.

It was at this period that the originally egalitarian texts of the Mahabharata and the Gita were corrupted with the Vedic idea of a divine intervention in human affairs and with the god ordained validity of social strata. Devotion, piety, rituals, holy talismans, sacred hymns, reverence of Brahmins and respect for gurus made the Brahmins very powerful. Now the idea of a supernatural, prayer answering, thought reading, sin punishing, divine force captured Indian minds.

According to extensive research by Phulgenda Sinha, R. B. Vaidya and others the original Mahabharata had 8,800 verses and had been called Jaya. It was now expanded to the Jayabharata with 24,000 verses and finally to the present Mahabharata with 100,000 verses. The original Gita with 84 verses was now expanded to 800. Even Yoga was corrupted. Patanjali's original text had 83 very practical Sutras. It was now enlarged with the addition of 112 new ones to make it an almost religious text.

Apart from Shankaracharya there was also Kulluka at this time who enlarged the Manusmriti to make the caste system so rigid and unforgiving. Now all forms of creativity were frozen into a series of rigid Shastras. All art, sculpture, music and literature were locked into ritualistic, repetitive and lifeless forms. The guilds of artisans and craftsmen who had been so honoured in earlier times were now reduced to the position of low caste workmen.

After the 8th century many huge temples dedicated to Shiv and Vishnu had began to spread North, East and West modelled on the fine examples from South India. By the 11th century there were many magnificent new temples in Maharashtra, Madhya Pradesh, Gujarat, Rajasthan, Orissa, Bihar and Uttar Pradesh. The great temples of Somnath, Kanauj and Mathura were to become especially famous. At this stage the Brahmins were content to condemn the non-Hindu tribals to a contemptuous low caste status. It was only in recent times when low caste votes began to be politically important that they began an evangelical drive to enrol them as Hindus.

By the 8th century religion, with its magnificent religious structures, had triumphed over commerce and human creativity. This was the real face of the Dark Age in the six hundred years between the great Gupta Empire and the Afghan and Mughal Kingdoms.

Temples rapidly became centres of great wealth enriched by the generous offerings of their millions of devotees. It was these spectacular riches in jewels and precious metals so conveniently found at one place, and not the wealth of the land, that attracted robber warlords like Mahmud of Ghazni.

Now there was blind worship and undiscriminating awe. The past became sacred and all that it produced, good and bad, was reverenced alike. Slavish imitation was inculcated as duty while novelty and originality became crimes.

54. ARE THE BHILS, GONDS AND OTHER TRIBALS REALLY HINDU?

The tribal inhabitants of the forested hills and plains had cultures that almost certainly predated the Brahmins. They worshipped spirits believed to reside in mountains, rivers, trees and other physical phenomena. They had many tribal gods and did not subscribe to the worship of Shiv, Vishnu or any other deity of the Hindu pantheon.

The tribals, like tribals everywhere in the world, were animists living dangerous lives in the forests. They were simple and superstitious and prey to many uncertainties. They had their own deities but welcomed all gods that might benefit them so they would not remove any idol thrust into their shrines by wandering Brahmin priests or sadhus for fear of offending these deities and inviting their wrath.

They were India's earliest people and were casteless animists and not Hindu as they worshipped no Brahmanical gods, observed

Duryodhana temple at Gangaur

A neglected little Shiv temple at Gangaur

no Brahmanical rites and had no Brahmin priests. They did not also subscribe to Vedic deities, rituals and prayers. With the opening up of tribal areas, Hindu farmers and traders, followed by their priests, soon entered and introduced their deities and tried to impose their beliefs, customs on the simple tribals who they usually looked down upon as dark, dirty and unevolved.

No forest shrine had any full-time priest so they were easy targets for Brahmins and many local babas that could get easy livelihoods from the offerings of devotees. Many such forest shrines that were considered to have miraculous powers attracted many devotees and were often taken over by wandering Hindu priests whose Hindu idols were often placed beside the original deities. They gradually became places of Hindu worship with Brahmins presiding over the rituals. Under the influence of visitors, films, TV and education, many of these tribals began to adopt Hindu customs in a casual way but most continued to retain their old deities and their carefree animistic ways. At Gangaur, a remote village near Har Ki Dun in northwest Garhwal, for example, the old tribal influence still remains strong and Duryodhana, the old Kaurava hero is still the presiding deity at many village temples.

An interesting detail in Akbar's celebrated land records shows that all lands were classified as Muslim, Hindu and non-Hindu. The large last category had a few Buddhists or Jains but many more who, as tribals, had not yet come within the fold of Hinduism five hundred years ago.

The Dalits and other Scheduled Castes may, therefore, have a valid point in stating that they are not Hindu at all. If this definition is applied, the number of Hindus, or Hindus subscribing to Brahmanical deities and rites, in India may not be 80 per cent of the population but probably around 50 per cent.

No old sage, prophet, philosopher or scripture required or created India's temples. They were all funded by royal or merchant patrons and were the creations of the Brahmin priests for legitimising their claims to divine power.

55. WERE THE EARLY INDIAN TEMPLES REALLY HINDU?

About 2,200 years ago Kautilya's Arthashastra writes of temples, manned by Brahmin priests to act as spies, being placed in the territories of their tributary vassals. These were made of wood and have all perished. Even the deities of worship are not clearly known. After the arrival of the Greeks, Buddhist monasteries and stupas in stone appeared followed by Jain and Hindu temples in stone as well.

There had been many local shrines for the worship of local spirits called by many local names like Bhumi Devta, Jal Devta, Same, Golu Maharaj, etc. Temples with resident priests or monks were to come much later. Some of the popular tribal places of worship were occupied by Brahmin priests and turned into Hindu temples. The famous Meenakshi temple at Madurai is, for example, still ruled by the ancient fish-eyed tribal goddess except for a brief period every year when she is ceremonially married to Shiv.

The even older temple of Chidambaram has a similar history. Many other temples like the temple of Jagannath at Puri in Orissa, Venkatashwar at Tirupati in Andhra or Vaishno Devi near Jammu had originally been shrines of local tribal deities till they were taken over by Brahmin priests. Though Vaishno Devi attracts millions of devotees today, it finds no mention in ancient literary sources though local priests try to convince devotees about various obscure ancient traditions. Some goddesses like Santoshi Ma were almost unheard of till popularised by a Hindi film.

56. How Did The Chains Of India's Caste System Evolve?

There is just one small reference to Varnas in the Rigveda and no evidence of immutable caste barriers in early Indian religious literature. The concept was to develop and gain strength very much later with the Puranas composed between the 4th to the 10th century AD. Manu (who has been dated to a period between 227 and 320 AD) wrote the Manusmriti but it was the commentary by Kulluka in the 7th century AD that was to make it so oppressive.

No great antiquity or religious sanctity can, therefore, be claimed for the deeply rooted caste system but it suited the higher castes to exploit it to the hilt. There soon developed elaborate lists of over 3,000 castes and sub castes. New concepts about pure and impure food, customs, marriage rites including the duties to Brahmins were defined with precisely detailed punishments for defying any of them.

One of Manu's injunctions states:

"No collection of wealth should be allowed by a low caste Shudra for it would give pain to a Brahmin and make him (the Shudra) arrogant and disrespectful."

This oft-repeated passage gave moral sanction for the continuous persecution of the lower classes and the enrichment of the Brahmins for untold generations. The upper castes believed that their better destiny was their just reward for good deeds in earlier lives and they persuaded the unfortunate lower castes to believe that they deserved their miserable lives as the fit punishments for sins in their previous incarnations.

The caste system was held together by strong interlocking concepts of pollution and the idea that a lower caste was dirty and disgusting proved far stronger than any logic. The carefree noble savages of the forests were not only considered inferior but were made to believe that they really were stupid, dirty and unevolved and people who could only progress by loyal service to the higher castes.

The terrible thing about the caste system was not that it compelled men to work against their will, because people always have to work against their will. The horror of the caste system lay in the fact that the human spirit was imprisoned within an unyielding cage of ritual and custom that persuaded them to work without reward or hope of reward for lifetime after lifetime and for generation after generation.

To make matters worse the Brahmin ethic allowed no concept of redemption. Once polluted, one was condemned for ever and could only redeem oneself in a future incarnation after austerities, sacrifices, good deeds and suffering. Loss of reputation, virginity or caste were a life sentences. Part of the appeal of Islam and Christianity to the lesser castes was the opportunity they offered to gain new status by accepting the new religions that allowed repentance and rehabilitation.

The Brahmins and Kshatriyas were the upper castes, separated by a virtual sanitary curtain between them and the lower caste Vaishyas and Shudras. Beyond these was another sanitary curtain separating them from the even more numerous castes of the untouchable sweepers, leather workers, butchers and other menials. Because all things emanating from the human body were considered unclean midwives and barbers were also listed in this last category.

All work done with the hands was considered unclean so most of the agricultural labourers, carpenters, stone masons, artisans and infantrymen were of the lower castes. So these creators of industry and commerce were looked down upon and India's economic growth faltered while economically useless temples, palaces and their assorted artifacts were wastefully constructed. Paradoxically the British use of untouchable castes like the Pariahs of the Madras army and the Mahars of the Bombay infantry were a key factor in their conquest of India.

The lesser castes therefore grudgingly carried out the orders of the higher castes but without the dedication, devotion and creativity that had marked their work in the earlier periods of India's greatness. Though this period of Indian history was outwardly the most prolific in the making of magnificent temples, forts and palaces, the arrogance of the higher castes and the degradation of the lower ones created a deep moral rot.

So under the magnificent exteriors lurked a deep decay as the spontaneous sources of creativity had been extinguished. Temples and cultural achievements were named after the high caste patron kings or deities and the low caste craftsperson's that had created them remained unrecognised unlike the Leonardo da Vincis, Michelangelos, Beethovens or Mozarts who were honoured in the courts of medieval Europe.

The upper castes arrogantly gave peremptory orders that the lower castes grudgingly carried out. They seldom got any encouragement from example or appreciation. With the passing of centuries, work became increasingly slipshod with little control over time and quality. The probable explanation for India's chronic dirt and unsanitary filth is because the upper castes refused to get involved in anything remotely unclean while the lower castes just did not care.

Unfortunately, the lower classes aspired to ape the higher castes and showed the same disdain for filth. As castes evolved many claimed higher caste positions for themselves than they strictly deserved. For example, many educated Vaishyas of Bengal eagerly took to teaching, medicine, law and professions and called themselves 'Gyan Kshatris' or Kshatriyas by knowledge. Similar self-promotion by successful lower caste groups who aspired to ape the higher castes occurred in many places and some dropped their caste names while others shamelessly created new names to suggest a superior caste.

It is very significant that slavery never took root in India. Even though Islam condoned slavery, even though it regulated its worst abuses, the Muslim noblemen found that the chains of caste were less demanding than the bonds of slavery. Slaves, like horses, cattle and dogs were personal possessions and thus objects of affection and concern that needed looking after and could not be thoughtlessly discarded. No such commitment or consideration was required for low caste menials. Those who claim that the caste system was just a division of labour are guilty of grave over simplification.

The caste system did, however, have some compensating features. Though oppressive, it allowed each caste a level of economic and social security with well defined rights and duties within the confines of a rigid system. There were also some safety valves like Holi, the spring harvest festival, where the low castes were briefly allowed to release their frustrations with moderate mockery and humiliation of their superiors.

By the time the Turks came to India in the 12th century, India's vitality and creativity had almost dried out. Kings ruled in their remote palaces and the priests preached in their temples while the artistes and craftsmen, demoted to the lower castes, were content to imitate and substitute words for action. Ritual and orthodoxy now dictated every detail of art, literature, mathematics, architecture of temples, palaces, houses, the details of sculpture and even military science. Shilpa Shastras codified these into elaborate rituals imbued with almost religious sanctity.

Wealth was the poison and arrogant pride the disease that sapped India's strength. For many generations, the creativity of India slumbered and then it died. Now there was blind worship and undiscriminating awe. The past became sacred and all that it produced, good and bad, was reverenced alike. Slavish imitation was inculcated as duty while novelty and originality became crimes. India quickly lost the manly virtues necessary to defend itself.

57. DID THE 'ONE GOD' RELIGIONS OF REVELATION INFLUENCE INDIA?

It seems quite amazing that Jehovah, the God of a small band of ancient Jews, who was to later become the model for the Christian God and the Islamic Allah, should end up inspiring worship by some 70 per cent of mankind. This 'One God' idea was however so powerful that it quickly supplanted the multiplicity of deities of earlier worship in every land. The earlier animist, pagan or kaffir deities who represented the spirits of the land or the forces of nature were usually benevolent though they were also sometimes malevolent. But they were easily approachable and easily appeased with simple rituals and sacrifices and did not dominate every human thought and action. They seldom had full time priests.

Until the arrival of Jehovah some 3,000 years ago, people in every land worshipped numerous deities that were originally considered to be spirits that inhabited every living and even every inanimate object. Every mountain, rock and river as well as the plants, trees, insects, animals and human beings were thought to have a 'Jiva' or living particle residing within them. The people of every land had originally believed that the terrestrial world was owned by these spirits and that Man was an intruder into their realm and had to seek their blessings in order to feed, procreate and prosper. Early prayer had been a simple ritual of bowing respectfully to these imagined spirits with the offerings of flowers, fruit or a little blood from their kills to seek their blessings.

The marginalisation of these pagan deities is all the more remarkable because this Jehovah was not a God that anyone could love. This god of the Old Testament was actually a most unpleasant character. He was jealous, destructive, vindictive, bloodthirsty, petty, unjust, unforgiving, capricious, malevolent and only interested in the Jews. Simply on the authority of a few prophets like Moses and Abraham, to whom Jehovah was believed to have revealed himself and his vision for humanity, the Jews were persuaded to believe that he was the only key to their long awaited destiny. This tradition of messianic revelation continued with Christianity and Islam even if the gods of these faiths were much mellowed down. But even this loving God of Jesus or a merciful Allah of Muhammad still retained the character of absolute and awesome power.

Unlike all the benign earlier deities Jehovah, God and Allah were awesome gods who, their followers believed, had huge powers to read thoughts, answer prayers, punish sins and perform miracles like getting the Jews their long awaited `Promised Land'. This all powerful One God idea was promoted by its priests to be a fearsome cosmic force with the divinely ordained power to control all creation and every little detail of life and behavior and with the ability to miraculously intervene into human affairs and the ability to read every worshipper's innermost thoughts.

Thus every childish indiscretion or even the mere thought of indiscretion would instantly generate a strong sense of guilt. This guilt was used to make followers cower in fear by the Jewish and Christian priests followed by Muslim clerics who quickly erected high walls of moral laws and rules that promised terrifying consequences for any deviation in 'God's judgment' in the afterlife to make their followers feel even more guilty, fearful and sinful. Thus the spontaneous joy of pagan worship with music, dance, intoxicants, sex and frivolity was sternly frowned upon and replaced with a dull, sombre, hypocritical morality that was paranoid about sin or even the mere thought of sin.

But these priests also offered huge rewards for those who wanted to escape from this ever present web of sin, guilt and fear, not only in the afterlife of heaven, but in the mortal life as well. Magnificent religious ceremonies and rituals in beautiful places of worship with elevating religious chanting and music were a soothing tonic for troubled consciences. They also offered to alleviate the sins of devotees by prescribing fasts, penances, sacrifices and pilgrimages. This great God was also believed to answer the prayers of the faithful to miraculously banish sickness, oppression and poverty or fulfil the wishes of the faithful. The pilgrimages and rich donations quickly enriched the priests and their places of worship and religions soon became a very big business with priests claiming to be their God's sole selling agents on earth.

The main reason for the success of the 'One God' idea was its ability to put enormous power into the hands of their full-time professional priests enabling them to command the absolute obedience of their followers. The earlier pagan deities had no priests to defend them and those who had worshipped them were mocked and ruthlessly persecuted so that the three Semitic religions with their armies of professional priests quite effortlessly gained dominance worldwide. This absolute faith also made Christians and Muslims aggressive proselytisers that made their religions very disagreeable to those of other faiths. Unlike the tolerant pagan faiths the legions of priests in these predominantly male religions could not tolerate the faith of any other with the result that more blood was shed in the name of religion than from any other cause.

These priests also legitimised their positions with a series of constantly rewritten sacred scriptures. In ancient times the difficulties of written communications and the need to constantly write them on perishable materials like parchment, bark, palm or papyrus leaves meant that many revisions were inevitable. The result was that each religion had a huge body of such obscure texts that priests were necessary to understand and interpret them. These texts all listed numerous rigorously enforceable laws in sharp contrast to the easy and loving worship of the earlier pagan faiths.

The 'One God' idea came to India quite recently mainly with the philosophy of Advaitya that was so actively promoted by Shankaracharya (788 – 820 AD). Earlier there had been widespread worship to a multiplicity of deities. India's earliest `Sankhya' philosophy had only believed in two realities of Purush (self) and Prakriti (nature) with the cosmic creator being a distant entity that would not concern itself with miraculous interventions in the affairs of mortal beings. It had believed that Man had an enormous ability to empower himself to achieve his goals of life by simplicity, discipline, avoiding injury to others and doing good deeds for all living things without any divine miracles.

Although Shankara preached throughout India during his short life, he had come from Kerala and could have been influenced by the `One God' idea that had taken root with the early Jewish and Christian settlers. But this idea that was so empowering to priests that it was very strongly taken up by the priestly class of Brahmins to make them a huge factor in India's future culture and religion. It was only now that Kulluka's commentary on the Manusmriti was to reshape and harden the caste system and make it so oppressive. It was now that the caste of Kshatriyas that had faded out during the thousand years of Buddhism was reinvented to create a powerful cadre of soldiers to enforce Brahmin wishes.

Vedic worship had basically been the exchange of sacrifices for miraculous boons through great 'Yagnas' or sacrifices. Though the 33 deities of the Veda had vanished from popular worship the power of miracles managed by professional priests was revived in a new worship focused on a One God in the form of Vishnu or Shiv. While their many lesser divine companions like Ganesh, Hanuman, Devi or Kali and several local deities based on earlier pagan worship continued to be worshipped, like the saints of Christianity, they were of much less magnitude. Krishna and Ram had not yet become objects of adoration. It was only now that the masses could be enslaved by the kings to provide the willing labour needed to build the thousands of temples that mushroomed throughout India between the 8th and 13th centuries. These soon became huge revenue earners as the gullible masses heaped their wealth before the deities in transactions with a One God that they believed could miraculously answer their prayers.

The new Brahmin power over all other castes is clearly evident from the huge land grants made to the Brahmins between the 8th and 13th centuries and their new power is demonstrated the paradox that while great temples were raised no magnificent palaces were erected at this time by the very kings who had endowed them. The Turks and Mongols who now entered India had little difficulty conquering the priest ridden and enfeebled Indian kingdoms that opposed them.

58. WHAT WAS THE IMPACT OF THE ARAB INCURSION?

Muhammad Bin Qasim's brief incursion into Sind in 712 AD left very little mark on Indian history but it created a new awareness in the West about the wealth and wonders of India that invited many other invaders. His expedition was not the first Arab attempt to enter India. In 636 a sea-borne attack under Mughaira was repulsed. The Jat Kaikanis again repulsed an attack in 667. Rashid Bin Amru was routed a few years later as were two further attacks in the reign of Khalif Walid I.

The Jat kingdom of Brahminabad (near the present-day Mohenjodaro) had been usurped by a Brahmin named Chhach who had earlier been a minister. He seduced the queen and his intrigues successfully divided and weakened his neighbouring Jat rulers. He was succeeded by his younger brother, known to history as Raja Dahir. Several Jat rulers troubled by his intrigues then invited Arab intervention and Qasim with a small army of 3,000 soldiers led an expedition to Sind.

India in 1,030 AD

Qasim's expedition was not purely military and, like Napoleon's expedition to Egypt eleven centuries later, contained many scholars, intellectuals and observers. His chronicles not only praise the military and scientific prowess of his Indian adversaries but also of their life and culture. Qasim found that though the locals were 'not people of the book' they were religiously and culturally advanced and even suggested the possibility that the locally worshipped Brahma, that phonetically sounded similar to Abraham, might have some significance. In these early days Islam was much less rigid and priest-ridden than it was to become during its centuries of decline.

A reply to his letters from his superior, the Governor of Kuwait is most revealing:

> "It appears that the chief inhabitants of Brahminabad had petitioned to be allowed to repair the temple of Budh and to pursue their religion. As they have made their submission and agreed to pay taxes to the Khalif, nothing more can be required of them. They have been taken under our protection and we cannot in any way stretch out our hands on their lives and property. Permission is given to them to worship their gods."

Sadly, the courageous and enlightened Qasim was falsely implicated for the molestation of two girls captured from pirates while on their way to the Governor's harem at Kuwait and he was slowly and painfully executed.

59. DID MUSLIM INVADERS ACTUALLY DESECRATE HINDU TEMPLES AND SLAUGHTER HINDUS BY THE THOUSANDS?

History has many examples of savage destruction for political, military or religious reasons. Timur Lang, for example, slaughtered 90,000 Muslims in Baghdad so religion had nothing to do with it. But the first Turk invaders from Afghanistan were crude robbers with little intellectual, cultural or religious pretensions. They simply came for loot and plunder and there is not a shred of evidence that they had any interest in the Indian people or desire to convert them to their own recently acquired religion. The glorified accounts by some Muslim court flatterers in much later times, may speak of conquest by the sword and the Quran, but there is little evidence that these rough Turks took their priests at all seriously. These accounts, usually flowery texts to flatter their patrons, unlike the accounts from local sources greatly exaggerated the extent of loot and bloodshed.

It is clear that the desecration of temples often had little to do with religion and a lot to do with loot and plunder. The huge donations given by millions devotees and patrons to the Hindu temples made them by far the richest targets for any plunderer. Paradoxically the wealth of the Indian temples revived soon even after the raids of Mahmud Ghazni. He was on occasion careful to spare several Hindu deities so that they could again attract wealth for looting at a later date.

Mahmud's seventeen almost annual raids lasted from 997 to 1,030 AD. He looted a city near Peshawar in 1,001, Bhatia on the Jhelum and even a Muslim city near Multan. In 1,008, he raided the temple of Kangra where the Shahi rulers had evidently accumulated 180 kgs of gold, 2 tonnes of silver and fabulous other booty. Thanesar followed in 1,010 "with plunder impossible to recount." In 1,018 he attacked Mathura and Kanauj the following year and reportedly returned with loot of 20 million Dirhams, 53,000 slaves and 350 elephants.

In 1,025 he attacked Somnath in distant Gujarat where 50,000 devotees reportedly prostrated themselves to save the temple but were slaughtered. If this brutal atrocity had actually happened it is unlikely to have gone unrecorded in any contemporary Brahmin, Jain, Sanskrit or local account. The horrible story actually came from Turkish and Persian accounts glorifying Mahmud written four centuries later. And this so-called slaughter at Somnath was coincidentally exactly similar to the alleged slaughter of 50,000 Muslim Shias by Ghazni at Qom in Iran.

But such exaggerated accounts from Mahmud's courtiers were to unfortunately become one of the main foundations for virulently anti-Muslim mythology of later times. The huge loot of the Somnath temple was probably true for his scribes also reported that the booty was so huge that his armies staggered back with great difficulty and were furiously attacked by co-religious bandits all along the way.

There is no evidence that Mahmud was a religious fanatic but he was perhaps one of the greatest bandits to have ever roamed the world. He even raised a Hindu army under a highly regarded Hindu general, a Brahmin called Tilak, who fought against Ghazni's own co-religionists in his battles in Central Asia.

The bloody slaughter of Delhi citizens by Timur Lang and later by Nadir Shah was not targeted at Hindus but were brutal reprisals for the murder of some of Mongol and Persian soldiers in which neither the Muslim nor Hindu inhabitants of Delhi were spared.

The British slaughter after the suppression of the Sepoy mutiny was as bloody and crude but has not been remembered with the same communal passion. In the succeeding centuries, there were many examples of loot and slaughter. But as soon as the Muslim rulers settled in India they needed the active cooperation of the local inhabitants and mostly tolerated their religious customs.

For nearly two centuries the Muslim sultans of North India spent their main effort in blocking the entry of Muslim Mongols. Alauddin Khilji had a standing army of 475,000 soldiers to block their entry into India. And the macabre towers of severed Mongol heads was a practice never inflicted on any Hindu adversary.

Exaggerated accounts of brutal slaughter were not alien to other cultures either. Persian accounts reported that Genghis Khan's Mongols had slaughtered a very precise 1,747,000 people at the battle of Nishapur and 1,600,000 people at Herat. Such ridiculously exaggerated numbers would require some 350 dead for every Mongol warrior.

People loosely speak of Islamic art or architecture as if religion had anything to do with it. Nothing could be further from the very basic Arabian architecture or cultural traditions than the highly sophisticated buildings and arts of ancient Persia. The Afghans and Mongols had no architectural tradition to speak of and mainly relied on Persian architects. Rajput rulers created architecture that fused together many elements like chattris and chabutras more suitable for warm climates into the Persian designs oriented to cooler areas. Climate had much more to do with the design than any question of race or religion.

Many people also very loosely speak of Muslim invaders without realising that there had been many other incursions or invasions of alien people into India for thousands of years. There had been the Aryas, Persians, Greeks, Scythians, Parthians, Kushans, Jats, Huns, Arabs, Afghans, Turks, Mongols and several European nations apart from the Burmese and Tibetans in the east. They were all absorbed quite easily into India's evolving ethos. They all came to India with different motives apart from the common quest for land or trade and the fact that Arabs, Afghans and Mongols were Muslim or that the European colonies were Christian does not mean that there was any Islamic or a Christian assault to Hinduism.

The Hindutva view of Indian history tends to be so focused on the Hindi-speaking heartland that they are often surprisingly silent about events in other parts of India. They have no problem in glorifying Samudra Gupta's conquest of South India up to Kanchipuram in the 4th century AD but are surprisingly silent about the conquest of North India under Rajendra Chola who conquered Benares in the 11th century. And they are so paranoid about Muslim invaders that they know nothing about the Tibetan empire of Songsten Gampo in the 7th century that had extended to many parts of northern and eastern India. It is very strange that the intellectual champions of a robust majority community should suffer from such an inferiority complex.

60. Why Did The Rajputs Fail To Stop The Turks And Mongols?

Many Turk and Mughal accounts praise the superb horsemanship, swordsmanship, military skills, and gallantry of individual Indian soldiers. They however also record that they could not combine effectively in team or group effort. Rajput armies, unfortunately, relied on one crushing victory and their pride could not face the ignominy of losing any skirmishes let alone smaller tactical battles in order to win a greater war. Their social conditioning gave them no preparation for the possibilities of a tactical withdrawal or temporary defeat. Becoming a captive unfortunately entailed an unacceptable loss of caste that made death preferable to defeat. So whenever the prospect of victory faded the morale of the Rajput armies would be totally crushed.

These proud but hollow standards of chivalry made the Rajputs vulnerable. When faced with defeat, they would drive their weeping womenfolk into flaming 'Jauhar' pits, or mass pyres, where they were burned to death. The administration of drugs may have made the tragic event only slightly less painful. The men, in their turn, would then discard their armour and ride drugged into battle with a determination to die in glory. Many years later, Babur was to remark: "The Indians know how to die better than how to fight."

Indian armies always advanced slowly in big blocks according to a fixed, and thus predictable, science that had hardly changed since it had been defined in Kautilya's Arthashastra. Pomp and show was more important than strategy. Enemies were to be awed by might and magnificence and shock had no place. Surprise, a key element in war, had little part in their set piece planning. They were proud of their colourfully decorated war elephants and their elite cavalry. Their brightly decorated tents and elaborate arrangements for food, religion and comfort required a huge train of camp followers with the result that they had to move slowly with a low ratio of fighting teeth to supporting tail. Their dependence on their magnificent elephants also slowed them down unlike their Turk and Mongol adversaries on their quick and mobile ponies.

Unlike the infantry-based armies of Alexander, the low caste Indian infantrymen and archers were not accorded much importance and were often casually sacrificed like pawns in a game of chess. Rajputs though highly skilled horsemen who were effective in a cavalry charge were vulnerable against the archers and infantry of their enemies in any close skirmish.

By contrast, their early Turk or Mughal adversaries usually advanced rapidly with an advance guard of fast light horsemen to harry and disturb ahead of the main blocks with another bloc of flexible reserves ready to be thrown into battle at critical points. With small baggage trains to slow them down they were mobile and flexible and mainly relied on fast mounted archers using short re curved or double bows. With teams of additional horses they could cover huge distances to surprise their foes. They also mastered methods of mock retreat, shock and surprise.

Astrology was also a major problem. The Brahmins in all the royal courts had no conception of the importance of the opportune moment and would not allow any military movement except at times that they deemed auspicious and after conducting the necessary rituals for success. During the third battle of Panipat, for example, the Marathas despite having superior French cannon were not allowed to move from their defensive position for weeks since they and their horses were sick and hungry. Many collapsed with the result even on the initial two mile charge when they eventually engaged the Afghans and were predictably defeated with a loss of 80,000 soldiers. Although Abdali returned to Afghanistan his armies settled down as the Rohillas on the plains of the Jamuna. This example shows the high price of just a single example of astrology.

The morbid fear of defeat predictably made the Rajput kings tend towards defensive warfare. Instead of mounting daring forays to secure their territory, they, with their large entourages, would seek the safety of well-fortified camps until the enemy was upon them and would then retreat into their fortresses with little concern for the common people in the city below. As in chess, this 'castling' allowed the king to remain safe and distant from the common soldiers on the battlefield. Chess is an Indian invention that still reflects these old traditions of Indian warfare with pawns for sacrifice, dashing horsemen and immobile kings on their ponderous elephants or safe in their castles.

Their enemies were, therefore, left free to cut their lines of communication and plunder at will. It was not surprising then that the poor defenceless common people in the plains below had little sense of loyalty to their highborn rulers let alone any sense of nation. One set of rulers was not much worse than another and had to be fatalistically accepted. It usually only meant just a change in the rent collectors.

The courts of Indian rulers were also hotbeds of intrigue where courtiers, priests and womenfolk jostled for position and influence. These efforts for selfish personal advancement meant a subversive attack on anyone with ability, sincerity or integrity. It was an environment that completely undermined the cooperation and teamwork so vital for sustained attack or defence.

Rajput pride and the chronic sycophancy of their courtiers were also barriers to learning any lessons from the past. Rulers were easily flattered to overlook their own weaknesses and to believe in their invincibility. Astrologers would assure victories but only allow attack at times that they deemed to be auspicious. New ideas were not welcome and there was great comfort in tradition. Truth was dangerous in the courts of sycophants and the bearers of bad news or good advice often lost their heads.

Corruption was also endemic. Intrigues ensured that there was no permanency in the land grants for noblemen to maintain their troops or services. They were also subject to arbitrary change so the beneficiaries would hold back part of the land taxes to provide for an uncertain future. As the rulers relied on subordinates to collect their taxes and tributes, there were inevitable leakages in the system.

Despite a long period of several hundred years from the first plundering raids to the time the Turks settled down, the Rajputs learned nothing from their setbacks but forgot no insult to their arrogant pride. Before the Mughal conquest, the revolutionary Chinese inventions of gunpowder and paper had been used in India but none of the Indian rulers displayed any inclination to depart from their traditional ways or showed any willingness to learn about new weapons or military science.

61. What Was The Impact Of Islam On India?

Six hundred years after the death of the Prophet, a succession of priests and scholars had made Islam an increasingly intolerant and priest-ridden religion. The rigid principles, inflexible codes and aggressive attitudes of the not very civilised early Muslim invaders were also a great shock to the people of North India. Islam was another social religion that was too simple for a complex, pluralistic and metaphysical people who had just defeated the social and material faiths of Buddhism and marginalised Jainism.

The Islam that reached India had undergone considerable change over the five centuries since its beginning. Muhammad (570 to 632 AD), living in a feudal and tribal time, was a simple Arab trader who proclaimed the socially revolutionary idea that before Allah all people were equal. This almost communistic idea appealed to people oppressed by the great despotic civilisations of Persia and Constantinople. It quickly spread from Spain to the borders of China in just 60 years. It could not enter India till much later except through the limited influence of a few Arab and Egyptian traders.

Originally, Islam had been a very simple religion with few pretensions of spirituality but had incorporated many elements of Jewish and Christian religious traditions. It laid out a detailed code for social, physical, moral and spiritual hygiene with clearly defined rules for almost every situation, thought and action. It unfortunately introduced the idea that martyrdom was a sure path to heaven leading to a romanticised fanaticism that was to affect both Islam and its enemies over the years.

For the first several centuries Islam was a much more gentle and rational religion than it became during the past 400 years. As the Islamic empires lost power and influence with the rising strength of the European nations, the Mullahs blamed the diminishing position of Muslim nations to departing from the strict tenets of the Quran, as interpreted by them, and made Islam increasingly intolerant and fanatic.

When the Sultanate Kings like Ghori, Balban, Iltutmish and Alauddin Khilji made the city of Delhi their capital in the 12th to 15th centuries, their empire was a thin strip of land in the Yamuna and Ganges plain from where they aggressively attacked the Rajput kingdoms around them. As they were few in numbers they were initially unable to hold areas far from their strongholds.

But for a short and bloody raid in the 13th century by Timur Lang the Mongols, or Mughals as the Persians called them, were successfully resisted and only arrived some 300 years after the first Afghan rulers. They were another band of initially crude people led to India by the colourful Babur in 1526 AD. They however quite quickly became the cultured and magnificent Mughals. By this time the numbers of Muslim subjects in India had grown sufficiently to make a centralised Empire possible. Even then, Akbar found it expedient to make alliances with the Rajput rulers instead of risking outright conquest into territories with large alien and potentially hostile populations. In a tradition similar to that of the old Mauryan and Gupta Samanthas, he would reinstate many of the defeated or compliant rulers back on their own thrones to rule as his governors on condition that they gave him generous tributes, taxes and contingents of soldiers to serve him. A few matrimonial alliances further cemented such bonds.

The Mughals, being fairly recent converts to Islam, were not initially at all rigid in their religious convictions. They mostly regarded themselves as professional rulers who had to rather reluctantly tolerate the increasing power of the Mullahs. Another moderating factor was the influence of women. Few women had accompanied the

Afghans, Turks and Mughals when they came to India so most of them took local wives. Though most of the women were converted to Islam, many continued to worship the objects of their earlier devotion and considerably softened the attitudes of their menfolk to Hindus and Hindu customs.

Akbar's Din-i-Ilahi may have been a self-glorification exercise or a half-hearted attempt to fuse the tenets of Islam with other religions but it does emphasise the fact that his commitment to Islam was by no means inflexible or fanatic. But all the Mughals were proud to be Muslim rulers in a Muslim land and took the role quite seriously though usually with magnanimous tolerance. Akbar's great grandson, Dara Shikoh was the most eclectic and was actually responsible for discovering the nearly forgotten Upanishads and having them translated into Persian from where it went into French and English before being discovered by a wider Indian public.

Surprisingly, there are many records to show that although Aurangzeb was a very devout Muslim, he had endowed at least 36 Hindu temples including the Someshwar temple at Banares as well as those at Mount Abu, Ujjain, Chitrakoot, Guwahati and Girnar. He did, however, order the destruction of the Kashi Vishwanath temple at Banares in 1669, evidently as a punishment for the ravishing of one of his guests, the Maharani of Kutch who, in a large entourage of Rajput guests were travelling with Aurangzeb. She was kidnapped and ravished by some temple priests within the temple precincts. Aurangzeb seems to have considered the temple a just punishment for what he regarded as a grave insult to his Imperial authority. According to Dr. Pattabi Sitaramayah it was the outraged Rani herself who had insisted on the demolition of the temple after which Aurangzeb had declared... "such an offence could not be in a house of God" and ordered it to be destroyed forthwith.

He also had the Mahant arrested and punished but very few people know that before the destruction he ordered the priests to remove the sacred idol of Vishnu. It was a clever political ploy for, without a sanctified idol, it was no longer a temple and what was destroyed was just a structure of brick and stone.

Aurangzeb's destruction of the Deo Matt temple at Mathura, the alleged birth place of Krishna, was actually a political reprisal for the

Bundhela raja of Orcha who had built it but had sided with one of his rebellious sons. So the destruction in 1661 AD was targeted at the raja and not at Hindus. The Katra Masjid was then built at the site. The myth of Krishna was probably not strong at this time because Mathura came under the rule of the Jats of Bharatpur for forty years and if there had been any strong Hindu feelings, the Jats would have had no difficulty destroying the mosque and building a temple again.

Aurangzeb's royal Farman dated February 28, 1659 clearly shows that he was no anti-Hindu fanatic. It clearly states:

> "It has been decided according to our Shariat that long standing temples should not be abolished but no new temples be allowed to be built. The royal court has received information that some persons are troubling some Hindus and some Brahmins in and about Banares, who have been granted the right to worship in the old temples. Our royal command is that you should direct that in future no person shall, in unlawful ways, disturb the Brahmins and other Hindu residents in those places."

The commonly held view that Aurangzeb reintroduced the Jezia tax on non-believers may have also been exaggerated. Most people believe that he reimposed the hated Jezia tax, evidently abolished a century earlier by Akbar and made his Muslim subjects pay a larger Zakat tax. But there is no actual evidence that this is true because a detailed examination of voluminous Mughal documents throughout the Mughal period by Professor Akhtar Ali reveals that the Jezia had never actually been levied in India. Kharj or land tax was the foundation of the Mughal revenue system and there was no administrative system for collecting Jezia.

He undoubtedly needed heavy taxes to fight his increasingly expensive military campaigns against the rebellious groups like the Sikhs and the more numerous Marathas and these were causes for resentment by all subjects. The last 40 years of his long rule were spent in Central India waging this bitter and ultimately futile war.

Aurangzeb was not just a devout Muslim but also a devout Sunni who repudiated the Shia faith that his great grandfather Humayun had adopted in exchange for Persian help. He considered it a great heresy and waged a more severe war against the Shias than against the Hindus. Surprisingly, Aurangzeb's mission to the south was not to fight the Marathas who had no political presence when he first entered the Deccan. His goal was to vanquish the apostate Shia rulers of Golconda and Bijapur.

Many Maratha soldiers, including Shivaji's father who had served with the Mughal armies of Bijapur, gained valuable battle experience in the long Mughal struggle for supremacy. These bands were to grow into stubborn soldiers after the daring and brilliant organiser Shivaji was able to unite them. So paradoxically Aurangzeb was himself the creator of the Maratha confederations that ultimately brought him and the Mughal Empire down.

In India, Islam had originally been much more tolerant than is generally known. After the savage initial pillage of temples by Mahmud of Ghazni, the rulers of relatively small Turk and Mughal communities could not settle here without the support of the local populations and had to respect their religious and other social traditions. Ninety per cent of the temples destroyed were either acts of war or occurred during the suppression of rebellions. With a few notable exceptions, few temples were actually destroyed even if new ones were discouraged or disallowed. And those few that were vandalised were usually political actions to punish rebellious local people. Though different trades and communities lived in separate mohallas or colonies, they generally lived in harmony with few instances of religious conflict. Muslims were the elite in most North Indian cities with Hindus mostly as agriculturists or petty providers of stores and services.

Many Hindu customs like sehras at weddings and the use of mehendi were widely adopted. Respecting Hindu sentiments, even the butchers of Delhi closed their establishments on Tuesdays and the Mughal rulers ensured that no drain opened into the Yamuna to pollute it.

62. WHY DID THE MUGHAL EMPIRE LAST SO LONG?

Most Sultanate and Turk rulers were unable to ensure lines of succession. This was mainly because Islamic nations had no tradition of primogeniture for succession and also because the democratic Muslim concept of Ummah, or community consensus, allowed anyone to challenge iniquity so there was no innate sanctity in monarchy.

The sultanate rulers had gradually lost the lean and mean military systems of their forbears and soon adopted the proud traditions of classic Indian warfare and Babur's adversaries the Lodis had become very different from his small mobile forces. The first use of cannon in India by the Mughals also had a decisive effect in panicking Ibrahim Lodi's elephants and gunpowder thereafter became a crucial element in Indian wars. But it was the other Chinese invention of paper and printing that had even greater effect. In the times of peace, it hugely advanced communications and record keeping necessary to hold together the complexities of managing a far-flung empire.

The first Mughal Emperor was Babur, a great- great grandson of Timur Lang and a descendant of Genghis Khan's second son Chagathai, after 13 generations, on his mother's side. So he was actually more Turk than Mongol. Though Genghis had died nearly 300 years before Babur the impact of his amazing rule lingered on.

Though Genghis had been an indigent nomad from one of the poorest parts of the world he had great practical skills and surprising moderation. He believed that no one could control more people than the 10 fingers of their hands. So he made the lowest units of command into small bands of ten under one leader to whom they had to give absolute obedience. The commander of a hundred had ten groups of ten and, a Hazari, or commander of a thousand had ten groups of hundred and so on. This ensured total obedience and flexibility of command. In some campaigns they would group ten captives under each soldier as a human shield ahead of his attacking forces. The system of ten continued with the Mughals with an Amir commanding 5000 as the highest command.

The Mongol armies were a originally lightly armed but a total cavalry force with light leather frontal armour and armed mainly with short recurved bows. They were not slowed down by any baggage trains so they could cover huge distance, had to eat off the land and pillage ruthlessly. With relays of back up horses their speed and

The Mughal Empire in 1707 AD

range of manoeuvre shocked and disoriented enemies accustomed to the conventions of war. He was also a master of psychological warfare and would release terrified captives ahead of his armies to demoralise enemy defenders further ahead. Genghis also made it a point to quickly destroy the aristocracies of his defeated enemies, who were now leaderless. So most of them quite readily joined his armies where they were offered equal shares in the spoils of war.

In just 25 years Genghis Khan's armies had subjugated more land than the Roman Empire had in 400, creating an empire that in the 200 years under his successors stretched from Beijing to Moscow. Though the Mongols built no structures, created no religions, wrote no great literature and achieved no technological marvels the Mongols, for the first time, encouraged commerce and ideas to travel freely from Asia to Europe enabling huge advances in technology and intellect that stimulated the renaissance and even contributed to the Industrial Revolution. When skilled bell metal engineers from Europe combined Chinese gunpowder with Arab flame throwers they produced the cannon that was to revolutionise warfare.

A major factor in Babur's grandson Akbar's success was the practical business of bringing of more lands under agriculture with new methods of revenue collection that augmented the revenues needed to field big permanent armies and build magnificent forts. Another huge expense was the constant cost of importing horses from Central Asia and Arabia as the horses bred in India had never been very good.

Babur and Akbar were ferocious battle leaders and even Humayun sporadically showed considerable courage and skills of war. Their military prowess and their practical alliances quickly silenced rebellions. Even Jehangir, Shah Jehan and Aurangzeb spent considerable time in military campaigns.

Babur and Akbar were ferocious battle leaders and even Humayun sporadically showed surprising courage and knowledge of the skills of war. Even Jehangir, Shah Jehan and Aurangzeb spent considerable time in military campaigns. The Mughals were mostly very pragmatic professional rulers who kept their main supporters in a state of uneasy balance.

The success of the Mughals was also because of a few key factors:

1. They created a composite governing class who had a vested interest in a continuity of service to the empire. Surprisingly nearly 30 per cent of the senior officers or Mansabdars were Hindu, and unlike the Muslim Amirs who only had temporary

tenures to keep them on their toes, they enjoyed continuity of tenure even to their successors. The Rajputs thus remained loyal and were held by gilded chains.

2. An elaborate and surprisingly honest administration mostly managed by Hindus at the large lower levels with well structured systems and elaborate documentation.

3. A stable monetary system with gold, silver and copper coins for convenient trading for valuable to common place items. A regularly paid army and administrative structure that was not subject to despotic whims.

4. The Emperors were also masters of public relations. The daily Jharoka Darbar at first light was like a morning prayer and their accessibility to all at public audiences for the redressal of grievances as well as the pomp and show of their ceremonies and travels endeared the Mughals to the masses. This majestic aura continued even after the decline of the Empire and even the Maratha rebels and the European adventurers wanted Imperial firmans to legitimise their activities.

The four pillars of the Mughal Empire had been the Turranis, Afghanis, Iranis and Rajputs. The Turranis were the Turk and Mongol clans like the Chagatai and Uzbek. The Iranis were the Persian purveyors of culture and civilisation who were the architects, painters, musicians, poets, writers, irrigation engineers, etc. The Afghanis were the descendants of the first Afghan migrants. The Rajputs Amirs were also a major force in the Imperial service.

All four groups held honoured positions in the Mughal service and many were Amirs of high standing but the Emperors constantly played one group against the other to prevent any faction becoming too strong so intrigues were endemic. By the end of the 17th century, continuous migrations of Persians, Turks and Afghans seeking employment in the growing imperial services had swelled the ranks so much that many newly arrived adventurers began to resent the powerful influence of Rajputs in the imperial service.

There was, however, a rising tide of Hindu assertiveness. The Mughal Empire was an aristocratic edifice built on the foundations of a substantially Hindu support base and a century of peace and prosperity under the Mughals had created a new generation who were not as willing to blindly accept Mughal authority and were beginning to assert their own identities and aspirations.

The Mughals were a very attractive dynasty of kings who took the business of ruling their mixed populations seriously. Their marriage to high ranking Hindu princesses and tolerance to most Hindu customs also reduced the feeling of alien rule to a great extent. The pomp of the courts, durbars and royal caravans also had a huge impact on the masses. They were the stars of their times and their durbars were great local events.

The Mughal court was also mostly on the move in the old Mongol tradition. A large mobile camp often 20 miles in circumference was a moving centre from where the Emperors sent orders to the far corners of their empire through relays of fast horses stationed at serais or inns every four miles on their main routes. Actually there were two duplicate royal camps with one being erected a days march ahead, identical to the previous one in every detail, including the location of the tents for individual noblemen, shops and services. Over a period of many months, the huge royal entourage would travel long distances every year from Kashmir to Bengal. Thus constant travel made all Mughal noblemen physically fit and adaptable. It also enabled the proud Imperial court to have a local presence from time to time in many distant provinces.

The Mughals took the training of their princes seriously with early introduction into military commands so that they were all battle hardened by the time they had made it to the throne after fighting and eliminating their brothers. So a succession of hardy rulers ensured a vigorous and able leadership. Aurangzeb, five generations after Babur spent his long life in almost continuous battle. But though Aurangzeb was pious and very industrious, he was not a good strategist. And in the end, the Mughal armies had become huge and unwieldy and undermined by corruption and intrigue. But it had taken over 200 vigorous years before the Mughals became soft and effete.

An account of Aurangzeb's army on the move illustrates this evolution from the light and nimble armies of their Mongol forebears:

First came 300 camels loaded with silver and gold, then came his hunting establishment with hawks and cheetahs, then eighty camels, thirty elephants and twenty carts with the official records, then a hundred camels with water and the royal kitchen. Fifty camels and a hundred carts carried the wardrobe and jewels of the Emperor and his womenfolk as well as presents for successful commanders. Next came the mass of the cavalry followed by the elephants of the Emperor's, establishment. Two thousand men with spades smoothed the ground before the cavalcade and another 1000 followed. Last came the rearguard of the infantry who, as in Rajput times, were considered inferior to the elite arms of the cavalry and artillery.

As with dynasties in other places and at other times there had been extensive psychological changes from generation to generation. In most of them the founders had usually been rude robbers who captured an early estate. The second generation were the administrators who consolidated or enlarged the territory. The third generation spent less time in war and administration and began cultivating arts and culture. The fourth were devoted to culture and building and needed heavy taxes to pay for their indulgences. The fifth generation was debauched and began losing control of their distant provinces that resented the taxes and had lost respect for the central authority. Paradoxically the cultures were most prolific in their times of decline. The Mughal Emperors show the steady progression from hardy horsemen to effete monarchs surrounded by luxury and depravity at the end of the great empire.

Once the rot had set in the magnificent Mughal armies were to prove themselves equally ineffective against small well-drilled and disciplined forces of Europeans that chiefly relied on infantry. Their armies with enormous baggage trains were no longer light and swift like those of Babur but had become burdened with huge baggage trains, lumbering elephants and slow and ungainly artillery.

63. Was It The Persians That Made The Turks And Mongols Cultured?

The Afghans, Turks and Mughals were originally hardy nomads and it was the cultured Persians who taught them the finer things of urban life and were the main contributors to the culture of medieval North India. Like the French in medieval Europe, they were the purveyors of civilisation in Asia from the 12th to the 18th century.

Persia had a long and very rich cultural tradition That had developed from the time of Cyrus the Great in 600 BC. The cultured Sassanian Empire declined after the Arab conquest in 627 AD but their great cultural tradition continued. Though they accepted Islam, they staunchly defied many orthodox Islamic restrictions and continued their proud old traditions of depicting portraits of people, animals and nature in their paintings and carpets as well as in the building of elaborate tombs. Their long tradition of miniature paintings, decorated woven carpets, costumes, musical instruments, cuisine, architecture and gardens were to profoundly influence North India for centuries even after the demise of the Mughals. After Aurangzeb forbade portraiture in his court, legions of jobless skilled painters came under the patronage of Rajput rulers to paint Rajput motifs into an essentially Persian painting tradition.

The Chakra, or spinning wheel is a Persian word and was a big improvement on the earlier Taqli or indigenous spinning top. The flat weaving loom or Kagha was another Persian innovation. The Persian Wheel with a moving chain of buckets to raise water from wells was a great aid to agricultural irrigation.

Their greatest contribution was perhaps to the language for their rich vocabulary and idiom was far in advance of Arabic or local Indian dialects in sophisticated expressions and poetic style. By the 12th century, Sanskrit had faded out of use to virtually become a secret though sacred language of Brahmin priests. Many Persian loan words became an intrinsic part of many Indian languages. Even to this day, Hindi cannot provide words for many subtle or emotional expressions, so Hindustani and Urdu with many Persian words became popular in Hindi films.

The marriages and interaction with Rajput noble families also brought in a rich infusion of local traditions. It took just a few generations for rough Mongol warriors to become effete courtiers. Nothing could be of greater contrast than the rough Genghis Khan and his cultured descendants like Shah Jehan in India or Kublai Khan in China.

64. WHY IS ISLAM SO INTOLERANT AND FANATIC TODAY?

Islam, that simply meant surrender to the will of God, was once much more tolerant than it is today. It was unprecedented in its time for its tolerance of race, colour, sex or class. Very few remember that Muhammad himself granted a charter to the Christian monks of Sinai that breathes goodwill if not actual love. When Khalif Omar entered Jerusalem, Christians urged him to spread his carpet and pray within the Church of the Holy Sepulchre but he refused saying that some ignorant Muslims, after him, might try to claim the church and convert it into a mosque. So he prayed at a site where the Mosque of Umar now stands outside the Masjid al Asqa.

The tolerant Islamic treatment of Christians and Jews in Spain for 600 years and many other countries was in sharp contrast to the brutal Christian re conquest of Spain where not a Muslim was left alive in Spain, Sicily or Apulia.

Muslim fanatics may quote one of the Prophet's exhortations against idolaters but how many know the sura al-nam where verse 108 says:

Do not revile those who worship other gods lest in their ignorance they revile your god.
Each people adhere to their beliefs they act as they please.
But in the end all shall return to their lord and will be told of the wrongs they did.

All religions preach the faith of their founders but they also carry a huge baggage of customs that are social rather than spiritual. Easter and Christmas were never part of the teachings of Christ while Eid and Ramzan were ancient Arab customs that long pre-dated the advent of Islam. Revenge was also an old Arab custom that has unfortunately become a part of the Muslim tradition worldwide. Revenge had been a necessary survival custom in the precarious times when small tribes of Arab Bedouins had to protect themselves from bigger or more powerful tribes who, without the fear of revenge, could easily loot or molest them.

Life in the desert was always very tenuous and there was fierce competition over the scarce sources of food or water. Individuals could not survive except with the protection of the bonds of blood within their tribes and through alliances with other tribes. This was expressed in the Arab ideology of Muruwah that not only meant manliness, pride and courage but endurance in suffering, protec-tion of the weak, avenging each and every injustice and boldly de-fying stronger enemies regardless of the consequences. This phi-losophy also glorified the most generous hospitality to friends and equally intense hatred to enemies.

Oppressors had to therefore be very careful for this well es-tablished tribal code made it certain that any injustice would be avenged at some future date. Regardless of power and position no one could ever be absolutely safe from attack and had to tolerate lesser tribes and be very careful not to incite any serious animosity. The American cowboy glorification of revenge arose out of simi-lar compulsions among numerous isolated ranchers who, far from legal remedies, had to protect themselves from their potential op-pressors. Paradoxically we today see America's cowboy spirit pitted against the Muruwah spirit of the Muslim world that views America as an oppressor.

This revenge philosophy has plagued Islam from its earliest days. The early Khalifs Umar and Uthman as well as the Prophet's own son-in-law Ali were all assassinated by vengeful factions. The predominantly Bedouin Kharajite faction, who were unhappy that Ali had not avenged the assassination of Uthman, mainly caused the split into Sunni and Shia sects that was to cause so much blood-shed over the centuries. These Kharajites had a very narrow and extremist view of the words of the Prophet. Their successors, espe-cially the Wahhabis after the late 18th century were to gain great importance when the Al Saud family captured Medina and Mecca in 1924 and then gained the huge power of oil riches discovered in 1938 to export their extreme brand of Islam that was later an intrinsic part of Taliban thinking.

Actually, many Wahhabi ideas were a heresy to the words and actions of the Prophet whose conquest of Mecca had been achieved without shedding a drop of blood through a year long, almost Gandhian, campaign of patience and moral principles. Muhammad preached peace, except in times of actual combat, and the very word Islam means absolute submission to the will of a merciful god.

The word Jihad is rarely found in the Quran but is referred to 199 times in the Hadith that was written two centuries after the death of the Prophet. The Wahhabis interpreted Jihad to mean a holy war even though Jihad had actually meant a striving and Mujahiddin was no holy warrior but only one who strives. For Muhammad there were two Jihads and the greater Jihad meant a struggle against one's own weakness while a lesser Jihad was to fight against injustice. Both enjoined adherents to struggle on regardless of the odds with the certain faith that Allah would come to the aid of the sincere devotee. But there were strict rules and Jihad could not be declared by anybody but only by an authority of widely accepted repute.

The Quran clearly says that killing in the name of Islam was the opposite of Jihad and had expressly forbidden an attack on anyone who had offered no offence. It was forbidden to harm or to kill women and children. It was also forbidden to take hostages or to torture or kill prisoners. Even suicide was forbidden. Muhammad also said that anyone who sets another... even an ant... on fire commits the greatest sin and is destined to the fires of Hell.

There was no need for such a philosophy of revenge in more affluent pastoral or urban communities and was thus unknown in the philosophies of China, India, Europe or in many other societies. In fact mature cultures understood that accommodation was preferable to violence. This was so well enunciated in Buddhism that preached that hatred can never be appeased by hatred but only by love. It asserted that the only lasting victories were the conquest of the heart because victories in the battlefield only caused the defeated to lie down in sorrow and wait for revenge making future peace impossible.

As time went by the Ulema gave Jihad a more and more fanatical meaning. So a true Jihadi would calmly enter battle without concern for his life and with the sure confidence that his sincere struggle would either get him victory or certain entry into heaven.

The glorification of violence is not only fostered by popular action films but is also endorsed by many religious traditions. Revenge is one of the most popular justifications for all the arson, torture, murder and mayhem that plague our world today. The slaughter of Sikhs after 1984, or Muslims after the Mumbai bomb blasts or in Gujarat after the torching of the Godhra train and even the American attacks on Afghanistan and Iraq were all justified by the idea of revenge. Evil things are never committed with such pride and joy as when they are done out of revenge and especially if they are done in the name of religion. Jihad may have been a good philosophy for military commitment but was dangerous and disruptive in the hands of illiterates, especially if they were armed with dangerous weapons. Even the dreaded word Fatwa never meant a draconian sentence but just a clerics 'Opinion'.

As the Muslim communities gradually slid into poverty and illiteracy, especially during the past 300 years, they came increasingly under the influence of ignorant and bigoted mullahs who used their own interpretation of their scriptures to channel the frustrations and bitterness of their adherents in frequently violent directions. By closing their doors to new ideas they condemned their followers to ignorance, poverty and frustration.

65. Were Forcible Conversions A Widespread Practice?

Hindu accounts of their sufferings were mostly derived from exaggerated and glorified Islamic accounts of their conquests that much later became part of a sad Hindutva mythology. Nowhere in the world have conversions survived without conversions of the heart. Unconvinced converts may outwardly accept conversion but will quickly revert to their personal faiths as soon as they are free to do so.

As with many 'Rice Christians' in China, many lower class Indians readily chose the religions of their new conquerors. As many had also earlier suffered oppression from high caste Hindus it may have been no great sacrifice.

From the 12th to the 18th century many generations had known India to be a Muslim country with Muslims in most of the high positions with Hindus as agriculturists, traders, clerks and poor supplicants for favours. At this time almost everyone had forgotten the past greatness of India's culture and religious traditions. Many better class or educated Hindus willingly converted as Islam and Islamic culture that must have then appeared to them to be superior to the rather degraded forms of Hinduism that prevailed over most of North India during the centuries of Turk and Mughal rule. Many Hindus, at the time, may have even believed that their all-conquering Muslim masters had a superior civilisation and perhaps even a greater god. During the period of British rule a similar conviction had led many educated Indians to become Christians.

Many Muslim clerics, like the Christian missionaries, firmly believed in the absolute perfection of their religions and were highly committed to convert those who they believed to be in darkness and ignorance and had not seen the true path.

The process of conversion to Islam was, however, very traumatic. The circumcision of men, being irreversible, was both painful and final. Being forced to eat beef, as seems to have been a common practice after conversion, made the Hindu subjects cross an irreversible boundary of moral and physical pollution. Having thus grievously sinned and been utterly polluted, in Hindu terms, it was difficult to ever again be accepted back.

The most powerful force for conversions to Islam was actually the numerous Sufi saints and mystics. Many of their tombs are still the objects of Hindu pilgrimage. Their gentle and mystic interpretation of Islam, abhorred by the orthodox Muslim Ulema, greatly appealed to a spiritual people. Many Sufi saints like Shaikh Salim Chisti and Nizamuddin Aulia gained many more converts than all the swords or laws of Islam.

66. DID THE SIKHS SUFFER TERRIBLE PERSECUTIONS?

Sikhism was deeply influenced by Sufi ideas. The Sufis did not pay much attention to superficial ritual but sought a mystical merging with the divine cosmic spirit. They believed the Vedantic

idea: "that God is everywhere and the whole world was a manifesta-
tion of the emanation of God." They respected the spiritual core of
Islamic ideas but had little time for orthodox customs and rituals
that they believed were the creation of the mullahs and not the
injunctions of the Prophet. Their fakirs believed in the mystical
significance of the sound 'M', similar to the sound 'Om' and of
singing the names or attributes of an all-pervading God in the style
of the recitation of the attributes of Hindu deities by sadhus.

Bullhe Shah (1680 - 1752), a Punjabi Sufi, wrote:

"Neither Hindu or Mussalman,
let us sit and spin, abandoning the pride of religion
Neither Sunni nor Shia, I have taken the path of peace and
unity
Bullhe! in all hearts I feel the Lord
So I have abandoned both Hindu and Muslim."

Waris Shah (1730 -1790), another Punjabi mystic, wrote:

"I am tired of reading Vedas and Korans;
My forehead is worn by constant prostrations in the mosque.
But the Lord is neither at Hindu shrines nor at Mecca,
Whoever found him, found him in the light of his own (God's)
beauty."
As another Sufi mystic was to state...
"Whoever worships God for anything,
(paradise, reward or punishment)
is worshipping for himself... and not for God".

These simple but profound observations apply to the pious of
all religions who devoutly make sacrifices, offerings, pilgrimages or
petitions at all the many places of worship. Many Sufis were killed
for their heresies. Like Christ, one martyr Hallaj was crucified in
922 AD for blasphemy.

Dara Shikoh, Aurangzeb's elder brother, was an enlightened
believer in the common essence in all religions. He wrote:

"Happy is he, who, having abandoned the prejudices of vile selfishness, sincerely, and with the grace of God, renouncing all partiality, shall study and comprehend the translation... shall become imperishable, fearless, unsolicitous and eternally liberated."

Some of his poetry reads:
"Here is the secret of unity, O friend, understand it.
Nowhere exists anything but God.
All that you see or know other than Him,
Verily is separate in name, but in essence is one with God.
Paradise is where no Mulla exists-
Where the noise of his discussions and debate is not heard."

Dara's death, however, also marked the defeat of a gentle philosophy that might have created a closer bond between Hindu and Muslim faiths and saved India from the hatred and carnage of later times.

As with the earlier reforming religions, Islam especially appealed to the lower castes oppressed by Brahminical tyranny. Sufism was far more compatible to the indigenous psyche than the austere precepts of the Prophet as interpreted by narrow-minded mullahs. The preceding centuries under the sword of Islam did not achieve nearly as many conversions as the gentle persuasion and spiritualism of the Sufi saints and fakirs.

Even if individuals like Aurangzeb were staunchly orthodox personally, they seldom interfered in religious practices except in matters concerning state security or revenue. It is sad to relate that while Sikhism might have become a great bridge of harmony between Hindus and Muslims, the reverse was to occur.

Guru Arjan Dev was no bigot as is clear from his composition echoing the precepts of both Vedanta and Sufism:

"I do not keep the Hindu fast or the Muslim Ramzan
I serve him alone who is my refuge
I serve one master, who is also Allah."

In its early stages, Sikhism seemed destined to be a gentle and devotional bridge between Hindu and Islamic religious traditions. The Sikhs began as believers in a gentle, egalitarian and tolerant religion but after persecution from the time of Jehangir they became bands of stubborn, resourceful, predatory and warlike rebels on their main routes between Delhi and Lahore. They were a terrible irritation to the Mughals who undoubtedly tried to exterminate these hardy rebels.

Initially, the persecution was purely political because the new emerging faith was not seen as any threat at the time. Though the Sikh religion had a strong underpinning of Hindu Bhakti philosophy it outwardly resembled Islam in many external ways. The worship of a holy book instead of idols, the shape of the domed Gurdwaras, the prostrations at prayer, the covering of heads at worship, the social egalitarianism and in the prohibitions against intoxicants, etc., were very similar to Islam. In fact Sikhism might have once been a Sufi sect for it is not absolutely certain whether the founder Guru Nanak was Muslim or Hindu. At his death his body was claimed by both his Muslim followers for burial and his Hindu followers for cremation till it miraculously disappeared. Most of the early verses of the Sikh holy book, the Granth Sahib, were composed by him, Kabir and a Sufi saint called Farid.

The conflict between the Mughals and the rebellious Sikhs was to escalate into a severe persecution. While the Mughal attack seemed to be against a religion, the purpose was purely political. The stubborn, and resourceful Sikh brigands were a continuing political irritation, which they ruthlessly tried to exterminate.

But as the sect began to attract a following, it also began to depart from purely spiritual matters and venture into politics. Some unfortunate alliances with rebel Mughal princes drew the wrath of the Mughal establishment as did some policies that threatened Imperial revenue. Similar to the 1/7th tax on Muslims, Guru Arjan Dev issued a directive that 1/10th of all income should go to the gurdwaras and this affected Mughal revenue collection and could not go unchallenged.

Though some historians have given a strong communal colour to the torture and execution of Guru Arjan Dev, very few know that his chief tormentor was no Muslim but a Hindu banker whose daughter Arjan had refused to marry to his son. Paradoxically his main defender was Mian Mir, a revered Muslim divine who is remembered for laying the foundation stone at Harminder Sahib or the Golden Temple at Amritsar. The increasing persecutions, however, turned a gentle Sikhism into a much more militant creed by the time of Guru Gobind Singh.

Even the Sikh turban and beard was not so distinctive at a time when most men wore turbans and beards but Guru Gobind Singh made it, among the five 'Ks' of the steel Kara or bracelet, the Kanga or comb, the Kaccha or underwear and the Kirpan or dagger as mandatory for Sikh warriors. These were howevers required of soldiers and not of ordinary civilians. But the Sikh priests quickly made it mandatory on all male followers.

Many Jat tribes who had settled in North India had been suspicious of the Brahmin priests, rites and sacrifices and found the practical simplicity of Sikhism and its freedom from caste appealing and were to become its main followers.

Unfortunately, even this simple and most practical of religions got thoroughly corrupted by revisionists over the years. Despite being a recent religion where most of the historical facts are on record, their priests soon preached a miasma of superstition, mythology and ritual to many uneducated followers that the founding gurus would have abhorred.

But as they grew stronger the Sikhs were also guilty of persecuting their foes. The Badshahi Mosque of Lahore was turned into a stable. The Sikh rule of Kashmir under Ranjit Singh was marked by a rapacity and brutality remarkable even in these savage times. The word Sika Shahi remains to this day a metaphor for such cruel excesses.

When some of Aurangzeb's minions were on a conversion drive in Kashmir, several Brahmin Pandits went to Amarnath for divine guidance. One of them dreamt of the pious and pacifist Guru Tegh Bahadur and so they went to his seat at Anandpur to seek his help. He agreed to help and went to Delhi with three Hindu companions, Bhai Mati Das, Bhai Sati Das and Bhai Dayala to peacefully appeal to the Emperor. They were immediately arrested and asked to abandon their mission. The Guru remained firm in his resolve even when he was threatened with the death of his companions.

On November 6, 1675, Bhai Mati Das was sawn in two at Chandni Chawk. Bhai Dayala was put into a cauldron of boiling oil the next day and Bhai Sati Das was wrapped in cloth and set ablaze the day after. On November 11, the Guru was beheaded and his head was taken to Sisganj where a gurdwara in his honour now stands.

304 years later, on November 7, 1979, the Delhi Administration, to honour the martyr Bhai Mati Das decided to install a plaque at the place where he had been killed. As Sikhs did not wear turban and beard till the time of Guru Gobind Singh, the image of a Hindu boy was quite correctly portrayed as a clean-shaven young man with short hair. Next morning it was discovered that some Sikh fanatics had smeared it with tar and later smashed it up because the image of this Sikh hero was not of a bearded Sikh in the tradition of later times.

Many Sikhs fervently sing a beautiful aarti that Guru Nanak had written after being appalled by the ostentation at the Jaganath Puri temple, an aarti that proclaims that 'the sky is the platter, the sun and moon the lights, the stars the jewels, the wind the flywhisk, etc.' Despite this, Sikh temples were soon vigorously competing in ostentation with gold-plated domes and other extravagances. Sikh priests, like those of many other religions, became powerful political forces who were unable to resist using the power of religion for political instead of spiritual purposes. Their gurdwaras, instead of being places of spiritual worship, often became hotbeds of intrigue, politics, violence and corruption.

67. Why Did So Many Hindus So Loyally Serve Muslims And Muslims Serve Hindu Rulers?

The Turks, Afghans and Persians were the main soldiers of the Sultanate and Mughal armies but there were several distinguished Muslim officers among the armies of the Rajputs, Marathas, Sikhs and others rulers. But these soldiers and officers were for the most part professional mercenaries and religion was no barrier to loyal service. So many Muslim and Hindu officers loyally served their masters because there was never any feeling of religious betrayal when politics and not religion was the purpose of most medieval Indian wars.

Not only were generals like Raja Man Singh Akbar's most trusted general but even the supposed champions of Hindu rebellion like Shivaji had many high ranking Muslim officers in his army led by Ibrahim Khan Gardi. Opposed to him was Raja Jai Singh of Jodhpur on the side of Aurangzeb. The armies of the proud and resolute Rana Pratap were commanded by a Muslim general Hakim Khan Sur. Raghunath Das was Aurangzeb's first Prime Minister and Raja Jaswant Singh his Governor in Afghanistan.

Two centuries earlier, Malik Kafur, originally a Hindu eunuch of low caste origin was to become Iltutmish's most outstanding general and a century later, Ranjit Singh's artillery was similarly commanded by a Muslim. Tipu Sultan's Prime Minister was a Brahmin named Purnea and another Brahmin called Krishna Rao commanded his armies.

68. WAS ISLAM EVER TOLERANT ?

Although Islam was avowedly a religion of peace it, like all religions, changed drastically over the 1400 years of its history. In the early years it was one of the most liberal of religions offering equality to all men and giving women better rights than had ever been known before. Few Muslims, let alone people of other religions, know verses 2:255 -256 of the Quran that explicitly states:

"let there be no compulsion in religion."

In the 17th century, Protestants facing persecution in Europe remarked on the tolerance to all religions in Turkey. Even the Jews severely persecuted by Christians in Europe commended the tolerance of Islam at the time.

Muslim hotheads in India and many other countries do not even know the meaning of Jihad. The Prophet conducted the first Jihad, or struggle, against cruelty and oppression to establish peace and the rule of righteousness. He specifically enjoined that women and children should not be hurt. He said that killing in the name of Islam is the opposite of Jihad.

The torching of a train at Godra, that triggered the Gujarat riots, was totally against the tenets of the Quran. Islam is not only against the burning of the dead but the living as well. The Prophet said it was a sin to even burn an ant because only God had the supreme right to fire that is imprisoned in hell, so it does not hurt anyone. Anyone who sets another on fire commits the greatest Muslim sin and is destined to the fires of Hell.

During the triumphant first two centuries Islam was very liberal, according to the traditions of the time, and encouraged new scientific thought and unhesitatingly accepted new ideas from others. The initial Arab conquest did use force against other states and rulers but it's, almost communistic, egalitarianism appealed to the people burdened by the heavy chains of the prevailing despotic feudalism, slavery and serfdom. If there had not been this support from the people, enemies would have regrouped behind them and the armies of Islam could never have swept so fast to cover an area from Spain to China in just a few years.

This spirit of inquiry encouraged science, alchemy, and mathematics and rescued the works of Homer, Aristotle, Plato and the great Greek thinkers from oblivion. Their six hundred year rule in Spain was perhaps one of the most enlightened. Christians and Jews lived in harmony with Muslims during this period and many Jews were recognised as its greatest scholars. It was an artistic and scientific culture that transformed a Europe of the dark ages and ignited the spark of the renaissance that was to later make European nations the masters of the world.

Up to the 12th century, the Islamic countries continued to prosper but they had by then abandoned the simplicity and tolerance of earlier times. The rulers quickly became rich, opulent and despotic. Turkish and other Muslim states waged unending wars against Christians and both sides used the banner of threatened religion to unite their ranks and perpetuate myths about the cruelty and treachery of the other. Priests of both camps goaded their kings and knights to whip up hatred for the enemy leading to the Crusades. Later on the Spanish Inquisition perhaps demonstrated the worst example of religious intolerance ever documented.

By the end of the 13th century the Ulema, on their own authority had declared that the doors to revision were closed. Thus the minds of their followers were shut to the huge technological, social and cultural developments that were sweeping through Europe with rapidly increasing complexity. This left Muslims in a quandary of having to try to reconcile their spiritual traditions to a new set of material values.

Where the bitter religious wars of the Crusades had failed, science and commerce succeeded. After the 16th century, the rapid rise of European maritime and economic power driven by their mastery of new technologies and ideas saw the decline of previously powerful Muslim Empires. As they slipped backwards they closed their doors to new ideas and consoled themselves with glorified nostalgia for their past greatness. Their mullahs made their followers believe that this decline was because Muslims had departed from the sacred tenets of their revealed and so unalterable religion.

By the end of the 19th century, Muslim countries had become the poorest in the world. Then the accident of oil suddenly made the rulers of many these countries very rich but did not lift the masses out of their illiteracy or the grip of their mullahs. Increasing poverty fanned the flames of bitterness and hatred and many eager young people seeking release through fanciful myths of past greatness were quick to rise in angry violence against all who they thought were their oppressors. Distorted myths gave justification to violence and oppression.

In an age of growing ignorance many purveyors of religion encouraged the glory of martyrdom. Miracles, talismans and curses, the inevitable refuges of the oppressed, were offered by an assortment of uneducated Babas, Fakirs and Pirs. As always these have been the refuge of the poor and superstition soon overwhelmed the simple social tenets of the Prophet. Religiosity again overcame the simple purity of religion.

In recent times some Muslim leaders, still rooted in mediaeval thinking, began to encourage and finance the fanaticism of their less fortunate Muslim brothers in other countries. Except for Turkey, most Islamic countries were content with the memories of past glories and unwilling to adjust to the challenges of the rapidly accelerating modern world.

The Muslim paranoia about being dominated by a Hindu majority undoubtedly led to the trauma of partition in India. But few know that the main architect of Pakistan, Mohammad Ali Jinnah, had never wanted Pakistan. In 1928 at the Calcutta session of Congress he had said...

"We are all sons of the soil. We have to live together. Believe me there is no progress of India until Mussalmans and Hindus are united."

It was not the Muslims but the Muslim League that had wanted Pakistan. Mani Shankar Aiyar aptly says...

"The Muslim elite voted with their hands for Pakistan but the Muslim masses voted with their feet to stay in India. That is the true measure of their loyalty to the land."

69. Are The Scriptures Of All Religions The Words Of God Or The Writings Of Mortal Men?

No prophet or founder of any religion wrote any of the scriptures. All of them were written long after their deaths by apostles, priests and pious scholars. They were also rewritten and modified frequently over time to suit changing social and economic developments or material needs and also in response to ideas from rival religions. In the process the original words of the founders and their philosophies were often diluted, altered and sometimes lost. Most of the scriptures were also so difficult to read with the severe limitations of writing materials, and in archaic languages that were so difficult to understand, that priestly scholars were necessary to make them comprehensible to their followers.

The scriptures of Buddhism were based on Buddha's discourses after his enlightenment while Judaism, Christianity and Islam were 'Revealed' religions where the prophets claimed to have had revealed to them the immutable words of God. But numerous pious sages, apostles and committed priests actually wrote the scriptures of all religions many years after the death of their founders, prophets or sages.

Buddha's actual words, known as the Dhammapada, were only assembled and put to writing more than a century after his death. The Pali canon, Tipitaka or basket of three disciplines covers discourses, monastic discipline and Dhamma. Over the centuries, hundreds of additional texts were added wherever Buddhism was preached. The Buddhist scriptures evolved and were mainly defined by three councils. The first was held after the Buddha's death, the second, two centuries later, in the time of Ashoka and the third a thousand years later under Kanishka, the Buddhist king in Kashmir. Later, the three main sects were to have their separate scriptures. Mahayana used the Theravada scriptures with many sutras added. They have five series of sacred canonical writings while Hinayana had nine. Vajrayana of Tibet, which only developed after the 8th century AD, added many tantric texts to the Mahayana scriptures.

The New Testament of the Bible has many similar examples. There is no record of the birth of Jesus till 30 years after the crucifixion. The four gospels attributed to Mark, Luke, Mathew and John were only written and circulated between 60 and 125 AD. The apostle Luke had only visited Jerusalem 42 years after the crucifixion and there is also doubt about Mark. The four gospels were only declared authoritative after the pronouncement of Bishop Irenaeus in 185 AD.

The apostle Thomas, the closest friend of Jesus, who was even called his twin, wrote an inspiring gospel but refused to believe in the divinity of his great and beloved friend. He was, therefore, called the 'Doubting Thomas'. This inspiring gospel was therefore expurgated from the Bible by the apostles and priests who took command of Jesus' legacy. The early accounts had been written in Greek but, as Jesus' native tongue was Aramaic and his apostles and followers were mostly uneducated common people and fishermen the actual words of Jesus have been lost forever. Even Judas wrote his gospel. Some Biblical scholars have estimated that only 12 per cent of the words attributed to Jesus are probably authentic.

Christianity only took formal root in the last days of Constantine who had been a pagan sun worshipper till then. In 325 AD he decided

to end the considerable sectarian strife in Rome by fusing many pagan rites and customs into Christianity that was made the new state religion. The tradition of Christ being the son of God was derived from the pre-Christian Sun God Mitras. The birthday of Mitras was on December 25 as was to later became the tradition of Christ. Egyptian sun disks became the models for haloes of Christian saints, The Virgin Mary with the infant Jesus was a carbon copy of statues of the Egyptian goddess Isis nursing her miraculously conceived son Horos.

The Jewish Sabbath had been on a Saturday but was now changed to Sunday. The pagan winter fest became Christmas and Easter their spring festival became the Christian Easter. A new Bible was commissioned raising the human Jesus into a divine Christ. All the earlier gospels and writings were gathered up and burnt.

There were references to reincarnation in the accounts of Old and New Testament till 325 AD when the Emperor Constantine had them deleted. It was only in the second Council of Constantinople in 553 AD that reincarnation was formally declared a heresy. Gnostics and many early Christians notably Clement of Alexandria, Origen and Saint Jerome believed that they had lived before and would live again.

The Christian faith is namely founded on the idea of the resurrection of Jesus, (not Christ that was a title just meaning 'anointed') but this concept that was completely alien to the Jewish tradition that Jesus had often declared as being his mission to restore. He had once declared that he was "sent but unto the lost sheep of Israel." He had no interest in the non-Jews or Gentiles who he once described as dogs. Paradoxically his religion is today almost entirely followed by non-Jews.

But even the Jewish faith had evolved over the roughly twelve hundred years since Moses led the Israelites out of Egypt. Nothing illustrates this drift better than the story of the Ten Commandments that almost everyone accepts as a sacred tradition. Few know that the old Jewish tradition had 637 commandments handed to Moses by Yahova and that these were whittled down to ten by the Jewish clerics over the ages. Jesus however departed from the Jewish tradition by introducing a concept of compassion and love that might have been influenced by Buddhism that at this time had reached Persia and even Egypt. If he had been in Kashmir during his years in the wilderness, as many believe, this could have also been the explanation.

The idea of resurrection, so important to the Christian tradition, was added much after the Crucifixion. It was actually a concept borrowed from the Egyptian rites of the dead that believed that the body (Ba) and the soul (Ka) were to separate at death and to be reunited the Day of Final Judgment. This completely non-Jewish idea was used as a device to raise Jesus from a mere mortal to the stature of a god. St Paul, in his first letter to the Corinthians states:

"If Christ is not raised, then our preaching is in vain and so is our faith". But the Jews considered Christianity's greatest heresy was the proposition that Yahova, the great and indivisible God, could be divided into a father, son and holy ghost.

Paradoxically while early Christianity had furiously attacked the multiplicity of Pagan deities, it was to later add the worship of Mary, hosts of angels and over ten thousands saints and petron saints who are worshipped for their individual qualities in exactly the same way as the old pagan idols.

While Christians and Muslims talk of the Final Judgment, very few know about the 'First Judgment' for how can there be a final one without a first one? According to the ancient Egyptian rites of the dead, the first judgment was held on the banks of the Nile immediately after death. Witnesses would ask the collected crowd of mourners if there were anyone who accused the deceased of any heinous crime and if they could convince the witnesses, that the deceased had done a grievous sin, his body would be denied burial in the caverns of the dead on the west bank of the Nile to await the Final Judgment and left on the sands to be devoured by dogs, crows or crocodiles. The Pharaohs, of course, were mummified in their special pyramids or cavern in the Valley of the Kings.

In the Last Judgment the soul would be weighed with feathers to be united again with its carefully preserved mortal body. The Egyptian fascination for the after life and the elaborate rituals to preserve the mortal remains of the deceased was to influence many other later religions and also began the fashion of building magnificent tombs among many other religions

As the history of the Bible has been assiduously researched, it is significant that the oldest texts are the Codex Vaticanus that are dated to the 4th century AD while the oldest surviving Hebrew manuscript is the Codex Petropoltanus dated to 916 AD. These and other venerated accounts, therefore, incorporated many later traditions as with the scriptures of all religions.

70. Were The Scriptures Of Islam Also Modified Over Time?

The history of the Quran, like the Bible before it, is quite well documented and gives interesting insights into the compilation of all scriptures. Few people know that the Quran only began to be compiled many years after the unexpected death of the Prophet in

632 AD at the age of 62. There had been several earlier versions of the utterances of the Prophet during the 23 years after he received the revelation from the angel Gabriel. At this time there were only eleven people in Mecca who knew how to write and Zaid Ibn Thabit, one of the Prophet's youngest companions, was given the task of writing it by Khalif Abu Bakr (632-634AD).

He dutifully wrote these out based on his recall and with contributions made by numerous other witnesses to Muhammad's words. These had been inscribed on bits of skin, wood, palm leaves and on the shoulder blades of sheep and camels. He compiled them more or less in the order of the largest accounts first. The Third Khalif, Othman (644-56) then ordered all the Suras, or verses, to be gathered in the definitive Madina version in 665 AD or 33 years after the Prophet's death. Many other versions of the Prophet's utterances that were in circulation were then declared to be inauthentic and were gathered up and burned. Only fragments of the earliest versions in the old upright Kufic script survive. The two oldest surviving copies of the Quran in the more rounded later script are in Istanbul and in Uzbekistan and are dated to about 200 years later.

But the Suras or verses of the Quran did not answer all the questions of a changing society so the Muslim clerics sought further scriptural authorities for interpreting Islamic law. Two hundred years after the death of the Prophet, several clerics especially the pious and celebrated Al-Bukhari, a devout Muslim scholar from Bukhara, travelled the entire Muslim world to write out most of the Hadith. Not surprisingly, he was appalled by the credulity of people who tried to make miracles out of trivialities, and on his own authority, he rejected 99.6 per cent of the 600,000 pious contributions that he had received. Thus, the Sharia, meaning path, relied on the Quran and the Sunna, or the teachings of the Prophet as well as the Hadith that contains stories and traditions from his life that were added much later.

Sharia law, had three levels of crime. 'Had' crimes were the most serious concerning murder, apostasy, theft, adultery, etc., on which the Prophet had declared the word of God and the punishments required. 'Tazir' crimes had not been mentioned in the Quran like bribery, charging interest and selling defective goods for which the

Qazis, or judges, imposed fines, flogging or seizure of property. 'Qesas' crimes allowed a victim's family retribution or retaliation. There was no distinction between civil and religious law in Islam, the Qazis, usually appointed by the rulers or their governors, ruled on religious as well as on all civil, personal, criminal and other matters.

Many additions came later. In the Quran Muhammad, for example, had never said that women must wear a veil (hijjab) in the presence of male strangers. The Surah 24: 30-31 simply states:

> "Enjoin believing women to turn their eyes from temptation and to preserve their chastity, to cover their adornments and draw their veils over their bosoms and not reveal their finery except to their husbands... close relations... and their slave girls."

But as the women of the Prophet's household, as in many tribal or rural societies, even in modern times, used to cover their faces in the presence of male visitors, this example was used as a model and rigorously imposed later on by chauvinist Islamic priests on all Muslim women.

On the Indian subcontinent, and nowhere else initially, a hideous head to toe tent like black or dark burkha with netted eyeholes was demanded by the local mullas. It is believed that the burkha was originally used by highborn Hindu women in Punjab and Kashmir to keep them hidden from the sight of common people. In most feudal areas, pretty girls were also at risk of being kidnapped or simply acquired by local rulers or influential people. So surprisingly, it came to be regarded as a distinctive mark of status.

The Quran also says nothing against alcohol though it speaks several times about the evils of intoxication that could be from wines, spirits or drugs. In later times, however, the clerics made draconian pronouncements against alcohol and tobacco in any form or quantity.

Few people can understand why educated Muslims do not speak up against Jihadi fanaticism. Most people also equate terrorism with Muslim fundamentalism and do not know that a fairly recent Islamic sect has succeeded in capturing the minds of most poor Muslims.

Islam had many changes over the centuries. The first schism occurred when the Shia sect split from the dominant Sunnis and though it affirmed its faith in the Quran it developed its own Hadith. But there were many other sects, with their own interpretations of Islam like the Fatimids, Sufis, Kaljrijites, Ismailis, Zaidis, Nizaris, Alawis and others.

In the late 18th century Abd Al Wahhab, an Egyptian cleric, began the Sunni Wahhabiya movement that while accepting the Quran and Hadith as fundamental texts virulently opposed all innovations, superstitions and deviances contrary to a very narrow interpretation of the fundamental texts in a severely puritanical and legalistic form. It even opposed the worshipping of Muhammad or other saints or praying at their tombs. It tried to enforce very strict restrictions on the rights of women, prohibited the wearing of charms, going to sorcerers, etc.

Many of their beliefs however went beyond the teachings of the Prophet. The Quran had expressly forbidden an attack on anyone who had offered no offence or to harm or to kill women and children. It was also forbidden to take hostages, to torture or kill prisoners or to commit suicide.

Unfortunately the Wahhabi al-Saud dynasty conquered Mecca and Madina in 1924 giving them control of the Hajj. This enabled their fiery clerics to preach their extreme version of Islam to the entire Islamic world. Then the enormous wealth earned from oil, discovered in Arabia in 1938, enabled them to fund the construction and repairs of mosques around the world and finance the madrassas, or Islamic schools, attached to them, so their radical influence quickly spread throughout the Muslim world. They were ardent proselytisers who quickly radicalised the people from Indonesia to Uzbekistan and other places where Islam had earlier been quite tolerant.

Though the Wahhabis were themselves quite a recent sect of Islam they furiously attacked other gentler Muslim sects like the Ahmadiyas. The CIA then decided that such fanatics would be helpful in expelling the Russians from Afghanistan and financed the Taliban. The children of over three million poor Afghan refugees studying in Pakistan madrassas created an army of indoctrinated and gullible youngsters. But the fanatics considered the Saudi surrender to The economic and political influence of America as a great heresy and the Al Quaida was born. Osama bin Laden was thus an American creation and the USA reaped a whirlwind of its own creation.

The destructive American attacks on Afghanistan and Iraq alienated many moderate Muslims who felt that these attacks were morally unjustified and many felt that words like 'Axis of Evil' confirmed the idea that the US and its allies were on a virtual Crusade to destroy Islam itself. Many moderates, including some well educated young men from good families, became much easier to recruit.

In India, the radicalisation of Hindus with the Jehadi rhetoric of Hindutva suited the Muslim radicals perfectly. Revenge is sadly an important element of the Arabian psyche and being a part of Muslim thinking inspired vengeance for the massacres after the destruction of the Babri Masjid and subsequent mayhem in Mumbai and Gujarat.

It is unlikely that the moderate Muslim majority will try to regain control of the mosques or places of religious education until the many poor Muslims can be educated enough or can earn enough to be liberated from their influence. George Bush's 'war on terror' may have been motivated by his domestic political compulsions or by a 'cowboy' spirit of revenge but this will paradoxically strengthen his enemies. Muslim extremists may not bow down before American weapons but could become more moderate if more Muslims could believe that Wahhabi extremism is a heresy to the preaching of Muhammad and true spirit of Islam.

71. WHAT ABOUT THE SCRIPTURES OF INDIAN FAITHS?

Like the priests of all religions the Brahmin priests and scholars continuously revised elaborated and modified the many forms of indigenous faith and worship. While they always claimed the sanctity of the Vedas, they very readily abandoned the Vedic deities and installed new gods, goddesses and lesser deities of the Puranas that had mostly evolved out of numerous local tribal beliefs. Very much later they also raised Krishna and Ram from heroes of legend to deities popular of worship as well. New traditions gradually incorporated many tribal deities and philosophies as well as many of the traditions and philosophies of Buddhism and Jainism into their evolving faith. Selective passages and verses of the Vedas were always used to sanctify the evolving traditions.

Though many originally tribal deities like Jaganath, Venkateshwar and Murugan had no place in Brahminical scriptures, the Brahmin priests had no difficulty in finding some obscure reference in their huge ocean of literature to sanctify them and had no hesitation in presiding over new forms of worship. Though Brahmins today account for a tiny percentage of the Indian population they have successfully moulded the greater Indian majority to become very Brahmanical in their thinking, taboos and customs.

The much more recent Sikh religion that is well documented also shows how quickly the simple original philosophies and practices became corrupted by myths, superstitions and ostentations that the early Gurus would never have approved of. Their holy book the Granth Sahib was compiled by Guru Arjun Dev, the fifth Guru and is mainly compiled from the poetry and utterances of Guru Nanak, Kabir and the Sufi Farid. All of whom were saintly pacifists and even revered as Muslim saints by some of their followers.

It was Guru Gobind Singh, the tenth Guru (1675 - 1708), who made the sect militant 200 years after the founder Guru Nanak and added his Granth with many poems in praise of the warlike goddess Devi although idols were never allowed. He also abolished the previous caste-based surnames and all Sikhs were now to be called Singh, meaning lion, instead of their old caste names. Caste prejudices were not, however, so easily abolished and many Sikhs still write their caste or village names after the word Singh.

He introduced new disciplines including the five 'Ks.' Today, social pressure however makes almost all Sikhs have uncut hair and a turban and there is great outrage if any of the first nine Sikhs or their followers are ever depicted with shorn heads or beard as they may have actually been.

Although the Sikh Gurus abhorred idolatry and religiosity, their priests quickly made compromises to cater to the pernicious residues of earlier practices. To avoid idolatry they only worship their sacred book, the Granth Sahib, but in practice it is often worshipped as if it were an idol to be awakened and put to sleep with special music and food, clothed in warm cloths in winter or cool muslins in summer. Some are even provided with their own air-conditioners. Professional priests even sing a long uninterrupted recitation, the Akhand Path, in the same way that many Hindus have proxy prayers chanted for them by professional priests.

Perhaps the most bizarre Hindu practice is the recent processions of Kanwarias carrying two pots of holy Ganges water to their towns and villages. A pious practice that has no scriptural precedent. Curiously most of these pilgrims are not doing this pious pilgrimage for bettering their own karma but are paid by patrons to earn punya by proxy for them. But the pious hordes have in recent years become a serious traffic problem in the area every August.

History clearly shows that none of the scriptures of any religion can be proved to have been the immortal or immutable words of God or even the original words of the prophets or sages. They were in every case the writings of many devout mortal men. None of them were as infallible, inflexible, immortal and unchanging as their priests always claimed but had been in a process of constant evolution as the social and economic conditions of their followers changed. They all also borrowed many philosophical concepts, customs and rituals from each other.

There had first been a long oral tradition then the Vedas, Puranas as well as the epics like the Mahabharata and Ramayana that were all written by mortal men, as were the Buddhist and Jain scriptures, the Bhagavad Gita and the Granth Sahib.

Priests, to secure their hold over their patrons, willingly endorsed many popular social practices that had no place in the original scriptures. Raja Ram Mohan Roy, appalled by the Sati (widow burning) that his widowed sister-in-law was being required to suffer, studied Sanskrit and all the old scriptures and found no sacred text to support the cruel practice. He concluded that the practice of Sati had been created by avaricious relations interested in seizing the property of a dead husband and he then fought to abolish Sati.

The priests of every faith, as the devoted salesmen of their faiths, predictably claimed that their scriptures were the faithful record of the words of their sacred sages or prophets that had to be scrupulously followed down to the smallest detail. As they were all imbued with sacred and almost magical import, there would be great outrage if anyone dared to question their origins or meanings. All scriptures contain words of great wisdom, beauty and universal application as well as many that are irrelevant in changing times and even destructive in the hands of unlettered bigots. As professional priests took control of religions, ostentations, religiosity, rituals and superstition soon overwhelmed the simple tenets of the founders.

72. WHY ARE BLASPHEMY AND SACRILEGE CONSIDERED TO BE SUCH SERIOUS SINS BY ALL RELIGIONS?

Although blasphemy, sacrilege, heresy and apostasy did no injury to man or to society they could undermine the sanctity of the carefully nurtured scriptures and so the power of their priests. Writings or investigations that questioned, challenged, mocked or denigrated the mythology built around the prophets or sages and traditions especially enraged the priests of all religions. Paradoxically, the gods could be insulted but never the prophets that perhaps were considered to be proprietary to each faith. History, however, has no room for priestly sentiments, as facts of the past are non negotiable facts and cannot be altered to suit the sentiments of believers. The records of past events have to be respected even if they might offend the opinions of many who are steeped in a romanticised version of the past.

Apostasy, or rejection of the 'true faith', after accepting it was especially abhorrent to priests of all colours. The ignorant believer of another faith could be more easily forgiven than one who rejected the tenets of a religion after it had been learned and accepted. It was such a bad a testimonial to any religion that the offender had to be severely punished, banished, reviled or even killed.

As the prophets and saints were raised by their priests from human to divine levels, they had to be presented in an image of unblemished purity and goodness. So blasphemous charges concerning the morals of any of the prophets or saints were especially abhorrent.

Predictably there are many contemporary accounts that the clerics completely expurgated from all holy texts. Not surprisingly, all religions wanted to closely control science and history so that they could not raise doubts about the validity of their scriptures. Freethinking, encouraged by liberal education, was an anathema to them all.

Most Christians will be horrified by the Latin text 'De Sectaculis' written about 223 AD that says Jesus was the son of a prostitute, or by the account of Origin in 248 AD that states that... "Jesus fabricated the account of his birth from a virgin when in fact, Jesus' mother had been driven out by the carpenter husband to whom she was betrothed because she had committed adultery with a (Roman) soldier named Panthera. Left poor and homeless, she gave birth to Jesus in secret. Jesus later spent time in Egypt, where he hired himself out as a labourer, learned magic, and so came to claim the title of God."

The Vatican was understandably quick to search for the Dead Sea Scrolls and other texts as soon as they were reported to protect their carefully nurtured beliefs and mythology from being subjected to historical review. They predictably condemned the popular novel the Da Vinci Code that claimed that Jesus had been married to Mary Magdalene.

Materialistic motives also had an influence. Some Islamic scholars believe that Muhammad's victory over the Meccans would not have been possible until he had declared that the Kaaba (meaning holy of holies) in Mecca to be the house of God instead of the holy temple on Mt. Moriah in Jerusalem that he had earlier advocated. Many early suras of the Quran refer to worship within Solomon's house of God that was clearly not possible in the solid rock Kaaba. The Meccans had evidently objected to Muhammad's teaching as the destruction of the 365 idols at the Kaaba would have deprived them of huge income from the rich offerings of the many pilgrims. But when numerous Muslim pilgrims were to come instead their objections were over. The idea of the Prophet being influenced by such a mercenary or political motive is clearly abhorrent to believers.

Muslims are also very emotive about the Al Aqsa mosque in Jerusalem even if history shows that the first mosque built there was in 638 AD, or six years after the death of the Prophet, by Khalif

Omar. In fact it had first been a Jewish temple built by Solomon in 956 BC and later destroyed by Nebuchadnezzar in 586 BC. In 538 BC, Cyrus the Great ordered it to be rebuilt when he freed the Jews from Babylon. Under the Byzantine rulers of Constantinople, the site had been a church of St Mary of Justinian. It then changed hands several times with the fortunes of the Crusades. Such a record makes Muhammad's dream flight on a winged horse to this mosque rather unlikely but many Muslims would be appalled if this widely believed tradition were to be treated as just a flight of imagination.

The priests as well as the fanatics of all religions are well aware that history can debunk some of their carefully cherished beliefs and spare no efforts to try to subvert or control anything that endangers them. Such facts are therefore considered heretical and faith is often made a justification to deny any inconvenient revisions.

73. DO ALL RELIGIONS BORROW IDEAS FROM EACH OTHER?

The priests of every religion shamelessly borrowed popular philosophies, myths, customs and rituals from each other especially in ancient times when it was difficult to compare the claims of rival faiths. Beads and rosaries were probably a Buddhist idea originally but are now found in every religion. There had been tribal religious festivals corresponding to the spring and autumn harvests from ancient times in every country. Large organised pilgrimages to places of worship, however, probably began with Islam.

The ancient Egyptian religious traditions still survive and continue to influence many religions. Their tradition of tombs to preserve the mortal remains of great people spread from Egypt to Rome, where many of the first Christian converts were Egyptian slaves. They influenced Christian and Islamic burials in later times. The tradition of magnificent tombs for great kings or noblemen is unknown in Arabia but came to India with the Persian influence. Recently, King Fahd of Saudi Arabia, although one of the richest men in the world, was buried in a simple unmarked grave.

Skull caps are now common among Jewish and Muslim worshippers but the practice probably began with the Magi priests of ancient Persia to prevent human hair falling into the sacred fire and contaminating it.

Many Egyptian elements are found in Roman Catholicism. The word Pope is derived from Pharaoh while his crown is the same shape as the twin crown of the Pharaohs and the style of the Pope's shepherd's crop and flail across the chest is almost identical to representations of the Pharaohs.

The worship of Mary or the concept of a mother and child was alien to the Jewish or early Christian tradition but the Egyptian cult of Isis and her beloved son Horos was copied as it appealed to the multitude of Egyptian slaves in ancient Rome. The idea of the Madonna only became Catholic dogma in 1854 AD. The festival of Christmas was unheard of in early Christianity but the priests were unable to discourage the popular Roman rites of Saturnalia or the winter fest. If Jesus was born in a manger, at a time when sheep had lambs, his birth would have had to be in September. But professional priests, always ready to take control of other faiths including some of the older traditions of paganism that they claimed to abhor, created the myth of Christ's nativity to continue the popular winter festival. They were quite willing to accommodate alien traditions as long as the worshippers remained subject to their control.

The Greek Orthodox Church only believed in the Father and Son, while Roman Catholics believed in the Father, Son and Holy Ghost. Early Christians, like the Jews, had abhorred all graven images including the crucifix. When the Portuguese came to south India, the 'Thomas' Christians who had been in India almost from the time of Christ were appalled by the crucifix, portraits and statues that the Catholic visitors carried in complete violation of the early tenets of Christianity. The Portuguese, in turn, regarded them as heretics and tried to force them to adopt their version of Christianity.

Although Islam is considered a religion based on the revelation received by Muhammad, the Quran and Hadith contain a huge baggage of Jewish and Christian ideas, beliefs and customs along with a huge baggage of ancient Arab traditions like Eid and Ramzan that long predate Muhammad.

Competitive rituals also crept into all religions. If Muslims recited 99 names of Allah, 99 or 108 names of Vishnu became a similar chant for many Hindus. Shias had their Muharram processions so Gangadhar Tilak began the Ganesh Chaturti processions in Maharashtra a century ago to unite Hindus in similar festive parades. Not to be outdone Sunnis recently started having religious processions on the birthday of the Prophet. A Hindu Navratra similarly may have been inspired by a pre - Islamic Persian Nauroz that later became part of Shia custom and marks the summer and autumn equinox. It is significant that these dates are based on the solar calendar even though all other Hindu festivals follow the lunar calendar.

Perhaps the worst competition is the sound pollution caused by loudspeakers perhaps beginning with the Muslim Azaan was soon a part of the loud sounds emanating from loudspeakers at every other place of worship. The tradition of a Muezzin calling the faithful to prayer dated from the time of Muhammad but the scriptures of no religion requires electronic amplification of the prayers or sermons in their places of worship. An omnipresent God is not deaf and will surely hear the prayers of every worshipper. Loudspeakers are not for the religious but are tools of competitive religiosity.

74. CAN HINDUISM LEGITIMATELY CLAIM TO HAVE HAD THE LONGEST TRADITION OF CONTINUOUS RELIGION?

Hinduism never had a continuous tradition and was not uniform. It was actually a shifting label that had meant many different things at different times over the 2,600 years since Cyrus the Great first used the word Hindu to define the people living beyond the Indus. While the old religious traditions of Egypt and Babylon died out the Zoroastrian faith, preserved by a small community of Parsis, is probably the oldest surviving unbroken religious tradition. The Chinese and Jewish traditions also have as long a continuous religious tradition as Hinduism.

Hinduism, as generally practised in India today, is very different to the forms of religion in earlier times. The dedicated Brahmin priests, however, managed most of India's religious evolution for roughly 3,000 years. In the beginning, as in all religions, this tradition was oral but was put to writing from about the time of Christ.

Their deities, beliefs and customs steadily evolved over the years as they assimilated many local customs over the centuries.

The evolution of worship in India evolved through several distinct stages:

1. The earliest was the tribal tradition of worshipping the spirits or 'jivas' believed to inhabit every mountain, river, tree, rock and other object. These animists had no priests but 'Shamans' who would organise sacrifices, including blood sacrifices of buffaloes, goats , chickens and even humans to gain the blessings of the spirits into whose domain people thought they were intruding. These customs still survive in many remote tribal areas.

2. Then came the Vedic tradition of the Aryas with their elemental gods of the sun, storms, earth, waters, fire, etc., with Brahmin priests chanting Vedic hymns and performing great sacrifices at fire altars with magnificent ceremonies in order to gain boons.

3. Buddhist and Jain philosophy coexisted with early Arya forms of worship in the beginning but Brahmin priests and their patrons were more forceful than the gentle Buddhist monks and Buddhism was successfully erased in India by the 9th century AD. Both Buddhists and Jains believed in peace, harmony and sanctity of all life. Their beliefs of reincarnation, Karma, Dharma and Ahimsa later became an intrinsic part of Hindu belief,

4. Towards the end of the 1,000-year period of Buddhist supremacy came another form of Hinduism with the Puranas that introduced a huge multitude of new deities into vastly elaborated Hindu beliefs and customs. Shiv and Vishnu only now emerged as great gods with new companions like Ganesh, Lakshmi, Parvati, Saraswati, Devi, Kali, etc. The elaboration of great myths like the Ramayana and Mahabharata were accorded near religious importance. This was also the period of India's great temples. Inspired by Shankaracharya there was now a strong Brahminical revival that tried to assimilate many local customs and eliminate competing faiths. A vigorous

Brahminical revival introduced a new idea of a 'One God' into a previously pluralistic tradition, the caste system hardened and a new caste of Kshatriyas was created who unleashed a wave of persecution on Buddhists and Jains.

5. In the Mughal period, the almost forgotten legendary heroes, Ram and Krishna were elevated to 'Man Gods' and became objects of deep personal devotion unlike the abstract and distant stone deities of the past. They had initially been the gods of the underprivileged and were later assimilated into the evolving Hindu belief. The Bhakti devotional cults such as Vedanta, and Sufiism continued to be preached by individual sages requiring no idols or places of worship.

6. After the 19th century, when the British had superseded the Mughal rulers and most of their customs, the increasingly educated Hindus, began to be aware that there was little knowledge about their own history, culture and religion. Little was known about any great Hindu King, and many religious scriptures like the Vedas, the Upanishads or even the Bhagavat Gita were not known as they were mostly in the secret records of a few Brahmin pandits. Only the Ramayana and Mahabharata were widely enacted folktales. The Upanishads were first discovered and translated into Persian by Dara Shikoh around 1650 from where it was translated into French and English before becoming more widely known in India. The Rigveda was extracted from a reluctant Brahmin in Benares by Coerdeveaux in 1767 and was eagerly studied by German scholars before being known in popular Indian languages. Even the Bhagavad Gita was first translated by Charles Wilkins in 1787 and was virtually unknown to the people of India till a century ago.

There was now a strong hankering for a unifying Hindu religion and Raja Ram Mohan Roy in 1826 first began the use of the word Hindu to describe a religion instead of it just being a label for the local people. Hinduism, as a religion, was only now born. This label, that tried to unify India's numerous local religious practices also needed a common scripture comparable to a Bible or Quran and the Bhagavad Gita was clearly the best choice. If Shankaracharya's Bhasya is traditionally regarded as the earliest commentary on the Gita it must have been added to the Mahabharata at a very late stage. The simple original text was edited by many Indian philosophers like Vivekananda, Sri Aurobindo, Tilak and many others and Radhakrishnan's version only appeared in 1948. Under the influence of the now popular European standards of ethics and morality, several casteist and obscurantist sections were quietly deleted and its inspiring philosophical core was strongly promoted.

7. A virulently revivalist Hinduism began with the freedom movement and increasingly strident Hindu leaders began to view India's religion, culture and history in a much more aggressive manner. As the history of the Harappans, Mauryas, Sungas and Guptas began to emerge and people became aware of India's great historic and literary heritage there was a growing belief that Hindus greatness had been deliberately suppressed by foreign invaders V. D. Sarvarkar (1883-1966) whose militant hostility led to a prison sentence of 50 years followed by K. B. Hedgewar (1889-1940) and M. S. Golwalkar (1906- 1973) were to add fuel to the flames especially among followers of linguistic groups like the Shiv Sean in Maharashtra. Their glorified Brahmanism not only bitterly opposed anything to do with Muslims or Christians but also began a vigorous evangelical campaign to bring millions of tribal people into the fold of their religious convictions. An expansion into politics followed with the formation of the RSS whose political arm the Jan Sangh evolved to become the BJP. The massacre of millions at India's partition in August 1947 greatly inflamed the religious hatred.

It seemed unthinkable to many that India had never been a really Hindu country. It had been mostly Buddhist for a thousand years from the time of Ashoka to Harsha and Islamic from the 12th to the 18th century and then British till 1947. As India's history became known and old religious texts were discovered and popularised there was an enormous resurgence of pride in all things Indian.

This pride extended to regional groups and there was soon a huge pride in the ancient local cultures of Bengal, Maharashtra, Tamilnadu, Kerala and other states.

It sometimes went too far and many inventive writers and scholars would embroider the available facts to promote hugely exaggerated ideas about India's literature and history. The theory of Aryans originating in India had not been consistent with the absence of horses in ancient India but two Hindu academics proudly displayed a depiction of two horses in the image of an alleged Harappan seal that was promptly printed in some history textbooks during the period of BJP rule. In 2000 Michael Wetzel of Harvard University showed how the computer-generated image of a real seal had been deliberately manipulated to show the image of the two horses. As the textbooks were not withdrawn this patent fraud has become established history to millions of students.

Many of these concepts overlapped each other and the practised forms of Hinduism contain many of these elements simultaneously. As the Brahmins assimilated the many traditions they wove a complex tapestry of mythology including the mystification of historical events and personages. These with elaborate rituals made a shallow and often baseless religiosity triumph over India's rich and pluralistic heritage of religious philosophy and tolerance. The advent of cinema and TV allowed many producers to elaborate and exaggerate many religious themes.

75. How Did The British So Easily Defeat The Mughals?

Mughal rulers had learned nothing from history and like the Afghans and Rajputs before them had gradually lost their lean and mean martial tradition and surrendered to India's love of pomp and luxury and were quite easily routed. By 1740, the Mughal emperors had lost much of their vigorous martial spirit, become too effete to command the respect of their subjects and were unable to control the numerous local rulers who sprang up in every area. India once again lapsed into a state of political uncertainty and anarchy. Although many smaller kingdoms had spun off and many aggressive adventurers created new ones, there was no longer any central command and control. The marauding Maratha bands ranging all over the country also disrupted many older kingdoms.

Though the British, like the French and Dutch, came as mere traders they quickly found that they could exploit the power vacuum by manipulating the easily flattered and avaricious local rulers to their advantage. Their leaders were not hereditary rulers but professional officers. The tradition of the Christian churches had created management systems where individuals rose through the ranks of command on the basis of their abilities, courage, intellect and management skills. So European officers conditioned to a multilayered organisational structure could take independent decisions without having to wait for commands from a despotic and often distant ruler. It also allowed teamwork and a continuity of command that was not dependent on a mortal and sometimes incapable individual ruler.

After the British had defeated or marginalised their European competitors they began to exploit the opportunities that came their way. They found that their small well-trained and professionally led armies could defeat many more numerous enemies. Unlike the Mughal, Maratha or Sikh armies opposing them, they relied on tight boxes of infantry armed with new quick firing muskets. These, time and again, broke the wild cavalry charges of their foes. These troops were also trained to execute complicated battlefield manoeuvers unlike Indian troops who were trained as individual soldiers and horseman but were not taught to move in well-coordinated groups. British officers also worked closely with their sepoys and led with personal examples of courage and endurance.

British cannon were also very effective. Unlike the immense and unwieldy Mughal cannons that could only be fired once every 15 to 30 minutes, they had light field guns that could be fired rapidly and moved from place to place.

Much of the native cavalry were on horses that were individually owned by mercenary soldiers who were therefore careful not to risk their precious mounts and thus their livelihoods, in close combat. British troops, on the other hand, rode company owned horses and were also regularly paid, and were therefore, far more loyal than

early successes, they became ambitious and went on a spree of conquest between 1750 to 1857 fighting determined opposition from Mysore, the Marathas, the Sikhs and the Gurkhas.

Just 200,000 Englishmen were able to dominate 300 million Indians at the time of independence but their success would not have been possible without the willing, even eager cooperation of millions of Indians as their loyal and devoted servants.

Their alliance with mercantile interests, especially the Bania/ Marwari community was another factor in British success. These financiers found their investments with the British a much better risk than those with the many native rulers. They not only funded many of the individual and collective adventures of their British masters but were willing agents in mercilessly extracting rent from the peasants regardless of the harvests with the result that the once prosperous Bengal was quickly turned into a barren land.

Farmers on large tracts were forced to grow indigo as a valuable cash crop instead of rice and so added to the shortage of food. It went too far and endemic peasant indebtedness dried out any reserves for survival leading to repeated famines.

Both Muslim and Indian rajas and amirs were used to serving a superior emperor so it mattered little whether the sovereign was British or Mughal. As for the common people who had no memory of Hindu rulers, except in distant myth so they had become accustomed to many centuries of subservience to despotic rulers thus having a Muslim or British ruler made very little difference.

India had invented the zero that revolutionised mathematics but gained little from this knowledge while the Europeans learned mathematics from the Arabs and effectively used it as a base for a new science. From China Europe learned about the magnetic compass and used it to take ocean navigation to new frontiers. From China it also learned how to make gunpowder and soon made guns and canon of increasing range, power and accuracy. From China it learned about paper and printing but made an improved printing press with moving type to rapidly multiply knowledge.

The Europeans were also excellent organisers who balanced individual achievement with group action to operate in effective

teamwork. This was in sharp contrast to the egocentric individualism, disruptive intrigue and personal aggrandisement of their despotic opponents.

British alliances with Indian rulers were another major factor in British success. But this policy changed with the growing strength of the position of the English. Before 1800, the alliances were mostly temporary marriages of convenience but after the defeat of Tipu Sultan in 1799, they became much more arrogant and interfering. Many portions of the territories of Awadh, Hyderabad and other states were arbitrarily annexed and British Residents at the courts of all princes began to interfere in internal affairs. While the object was supposed by to curb evil social practices like Sati and despotic oppression, they also acted in the interests of British politics and trade. But when they began interfering in the succession of various kingdoms and wanted their pliant nominees to succeed the princes desired by rulers without heirs, it became intolerable to many rulers and was a major factor in the revolt of 1857.

The great upheaval of 1857 was a huge shock to the increasingly arrogant but complacent British rulers. Many mostly leaderless rebellious groups with different agendas rushed to Lucknow, Kanpur and Delhi and many did indulge in the bloody killing of many British men and women. So when the rebellion was suppressed the British indulged in even more savagely vengeful massacres. Rebels were strung from trees or blown from canons to make an example of the price of defying the British. Although the senile last Mughal Emperor, Bahadur Shah Zafar, was only a feeble and helpless bystander to the events, the British were determined to eradicate every vestige of the Mughal lineages. The old emperor was exiled to Burma and the royal princes and many courtiers were cold bloodedly slaughtered.

But this mutiny of the company sepoys that soon attracted numerous other malcontents was a rude shock to the British even if new recruits mainly from Punjab, ultimately suppressed these hired employees. But it stopped the British spate of annexations and the British abruptly confirmed the remaining 562 kingdoms controlling one-third of Indian territory. This new found security and gratitude of their subjects ensured that they would not have any trouble in the areas of their rule.

The opening of the Suez Canal in 1869 allowed cheap ocean passages to bring droves of Christian missionaries and shiploads of young British ladies whose Victorian values shattered many existing relationships between many British officers and their Indian consorts.

Many Indians with some level of education now began to enter British Government service with devoted loyalty to their masters. The British Raj now became a joint venture with many willing Indian stakeholders.

Until General Dyer's brutal massacre at Jallianwalla Bagh in 1919 most Indian leaders believed in the innate decency of the British rulers and were content to aspire to nothing more than a chance to debate policies for better rule by the British. Gandhi was to later lament :

> "The English have not taken India: we have given it to them. They are not in India because of their strength but because we keep them. it is truer to say that we gave India to the English than that India was lost."

Britain's greatest betrayal of India was undoubtedly the events leading to the bloody partition of August 15, 1947. The Viceroy Lord Louis Mountbatten was in such a hurry to be rid of his responsibilities in India, to gain his life's ambition of becoming the

First Lord of the Admiralty, that he brought forward the date of partition by eight months. This left just two months for the huge exercise to be organised. The hastily drawn Radcliffe Award defining the line between Hindu India and Muslim Pakistan was presented to the Viceroy a week before the partition and had not even been distributed when over 14 million Hindus and Muslims tried to leave for what they thought would be safer areas. This line went through the middle of many cities and no one even knew if Lahore was to go to India or to Pakistan.

The British then withdrew their soldiers to their garrisons for quick repatriation to Britain. Indian and Pakistani army units were in complete disarray as many officers and soldiers left to try to find new posts in their new countries. Law and order, left in the hands of Hindu or Muslim dominated local policemen, was a recipe for certain disaster. The unchecked slaughter that followed was to hugely raise old religious suspicions to a level of vitriolic hatred.

76. WHY DID SO FEW INDIANS OPPOSE THE BRITISH?

When they were founded, the Congress and Muslim League were no hotbeds of nationalistic rebellion but clubs of the rich landlords, leading lawyers and effete nawabs who were staunchly loyal to the British on whom their prosperity depended. They were little more than elegant English-speaking debating societies with members aspiring to positions or business opportunities or to place numerous 'Humble Petitions' before their British masters.

After 1857, the British bestowed numerous lavish honours on loyal subjects to ensure their grovelling obedience. Special Coats of Arms were designed for 102 rulers in 1877. Knighthoods, Orders of the Crown, Orders of Merit, Kaiser-i-Hind and many new titles as Nawabs, Khan Bahadurs, Talukdars, Zamindars, Darbaris, etc., were liberally showered on subjects eagerly vying for Imperial recognition. A multitude of glorious medals kept the officers and soldiers of British Indian army proud and pleased at minimal cost.

Though the Muslim noble families, earlier regarded as India's main leaders fell from grace after 1857, the community was pampered after the First World War after increasing numbers of Hindu leaders began to assert themselves. Most Rajput rulers, who proved themselves as pliable and loyal to the British as they had earlier been to the Mughals, were also supported and encouraged.

Many Muslim leaders including Jinnah clearly believed that the British would be their saviors defending 100 million Muslims from being swamped by over 200 million Hindus. This was not only resented by the Congress but even by some Muslim leaders like Fazlul Haq of Bengal and the Nawab of Dhaka who accused Jinnah of the grossest treachery.

Everyone vied for sycophantic attention. The poet Muhammad Iqbal may be remembered for his lyrical song, 'Hindustan Hamara', but few know that he wrote flattering poems praising Queen Victoria and Sir Michael O'Dwyer and was even elevated to became Sir Muhammad Iqbal. Even Tagore's Jana Gana Mana, that became India's national anthem, was originally written in praise of Britain's benevolent rule of India.

During the First World War, the Gaikwad of Baroda gave Rs, 350,000, a huge sum at the time, to the Governor's war fund. The Maharaja of Travancore purchased a patrol boat for the Royal Navy, the Maharaja of Kashmir provided 18 field ambulances, The Nizam of Hyderabad paid for three squadrons of warplanes. Maharaja Gopal Narain Saran Singh served Field Marshal Haig as a dispatch rider. Sir Pratap Singh of Jodhpur led his Jodhpur Lancers in battles in France and Palestine.

Only Fateh Singh of Udaipur refused to be subservient but he too, ultimately succumbed to the offer of a Knighthood. About 300,000 volunteers from princely states were provided to the allied armed forces and rulers bought war bonds worth Rs. 180 million. India provided the British with the largest volunteer army ever raised totalling to over two million soldiers. No empire had ever been served so loyally by so many soldiers so willing to die for a cause that meant nothing to them as a nation.

But things were beginning to change. Like the emerging Hindu identity at the end of the Mughal Empire, a century of peace and prosperity under the British had produced a younger generation that began to assert its own identity and aspirations. The British were correct in stating that the natives were getting restless.

77. DID THE BRITISH EXPLOIT INDIA'S WEALTH?

Several British officials, officers and adventurers returned to England after amassing huge personal fortunes in the 17th and 18th centuries. A few treasures like the Koh-i-Noor were acquired and transferred to the Crown or to British museums but these were a tiny fraction of the wealth generated every year in India. Actually, the cost of the large British administration and armies in India absorbed most of the revenue the British earned from Indian land taxes up to 1900.

Though the British introduced railroads, better roads, harbours, wireless and good internal security, they were preoccupied with their own priorities and, relying on rent collectors lost their sensitivities to the state of the farmers. So they were unable to implement measures to avert the periodic famines or epidemics. The number of famines soared from seven between 1800 and 1850 to twenty-four between 1850 and 1900. Officially 28.8 million people perished in famines between 1854 and 1901. The actual number of deaths must have been much higher than the figures reported. The British neglect of education outside the big cities was, however, a big lapse, resulting in a long-term impoverishment of the country.

They did not interfere much with the religions and customs of the people and allowed the structures of the caste system to continue. In the management of the Army, they departed from their own military traditions and created an intermediate layer of junior commissioned officers (JCOs) between the aloof officers and the common soldiers. This system has continued throughout the Indian subcontinent even after independence.

One of Britain's great failures was their unwillingness to pass on the technologies of the Industrial Revolution. They clearly wanted India to remain a predominantly peasant and mercantile economy while they reaped the rewards of mass production techniques. So there was opposition to modern textile mills in India that led Gandhi to boycott imported fabrics. It was the same with other industries and it came as a great surprise to everyone when a hitherto relatively unknown Jamshedji Tata, who had earned his fortune trading in opium with China, started Tata Steel in 1907. But in 1947 there were very few industries and even fewer Indian entrepreneurs willing to risk the investments needed to set up modern industries. So industrialisation through the Public Sector, for all its shortcomings, was undoubtedly an important factor in India's subsequent industrial advancement.

During the two World Wars, India not only provided the bulk of the British army's cannon fodder in a number of war theatres but also donated huge sums of money. In 1904-05, 52 per cent of the Indian budget was committed to the military. In 1943-44, money supply was raised from Rs. 3 billion to Rs. 22 billion resulting in inflation and shortages. Between 1939 and 1945, Rs. 3.5 billion was spent on the defence services in India. These were a far greater drain on India than a few jewels, baubles and treasures.

78.   DID FREE INDIA'S LEADERS FAIL THEIR COUNTRY?

Intellectual agonising about colonialism, socialism, capitalism, materialism, labour unionism, Nehruvanism and numerous other ism's generated oceans of debate that wasted legislative time and frustrated executive action. Pragmatism, unfortunately, was not an Indian virtue. So shrill words were the usual substitute for decisive action.

Gandhi was a rare exception with an ability to act instead of just relying on words. His Salt March, boycott of British goods and personal example in personally cleaning toilets and undertaking fasts to death during riots was a total departure from the customs of high born Hindus. He also rejected the clothes and marks of class and deliberately dressed as the poorest of the poor. It was his decisive but principled actions that were the main factors to change the old Congress party from a docile debating society into a purposeful political movement.

The rulers in India's history and literature as well as many modern political leaders who followed them tended to model themselves on proud mythological stereotypes of exalted authority and individual brilliance. Teamwork was unknown. When a leader died or fell from grace, the complete management edifice would quickly collapse because there were seldom any organisational structures necessary for continuity. By way of example, when the Congress, United Front or BJP Governments fell, the parties often fell apart completely. The concept of a second line of command was quite alien to Indian tradition.

As with the Rajput or Mughal courts, chronic intrigues and sycophancy had also corroded the motivation of the officers in government or even in business. Sincere, able and honest officers were undermined and superseded by others with greater charm, connections, manners and flattery. Truth was not welcome and the bearers of bad news, as in most despotic societies, often faced ridicule or punishment. Instead of facing unpleasant facts, it was so much easier to find excuses and to blame others or to fatalistically surrender to destiny.

This mythological model even rules day-to-day values and defines the roles for many in Indian organisations. Postures, brave words and symbolic actions are often more important than firm decisive action. Retreat into orthodoxy or tradition is a convenient refuge for those unwilling to act. This mythological setting is even seen in many traditional Indian homes where, even if the women actually dominate the household, the master of the house acts, and is outwardly treated, like a maharaja. Boys, popularly called little rajas, are pampered and girls learn early the need to pretend total obedience while using charm to get their way. Boys are typically denied nothing and grow to become spoiled brats unable to tolerate any denial of their demands. Weddings and festivals are made to look like popular representations of great mythological events with loud music, huge processions and glittering decorations.

The chambers of India's political leaders, senior government officials and many Indian business magnates often resemble mediaeval courts, or durbars, complete with proud corporate warriors, whispering vizier's, secretive treasurers, and sometimes even court jesters. Appearances and rituals of command are often considered to be more important than a clear vision of the future or a commitment to decisive action.

Surrounded by grovelling sycophants, ministers, government secretaries and many business leaders are easily persuaded to ignore the opportunities of new technologies or the dangers of the world outside. Lacking inner confidence, they often lose interest in a project as soon as it faces obstructions. There is seldom the tenacious resolution to overcome the odds necessary for real achievement.

Brave words often became convenient substitutes for resolute action. Symbolic or ritual actions were substituted. Instead of decisive action to solve problems the government will usually use symbolic actions like grand tours, commissions of inquiry, loud pronouncements or the ritual of passing laws, even with the full awareness that many laws like the abolition of child marriages are often incapable of implementation.

Though they deport themselves with proud arrogance, Indian leaders were usually inwardly insecure and thus unable to take any bold or decisive action. Vindictive punishments, carping criticism, mockery and humiliating abuse are the usual substitutes for calm and courageous reform and restructuring needed for getting results. And if any bold action is proposed, opponents will be quick to voice strenuous objections.

As for the lower classes, their motivation had been eroded by the long conditioning of an oppressive caste system with the result that the orders of superiors were routinely executed in a shoddy and half-hearted manner. They were confident that their bosses would only speak or shout at them from their elevated positions but would never actually get down to their level to lead by example. They expected little reward and feared no punishment and knew that even their shoddy work was essential for their superiors making them virtually safe from any rebuke or punishment. They would go through the rituals of pretended obeisance and respect for the higher classes but would carry out their orders at their own convenience and refuse to be hurried or corrected.

There was little respect for the precision, commitment and punctuality so necessary for an organised modern technological world. The intellectual was admired while the manual worker was scorned. The upper classes would languidly disdain any regime of discipline while the lower classes did not care. There was little sense of accountability. Failure was accepted fatalistically and there was seldom the resolution to try and try again.

India's freedom resulted in the sudden empowerment of numerous regional, linguistic, religious, caste and other sectarian interest groups. While this democratic step may have been socially desirable, it suddenly opened the floodgates of opportunity for thousands of groups who eagerly rushed into politics for personal and sectarian gain with little concern for the greater good of the country. The spoils available from exploiting government projects and funds were soon seen to be much more attractive to many including powerful criminal groups.

As education was not a requirement for legislators, they rarely had any vision of national, technical or global issues. They wanted to become legislators not to make laws but find ways to bend the laws for their sectarian advantage. In the name of poor farmers, the rich landed interests quickly abolished land revenue that had been the main source of government taxation in India since the days of Chandragupta Maurya.

So this rich traditional source of revenue fell into their grasping hands of the rich rural families and was controlled by them through the petty district and village officials well away from the sight of the public or government administrators. They then obtained huge subsidies on the prices of food, fertilisers, diesel, water and power that enriched them as it impoverished the rest of the nation. This not only over burdened the urban taxpayers but also has enabled them to comfortably subsist with less work and lower output while poverty assured docile labour of the weaker sections continuing. They, with the help of a petty bureaucracy beholden to them, effectively undermined all efforts at poverty alleviation as that would drastically alter their indolent lifestyles.

79. WHY WAS INDIA'S PROGRESS AND DEVELOPMENT SO SLOW?

Hypocritical morality was often used to justify draconian or economically unwise laws. The Indian Mafia eagerly promoted prohibition in many states but actually did very little to stop people drinking and siphoned off huge sums (amounting to about 90 per cent of the price of a bottle of spirits) into their own pockets making all areas that had been under prohibition into major centres of organised crime. As with the Kennedys in the USA, during the prohibition of the 1920s, such huge funds also propelled many ambitious politicians. Initially supported by women's groups and morality squads in several states the attempts were soon abandoned except in Gujarat where the liquor mafia cooperated to lubricate their political supporters and kept their smuggling, land deals and other dubious activities out of the public eye.

New political power quickly undermined and corrupted the administrations and even the judiciary. Politics soon became a big, popular and profitable business. In the babble of ever-louder egotistic voices, everyone was concerned with their own words and opinions and there was seldom the serious thought, debate and meditation necessary to diagnose, let alone solve problems.

The ever growing demand for more jobs for the rapidly growing legions of badly educated aspirants for jobs made the government become a huge octopus ultimately ruled by its legions of petty bureaucrats who complacently considered themselves safe from any punishment. Government ministries and departments were accustomed to refer all matters to numerous other ministries and departments and never felt committed to 'own' a problem, let alone to solve it quickly.

The continuation of an obsolete British system of checks and the balances ensured that there was high accountability for smallest action taken but very little for inaction or delay. Flexibility and the ability to adapt to changes and crises were almost impossible with such a large, unwieldy and complicated bureaucracy. Like the cumbersome Rajput and Mughal armies of earlier times, India's administration quickly became a fat cat with more tail than tooth and was unable to move decisively in any direction. Thus governments were incapable of responding to sudden disasters except with the usual 'knee-jerk' responses of inquiries and commissions.

While a few thousand IAS and other senior officers were pacified with a VIP status that made them full of the importance of being important, the millions of petty bureaucrats came increasingly under the direct orders of politicians who wanted to serve their sectarian interests rather than the good of the country. The multitude of section officers, thanedars, tehsildars and patwaris went through the motions of service but could not be made to work as they were beyond the reach of any effective system of rewards or punishments. They gained nothing from honesty and hard work but could reap huge benefits from corruption, sloth and misuse of power. Privatisation has helped make many government and public sector organisations more efficient but if effective rewards and punishments were introduced into all government bodies they could all become much more efficient.

Multiple layers of bureaucracy required files on almost any subject to move from the dealing assistant to section officer to deputy secretary to under secretary to secretary, other departments and ministries and often involving the ministers and then back down the long ladder. This not only caused endless delays but needed agents and lubricants to speed the files on their circuitous routes. Small gratuities to speed the files were not considered as bribes. So though there may have been many honest government officials, the Indian government was 100 per cent corrupt. Compared to many Asian and African countries, the quantum of corruption was not exceptionally high but corruption in India was most inefficient because even the recipients of 'speed money', were usually unable to overcome all the bureaucratic and political hurdles.

As any decisive action by any government officer immediately attracted departmental inquiries and even questions in Parliament there was security in the fact that if they did nothing they did nothing wrong. Leadership was difficult because politicians found it difficult to move the government that was a huge rickety machine with a multitude of brakes but no accelerator.

These factors were aggravated by a federal system under which the writ of the central government did not extend far to the states. So crucial areas like agriculture, forests, education, health, etc., were left to the states with central laws and goading having very limited effect. As the states were under huge pressure to find jobs for their supporters and faced chronic financial pressures it resulted in funds going to salaries instead of development. Endemic corruption was a further aggravator.

The weakness of legislators and the failure of administration was aggravated by an obsolete legal system that made redress of injustice tortuous and slow, if not actually corrupted. This all too often became an instrument of the rich and politically influential to oppress their less fortunate opponents.

India's greatest failure was probably in the area of rural development. Two thirds of the population live in villages but they contribute to less than a third of India's national product. The big landowners officially hold only about 2 per cent of the land holdings but continue to control nearly half the land. The best land. They also are a powerful force in politics. With great difficulty India adopted the High Yielding Varieties strategy of the Green Revolution and achieved the food security in the 1960s. But it succeeded too well and there was later a huge over production of wheat and rice that depleted the water table and soil fertility of India's most productive agricultural areas. The indiscriminate and excessive use of fertilisers and pesticides is now poisoning the land in many areas.

As most of the wheat and rice is grown in irrigated areas that account for just 20 per cent of the districts there was a consequent neglect for coarse grains that predictably mean the neglect of the remaining districts. The government warehouses often have more stock than they need and has to pay huge sums every year for stocks it does not want. But as it had evolved no alternate strategy and as it cannot also dare to alienate the huge peasant vote bank it is helpless. The recent spurt in land prices also tempts many farmers to sell their lands with the result that grain production is now falling.

To push up procurement the government had also lowered the quality standards and their agents accept anything that is FAQ or Fair Average Quality so there is little incentive for producing good quality. And as grain is purchased by weight, instead of by volume as is the international practice, farmers add weight with water that causes fungus and decay.

Agricultural development has relied on the generally feeble efforts of government agencies, technology and inputs little realising that agriculture's greatest resource was the farmers themselves. If they could be motivated to invest more into their lands and work them harder, India could double its farm output in a few years. China had the courage to reverse policy in 1980 and by empowering farmers through 'Farmers Contracts' allowed farmers use of cultivable land in exchange for defined levels of crop output instead of collective and cooperative farms. This step accelerated China's crop output by 33 per cent in just four years. This increased rural income triggered enormous economic growth in all other sectors of the economy and quickly made China a great economic force. India also needs to study the success of many other Asian countries that have made a success with commercial marketing of higher value crops like fruits, vegetables, fibres and agro fuels.

Over the centuries, the real wealth of India had come from its abundant agricultural resources and the industry of an intelligent hard working people. India's history shows that not very much gold or precious stones were actually mined in India but that huge quantities had been imported in exchange for the pepper of Kerala, the Muslins of Macchlipatnam, the calicoes of Calicut, cotton, spices, crafts and timber. Agriculture needed people to effectively work the land. Industry and crafts needed disciplined workers. Thus India's real wealth was only available when there were times of security and good rule with disciplined and industrious workers. When this weakened, India quickly became a poor, quarrelsome and disorganised country.

India's second major failure was in the area of education. Being a state subject it focused on a low-grade intellectual literacy in government schools with underpaid and demotivated teachers and an emphasis on local languages. The two million government schools therefore created a huge mass of semi literates who were insufficiently educated to hold any job. It ultimately just produced millions of young people with worthless degrees who were unwilling to work in the villages and unfit to work in the cities.

The Brahmanical love of higher learning had also resulted in ridiculously cheap higher education in absurd contrast to very expensive private school education. So many thousands of badly educated BAs, MAs and LLBs are churned out by thousands of rather dubious state colleges and universities to form a frustrated and unstable mass of discontented youth.

If the education of every youth had included 'hands on' crafts, like carpentry, plumbing, masonry, electricals, sewing and elementary mechanics every youth would have gained some real means to earn and would never starve. The Brahmanical aversion to working with one's hands created a contempt for manual labour. So teachers do not want to teach low caste crafts and today's youth want jobs and not work. Preferably comfortable government jobs with prestige, security, and very little work.

Thus frustrated youth now flood from rural to urban areas influenced by the role models of film and TV stars whose lifestyles they want to imitate. The glitzy glamour of the cities and the craving for quick wealth, sex, song, intoxicants and violence caused disorientation, widespread frustration and has created a rapidly increasing lumpen mass that can be easily swayed by religious fanatics and a lust for loot that fuels the riots that occur with horrifying regularity.

Half a century of peace and prosperity after independence had again generated a generation of restless youth who are becoming as assertive and demanding as their predecessors at the end of the Mughal and British periods and as unwilling to blindly accept government authority.

The government had also jealously guarded its turf and was hostile to the private sector with the result that many areas like industry, roads and telecommunications were allowed to languish. The recent winds of change, driven by the need to become globally competitive, has belatedly had some effect but much time and progress has been needlessly frittered away.

There was comfort in staying with old systems and traditions, even if they were irrelevant or wrong and a reluctance to face the predictable resistance to any change. People are quick to protest, strike or institute legal suits but are reluctant to actually do anything constructive. Instead of efforts to correct deficiencies, there was a ready eagerness to place the blame of failures onto others.

Many in India had closed their doors to new ideas or knowledge and consoled themselves with the thought that everything it needed to know could be found in their ancient texts. While India slumbered, the rest of the world raced forward to progress and prosperity. while many young people were eagerly looking west to modern idea there were many obscruntests who deplore western ways.

A distortion of history provided many excuses or alibis for failure. Unfortunately, the exaggerated lifestyles, the stereotypes of mythology as well as the mythological reliance on miracles, so much a part of popular films and TV, influenced mass behaviour. Violence and abuse were poor foundations for constructive development or nation building.

The poverty of India cannot be blamed on foreign invaders but on pervasive caste divisions and the inability of most Indian leaders to resist intrigues or sycophancy, to learn new technologies, and to effectively manage their people and their huge natural resources.

The phenomenal success of millions of Indians in every foreign land clearly shows that they thrive in environments where there are rewards for intelligence, hard work and integrity and instant punishment or dismissal for failure. Many Indians have cut through the ranks of top international corporations in leading edge technologies like computers, medicine, aerospace, etc. In India the situation is reversed and the hard working and honest suffer, while the dishonest and lazy are rewarded.

Though the nationalised banks had opposed computers for decades, until workers gradually discovered that modernisation and productivity were opportunities and not threats. It is now time for the government to dismantle its multi-layered bureaucracy and install a computerised transparent system of governance where every project and application is open and public and free from political or personal interventions.

It has been said that there are only two kinds of people. Doers and talkers. India seems to have become a nation of talkers. Only when India's leaders can teach their people how to work will India be able to regain its rightful place as one of the richest countries of the world.

But things are finally changing. Despite the pressures of populism and the push and pull of conservative and communist ideologies, India has somehow made fairly good progress. The winds of global change are also blowing away many old cobwebs. To the horror of Hindi language chauvinists, the recent boom in IT, business outsourcing and call centres has suddenly made India proud that the English proficiency of so many Indians has opened gigantic avenues of good employment. Bright students with private tuition from many small towns are outclassing students from government educational institutions for admission to the top IITs, IIMs engineering and medical schools of the country.

The communications revolution with cell phones reaching most villages has been a huge stimulus. The huge and rapid expansion of television has been hugely educative even if it had made young people yearn for the lifestyles of the people in the programmes. There may be incitements to violence as well as to the false values of cine glamour but increasing numbers of modern young people are no longer as attracted to the obscurantist ideas of their elders. The '1sting' and other investigative reporting is also having a salutary effect in showing up the failures and hypocrisy of many previously unaccountable government or political organisations.

Foreign investment has stimulated industry and big foreign brands in big consumerist malls are generating both jobs and excitement among the young without any surrendering of national interests. Even the sceptics are willing to believe several reputable studies that forecast that India with China will have the strongest economies and per capita incomes in the next four decades. These are the dreams of the increasing numbers of the young and India's 'Dollar Millionaires' are increasing at nearly 30 per cent per year. But sadly our planners and politicians are still in a time warp of past penury and readily surrender to the demands of declining numbers of the poor who want free electricity and subsidies. They are not sufficiently planning for the future drivers that need stable power and a better infrastructure.

80. Has Communalism Ever Been Politically Successful?

Paradoxically, despite the huge passions that religious and racial communalism generates, communalism has never been very successful politically. The Jews had wanted a Jewish state that the British Government obligingly carved out for them out of Palestine after the First World War but far from being the Promised Land that they had hoped for Israel remained afflicted by unending violence and anger as the Arab and other minorities were not willing to be totally subjugated.

The province of Punjab had once been the largest and richest in the British Empire till the Muslim demand for an Islamic state led to the partition of India. But later this pure Islamic state was to be no paradise and fellow Muslims from East Pakistan resenting the Punjabi dominance soon split away. But even in West Pakistan the nearly pure Islamic state faced an unending spate of communal upheavals with conflicts not only between the Sunnis and Shias but also in conflicts between Biharis, Ahmediays and other Muslim minority groups and ethnic groups like the Sindhis and Baluchis.

Then Sikh communalism resulted in a further splitting of India's post-independence Punjab and the non-Sikh states of Himachal and Haryana were created. But even in the rump state, the Sikhs though the largest group, were hardly united and there were conflicts not only between the Sikhs and Nirankaris but between several other factions as well.

Hindu fundamentalists had similarly longed for a pure Hindu state and the doctrine of 'Hindutva' tried to define a Hindu paradise of pristine purity free from the corrupting influences of the descendants of so-called Muslim and Christian 'invaders'. Unfortunately they also wanted to change Hinduism from a gentle and tolerant faith into a Hindu Jehadi movement. On the basis of very dubious history from writers like Savarkar and Golwalker, who were better at rhetoric than history, there was soon a deliberate demonisation of many historic figures like Ghazni, Aurangzeb and Jinnah to say nothing of leftist historians, Nehruvian thinkers and moderates who were considered the enemies of their dream nation.

Hindu communal organisations like the Rashtriya Sarvaseva Sangh (RSS) began to organise cadres of dedicated followers rather on the lines of the Nazi youth organisations and laid out a detailed dogma for their cadres. These promised a Hindu paradise of a Ramrajya where the pernicious influence of Muslims, Christians and English-speaking modernists could be purged from their system. But this aggression movement mainly appealed to people in the Hindi-speaking areas of India and was resented and even feared by linguistic and ethnic minorities in Tamil Nadu, Kerala, Andhra, Bengal, Assam and elsewhere.

The RSS, however, had a big following among many semi-literate quasi religious groups in North India and spun off several militant organisations like the Bajrang Dal, inspired by the devoted and destructive monkey god Hanuman, and the Vishwa Hindu

Parishad who were always virulently outspoken and sometimes violent. Their's was a world of love and hate with little conception of moderation. Their political wings like the Jan Sangh that later evolved into the Janata Party and later the Bharata Janata Party (BJP) rose to prominence after 1991 when the movement to destroy the Babri Masjid and replace it with a Ram temple at Ayodhya gathered strength. Though there is not a shred of historic evidence that the god Ram was born at that precise place the movement appealed to many lumpen poor. The inept and hesitant attempts of the ruling Congress Government to counter this movement allowed the BJP to become a political force. But it was never strong enough to act independently and had to moderate itself to accommodate their many political allies.

In Ireland, Sri Lanka, Bosnia, Ethiopia and many other places demands for a 'homeland' far from materialising have only resulted in violent bloodshed as the strong communal passions of the dominant group was opposed by equally strong counter passions from their opponents.

Sadly, religious passions always divide as they can seldom unite with those of other faiths. Efforts at 'ethnic cleansing' have often been attempted but world opinion today under the vigilant eyes of TV and media coverage ensures that they will never be allowed to succeed. For bigots it is hard do accept the fact that it was only when the dominant religious or racial groups recognise that they have to live and let live with other minority communities that lasting peace will ever be possible. The male libido that loves guns and violence thrives on extremism and does not care for the wisdom of Buddha who believed that the only victories were the victories of the heart.

What do we learn from these questions?

1. That faith in a great cosmic creator gives comfort and inspiration to people in every land.

2. That the prophets, sages or founders of all faiths love all humanity but that the professional priests, who often encourage hatred for other creeds, have few compunctions about using violence to maintain their religious dominance. They nurture fantastic myths, magnificent ceremonies and superstitions to enslave their followers using exaggerations of past events and personalities.

3. That the historic accuracy of most religious writers is usually very distorted. So most Brahmin religious and literary sources are highly flawed and the historical foundations of many of India's popular beliefs are often shallow, unscientific, inaccurate and biased. Many popular assumptions about Indian traditions, castes, tribes and minorities are erected on shallow foundations.

4. That no prophet or founder of any faith ever demanded any church, mosque, temple, idol or sacred relic. So none of these have any innate sanctity except as tools to perpetuate the power of the priests.

5. That the sacred scriptures of all religions were written by apostles and priests many years... even centuries ...after the deaths of the founders and are thus usually the selective words of the priests and not the sacred words of the founders or of God.

6. That the distinctive icons and costumes of religions like crucifixes, crescents, tridents, beards, long hair, veils, caps marks, etc., were never the demands of the prophets or founders but the commands of the professional priests to give their followers distinctive appearances as if they were brands on heards of cattle or sheep.

7. That faiths become religions when organised armies of professional priests take control and the define the scriptures, dogma, doctrines and rituals to capture mass followings, by propagating the idea of an all powerful all seeing, sin punishing, prayer fulfilling supernatural god.

8. That the priests of all religions, are an economically unproductive burden on the masses. India is estimated to have about ten million professional priests in a population of about 210 million households.

9. That industry and trade in periods of security and creativity had created India's real greatness. These were more stifled by caste, social and religious restrictions than by foreign invaders. Countries prospered when they opened themselves to new people and ideas and withered when they closed their doors. Industry and trade had been the foundation of India's real greatness while culture that had flourished in its periods of decadence was its tombstone.

10. That despite the huge passions generated by religious and racial communalism, fanaticism has never been very successful politically and had never succeeded in creating a religiously pure country.

SEEKING THE COSMIC SPIRIT

All life forms are bundles of energy carried by a great cosmic river that flows through them, around them and are a part of them. Charged by it, the humblest plant sends up thousands of lacy tendrils eagerly seeking the energy of the sun and many miles of rootlets downwards hungering for the moisture and nutrients that are necessary to feed its life mission to grow and passionately propagate itself.

A nameless formless cosmic energy flows silently, sinuously and joyfully through all life forms in its ceaseless quest unaffected by the material achievements, sorrows and fears that affect higher animals that are mainly stimulated by what they see, hear, smell, taste or feel of things around them. This conscious mind so dominates the quiet but deep springs of our unconscious awareness that we often blind ourselves to the real beauty of inner selves

Man, the highest animal, is especially troubled as he alone among all God's creatures is tortured by the fears created by his own turbulent mind. Man can seldom rejoice in moments of present contentment, as he is constantly troubled by the fears or the hopes of the future. Dogs, cats, crows, cows, tigers, birds, fishes and all other living things have excellent memories of the past and will recognise their foes or friends and will respond immediately and intelligently to the stimuli of the present in the form of danger, food or sex but they all sleep easy, untroubled by anxieties about what the morrow might bring.

Every quality that we admire or despise about Man is based on their response to the future. The man we call a coward shirks from present danger while the brave will boldly stand up to face it. The greedy will grab future opportunities while the unselfish will regard them with detachment. The noble will stand by their principles while the base will have little concern for morals, ethics or decency.

Man however is tormented by anxieties concerning all the many things that could happen in the future. Even if he has a secure home and income he will endlessly agonise about health, family pressures, careless words or business uncertainties.

His contentment will be disrupted if a friend, colleague or relative suddenly becomes more famous or richer than himself. He can adjust to however little he has but can be upset when others become more fortunate.

Greed for possessions can be an obsession. Denial can lead to bitterness and anger. If someone secures what he wants by lies or cheating or does injury to another he may suffer inner guilt. And to blind himself to the wrongs he has done he may shift the blame even upon those who he has made to suffer. Love and hate are very simple emotions, anger the reactions of the immature, greed the response of the undisciplined but envy and guilt can seriously erode mental peace. Man is also troubled about the uncertainties of life after death and often seeks the succor of religion, rituals, offerings and penances to try to atone for the guilt and anxieties that increasingly afflict his conscious mind.

So we all need to loosen up. Let go of the attachment to all the possessions and passions that so dominate our conscious minds. We need to tap that huge reservoir of cosmic energy and allow it to flow through ourselves and replenish the depleted wells of our inner strength. We must allow the deep wisdoms of our unconscious minds to direct us to what we instinctively know we should be. Recite just one `mantra' ... "Hang loose... Let go... Let the cosmic energy flow". Perhaps it may help you unleash the power of our own subconscious minds.

Our little world is just one out of many billion, planets, suns, moons and other solid bodies separated by vast distances of space. Science today shows us that even this solid world that we live on is actually made up of many smaller elements arranged in molecules, like planets in a galaxy and separated from each other by vast distances of relative space. These atoms are further composed of still smaller electrons and protons moving through even smaller expanses of space in charged energy fields. Man does not yet know if this vast world we live in is not just a small particle in a still greater cosmos nor even whether there will some day be the discovery of even smaller worlds than the smallest electrons that science has, so far, identified. All observable matter is, thus, no more than insubstantial fields of energy moving in a great void. The great `Shunya' or the great emptiness that pervades and surrounds everything.

All objects and all living bodies thus have no substance except through energy. All the great edifices of man, all our proud possessions and all observable objects are doomed to decay and die. All our hopes, fears, dreams, philosophies, arts, literature and historic achievements are nothing but a transitory mist floating on the endless ocean of the cosmos.

MAN'S UNANSWERED QUESTIONS REMAIN

What or who is the subject which directs these objects ?

Who guides the microscopic and macrocosmic cycles of their movements and changes?

What or who is the subject within all living things that directs a continuously changing process of birth, growth, decay and death?

If all observable matter is subject to change, could there be some greater changeless force that directs them through the cosmic cycle from birth to extinction?

Is this subject within all animate beings and the inanimate things, a separate entity, or are they just drops in some great encompassing cosmic river flowing, in eddies and swirls, towards some even greater cosmic ocean?

All our transitory possessions, objects, passions, ideals and even our mortal bodies are destined to be deserted by this mortal spirit as it moves uncertainly towards some unimagined destination. In it and around it is the unchanging void. The nameless, formless, Nirvana. The great inert stillness where nothing changes may be the only constant.

For each individual, our seemingly momentous passions, thoughts, traditions, pleasures and pain are mere expressions of a lonely transitory spirit on an often tiresome though sometimes joyous journey through an allotted passage of life. A spirit that comes to the world alone and leaves it alone but never is alone as long as it regards itself as being a part of some greater subject.

The cosmic creator, without name or form may be a great stream of cosmic energy in which every living soul is but a tiny droplet. A stream which surges over, under and through us as it joins other streams to flow into some greater cosmic ocean from where droplets evaporate again to resume the cycle of creation,

An increased awareness of our inner spirituality may mark a new consciousness because evolved spirits will find no purpose for the wood, brick or stone of its deities or places of worship. They will need no priests who pretend they are the sole selling agents of their brands of God who can insure the future for the fearful or the superstitious by claiming a magical ability to intercede with supposedly sacred words, beautiful images of deities or glorified concepts of God. If education and guidance can teach people how to find the glory of a spirit within themselves it will mark the triumph of inner spirituality and the end of raucous religiosity.

CHALTI KA NAM* HISTORY

JUG SURAIYA

As a people, we Indians - whatever we interpret that to mean - have long had scant regard for history that old has-been. It's perhaps because we have had too much of it that we have squandered it with profligacy, as witnessed by the collective amnesia of ruined, neglected monuments and a few scraps of fly-blown texts where only spiders and propagandists weave their webs of insidious intent. But for most of us - you, me and the homemaker next door - history has largely been a lot of left over junk, best handed over to the next passing *raddiwala* (the local garbage collectors of every Indian city).

Broadly, there have been two types of historical *raddiwalas*, people who have specialised in recycling bits and pieces of the past to fashion from them a rudimentary juggernaut - rather like that old stalwart of the Indian roads, the Ambassador car -which will take us to a programmed destination. The so-called saffron model starts with the promise that in the dim but nevertheless glorious past there was in India long before India existed a unifying Hindu way of life which was rent asunder by the invading sword of Islam; it ends with the proposition that Mother India can be rendered whole again only through the healing ministrations of the *Sangh Parivar*.

The so-called secular model (also known as a left-hand drive) starts with the premise that India was a global commune before India or global communes existed, that Hinduism was itself an import among many others, in a pluralistic harmony which was vitiated by the divisive advent of the British; it ends with the proposition that instead of Bal Thackeray, John Major- the then occupant at 10 Downing Street - should be challenged by his remote-control rule in the 1992 Muslim riots.

---

* *Chalti ka nam gari* was an old Hindi film but is now a metaphor roughly meaning moving along somehow.

Given these two options, many if not most of us might prefer to take a walk instead of being taken for an historical ride. Now, however, there is a third choice. *Called India Unvarnished: An Unemotional Examination of Some of the Main Questions about India's History'*, the new model comes in the form of a privately circulated catechism comprising 58 Q and A responses, (now expanded to 80). The author is Murad Ali Baig, better known as India's foremost motoring correspondent, who has taken time off from test driving automobiles to tackle the even more hazardous task of navigating our past, that unfolding landscape of the future as viewed through the distorting rear view mirror of the present: where we want to go determines where we come from.

The Murad model valiantly tries to steer a middle path between the saffron and the secular prototypes. In his intro, Murad notes that diverse interest groups - the British, the communists, Muslims, Hindus, etc - have tried to 'twist or distort facts to suit their preconceived notions'. His own exploration of the past is based on 'unvarnished' facts, such as archaeological remains (buildings, coins, weapons), which can be 'fairly accurately dated by radio carbon... and other scientific methods'. Certainly the chronological facticity of an arrow head or potsherd can be scientifically established. But how does one carbon date the facticity of dual proposition such as, for example, that of the Taliban and many others... Osama bin Laden is a soldier - saint while to Washington he is Public Enemy No 1? Moreover, isn't the inclusion of some 'facts' at the expense of other facts itself a non-factual foray? If Mallory hadn't the 'preconceived notion' of climbing Everest would he have noticed the 'fact' of its being there? Notions make facts as much as facts make notions.

Murad's route map includes some controversy - charged 'facts' and 'notions' of our past. Who were India's original people? (Proto-Australoids, Negritos), Who were the Harappans? (Probably the Dravidian settlers from the west.) Were the Aryans a race or a tribe? (A nomadic tribe from West Asia whose language was similar to old Persian and old Sanskrit. Murad skirts the contentious issue as to whether the Aryans were invaders or nomadic settlers. However, his statement that 'they were the first people to domesticate horses and their chariots were fearsome' suggests belligerent incursion.

What was the influence of Buddhism? (Buddhism held sway over most of India for over a thousand years from the time of Ashok; key concepts of later Hinduism like Karma, Dharma and reincarnation were of Buddhist origin.) When did the chains of India's caste system harden? (Probably after Kulluka's 7th-century commentary on the Manusmriti, 300 years earlier.) What was the impact of Islam? (Islam was a very simple religion with few pretensions of spirituality... It unfortunately introduced the idea that martyrdom was a sure path to heaven leading to a fanaticism in later ages... True Aurangzeb introduced the odious Jezia tax on Hindus; but Muslims paid an equally heavy Zakat tax. True he demolished the Kashi Vishwanath temple because a Hindu guest of his was assaulted there, but he endowed 36 other temples. Were there forcible conversions? (The agonised local accounts are as inaccurate as the glorified Islamic accounts of their conquests).

Did colonial Britain exploit India's wealth? ('The cost of their administration and armies absorbed most of the revenue they earned... A few treasures like the (acquired) Koh-i-Noor... were a tiny fraction of the wealth of the country. The real impoverishment of India by the neglect of mass education.) What was the impact of independence? ('It suddenly opened new avenues of opportunity for many thousands of caste, linguistic and regional groups who rushed into politics (without) ... any vision of national, technical or global issues but wanted to ... use their positions... to the advantage of themselves'.)

All in all, the Murad model provides a zippy drive. Good pick-up, impressive maneuverability around tricky corners and commendable fuel-efficiency through the minimum utilisation and/or emissions of hot air and other gases.

What worries me is the suspension: the suspension of disbelief when mounted on unvarnished truths instead of the soft-sprung undercarriage of honest prejudice, the only 'fact' of life we can ever really hope to know. And endlessly argue as we make, remake or unmake our history. Like the tinkering roadside mechanics keeping a rattletrap jalopy on the road.

SELECT BIBLIOGRAPHY

Aggarwal, Vasudeva S. *The Heritage of Indian Art*. Publications Division.

Aiyar, Mani Shankar. *Confessions of a Secular Fundamentalist*. Penguin Viking, 2004.

Allchin, Raymond and Bridget. *The Birth of Indian Civilisation*. Penguin Books, 1993

Ardrey, Robert. *The African Genesis*, Macmillan Publishing Co. *The Social Contract*, Macmillan Publishing Co.

Armstrong, Karen A. *History of God*, Mandarin (UK), 1993. *Islam : A Short History*, Modern Library. Buddha, Phoenix, 2003

Baig, M.R.A. *The Muslim Dilemma in India*. Vikas, 1974.

Barth, A. *The Religions of India*. Low Price Publications. Delhi, 1990.

Basham, A.L. *The Wonder that was India*. South Asia Books.

Beal, Samuel. *Travels of Fa-Hien/Sung-Yun*. Rupa and Co., 2003

Bronowski, Joseph. *The Ascent of Man*. Litle Brown and Co.

Bryson, Bill. *A Short History of Nearly Everything*. Black Swan (UK), 2003.

Burger, Julian. *First Peoples*. Anchor.

Campbell, Joseph. *The Hero with a Thousand Faces*. Mythos Books.

Chaitanya, Krishna. *Betrayal of Krishna*. Clarion Books, 1991.

Chaudhuri Nirad. *Hinduism, The Continent of Circe*. Jaico Publishing House, 1965

Chatwin, Bruce. *What Am I Doing Here?* Picador. Songlines. Picador.

Dahiya, B.S. *Jats, the Ancient Rulers*. Meghna Malik Partner (Sonepat), 1990.

Dawood, N.J. *The Koran*. Penguin Books. 1997.

Dawson, John. *Classical Dictionary of Mythology and Religion*.

Daya, Krishna *Indian Philosophy*. Oxford University Press, 1991.

Debroy, Bibek, *The 18 Puranas*. Books for All.

Dey, U.N. *Some Aspects of Medieval Indian History*. Low Price Publications, 1990.

Diamond, Jared. *Guns, Germs and Steel*. W.W. Norton (NY), 1997.

Dubois, Abbe J.A. *Hindu Manners, Customs and Ceremonies*. Oxford University Press.

Dumont, Louis. *Homo Hierachicus*. Paladin (UK), 1970

Du Ry, Carel J. *Art of the Ancient Near and Mid East*.

Dutt, R.C. *History of Civilisation in Ancient India*. Indus.

Easwaran, Eknath. *The Dhammapada*. Penguin Books, 1986.

Editors *The Making of Indo-Persian Culture*. Manohar, 2000.

Elwin, Verrier. *The Tribal World*. Oxford University Press. The Baiga, Wyman and Sons 1939.

Embree, Ainslie. *Sources of Indian Tradition-I*. Penguin

Frazer, James George. *The Golden Bough*. Macmillan and Co. 1951.

Frykenburg, R.E. *Delhi through the Ages*. Oxford University Press, 1986.

Ghose, Sarnujit. *Legend of Ram*. Biblophile South Asia in association with Promilla & Co., 2004

Griffith, Ralph. *Hymns of the Rigveda*. Motilal Banarsidas Delhi, 1991.

Harvard Oriental series: *Vedas and Other Scriptures*. Harvard University Press.

Hay, Stephen. *Sources of Indian Tradition*. II Penguin.

Henley, John F. *The Early Alphabet*. British Museum Press.

Hoffer, Eric. *The True Believer*. Harper Perennial Modern Classics.

Huntington, Samuel P. *The Clash of Civilisations*. Penguin Books. 1996.

Indien, Ronald. *Imagining India*. Basil Blackwell, 1990.

Ions, Veronica. *Indian Mythology*. Newnes Books (UK), 1983.

J .Barthelemy Saint-Hilare. *Hiouen Tsang in India*. Rupa and Co., 2003.

Jain, Girilal. *The Hindu Phenomenon*. UBSPD Publishers, 1994.

Jayakar, Pupul. *The Earth Mother*. Penguin Books, 1980.

Jha, D. N. *The Myth of the Holy Cow*. Verso. London 2002

Keay, John. *India Discovered*. Harper Collins. *A History of India*. Harper Collins (UK), 2000.

Keller, Warner. *The Bible as History*. Bantam Books, 1982.

Ketkar, S.V. *History of Caste in India*. Low Price Publications, 1990.

Khilnani, Sunil. *The Idea of India*. Penguin, 1997

Kinsley, David. *Hindu Goddesses*. Motilal Banarsidas, 1987.

Kochhar, Rajesh *The Vedic People*. Orient longman, 2002.

Kosambi, D.D. *An Introduction to the Study of Indian Culture Civilisation of Ancient India*. Popular Prakashan

Kulke and Rothermund. *A History of India*. Rupa and Co., 1994

Lal, P., *Ramayana of Valmiki*. Vikas Publications.

Lannoy, Richard. *The Speaking Tree*. Oxford University Press, 1987

Larousse, *Encyclopedia of Mythology*. Hamlyn, 1986.

Luce, Edward. *In spite of the Gods*, Little Brown, 2006

Mahajan, V. D. *Sultanate of Delhi*.

Mani, Veitam. *Puranic Encylopedia*, Motilal Banarsidas.

Mansingh, Surjit. *Historical Dictionary of India*. Vision Books (Orient).1998

Mason, Philip. *A Matter of Honour*. Penguin, 1974

Mueller, Max. *Sacred Books of the East*. Manohar.

Muller, Herbert J. *The Loom of History*. Oxford University Press.

Mckie, Robin. *Dawn of Man*. Dorling Kindersley Publications Inc. 2000.

Mithen, Stephen. *After the Ice 20,000 to 5,000 BC*. Phoenix Paperback, 2003

Molyneaux, *The Sacred Earth*. Duncan Baird Publishers, 1995.

Moreland, W. H. *India at the Death of Akbar*. Low Price Publications, 1990

Mujumdar, R. C. *Ancient India*. Motilal Banarasidas.

Nehru, Jawaharlal. *Discovery of India*. Oxford University Press.

Oak, P.N. *Some Blunders of Indian Histtorical Research*. Hindi Sahitya Sadan.

O'Hanlon, Rosalind *Caste, Conflict and Ideology*. Cambridge University Press.

Panikkar, K.M. *Hinduism and the Modern World*. Kitabistan, 1936.

Piggott, Stuart. *Prehistoric India*. Pelican Books, 1950.

Pratt, James Bisset. *India and its Faiths*. SBW Publishers (ND).

Radhakrishnan, S. *The Foundation of Civilisation*. Orient Paperback, 1990. Indian Religions. Orient Paperback, 1992.

Roebuck, Valerie. *The Upanishads*. Penguin Books, 2000.

Reade, Winwood. *The Martyrdom of Man*. Watts and Co (Lon), 1872.

Rhys, Davids T. W. *Buddhist India*. Munshiram Manoharlal Publishers, Originally T. Fisher Unwin (L) 1903.

Richards, John F. *The Mughal Empire*. Cambridge University Press. 1975.

Richman, Paula. *Many Ramayanas*. University of California Press.

Sastri, Nilakant. *A History of South India*. Oxford University Press.

Selincourt, Aubrey De, *The World of Herodotus*. Little Brown and Co. 1962.

Sen, Amartya. *The Argumentative Indian*. Penguin Books. 2005

Sinari, Ramakant. *The Structure of Indian Thought*. Oxford University Press.

Sinha, Phulgenda. *Sankhya Karika of Kapil*, India Heritage Press, 1991

–– *The Gita as It Was*, Open Court, La Salle, 1997.

Sherning, M. A. *Hindu Tribes and Castes*. Cosmo Publications (D). 1974

Spear, Percival. *A History of India*. Penguin Books.

Stavrianos, L.S. *A Global History*. Prentice Hall Inc. NJ, 1983.

Talageri, S.G. Aryan Invasion *Theory and Indian Nationalism*. Voice of India.

Tarapore. I. J. S. *The Religion of Zorathushtra*. Arun Naik (Bombay).

Thapar, Romila. *Early India*. Allen Lane (Penguin), 2002.

    A History of India. Penguin, 1966.

    Past and Prejudice. National Book Trust India, 1975.

    Recent Perspectives of Early Indian History. Popular Prakashan, 1998.

    Somanatha. Penguin Viking, 2004.

Thomas, Epics. *Myths and Legends of India*. B. D. Tarapore and Co. Pvt. Ltd. 1980.

Tod, James William. *Annals and Antiquities of Rajasthan*. Low Price Publication, 1995.

Toynbee, A. L. *A Study of History*. Thames and Hudson, 1988.

Trautmann, Thomas R., *Aryans and British India*. Vistaar Publications (ND) Sage, 1997.

Upadhyaya, B.S. *Ancient World*. S. Chand and Co., 1954.

Vaidya, R.V. *Study of the Mahabharata*, AVB Prakashan, 1967.

Verma, Pavan K. *The Great Indian Middle Class*. Penguin, 1998.

Vishvanathan, Susan. Legends of St Thomas. *IIC Quarterly*.

Weatherford, Jack. *Genghis Khan*. Three Rivers Press, (NY).

Woodruff, Philip. *The Men Who Ruled India* Vols. I & II. Jonathan Cape, 1971.

The Times Concise Atlas of World History. Times Books, 1992.

BBC, National Geographic, Discovery and History TV channels.

INDEX